The English Garden

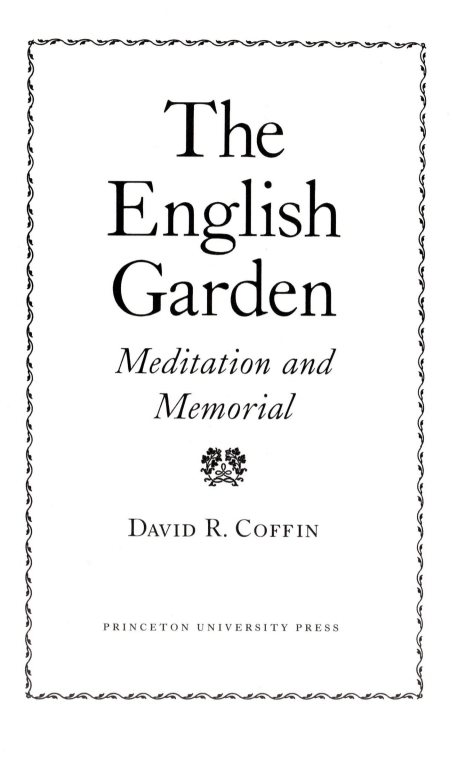

The English Garden

Meditation and Memorial

DAVID R. COFFIN

PRINCETON UNIVERSITY PRESS

Copyright © 1994 by Princeton University Press
Published by Princeton University Press, 41 William Street,
Princeton, New Jersey 08540
In the United Kingdom:
Princeton University Press, Chichester, West Sussex

Library of Congress Cataloging-in-Publication Data
Coffin, David R.
The English garden : meditation and memorial / David R. Coffin.
p.   cm.
Includes bibliographical references and index.
ISBN 0-691-03432-X
1. Gardens, English—History—17th century.   2. Gardens, English
—History—18th century.   3. Gardens—England—History—17th century.
4. Gardens—England—History—18th century.   5. Gardens—England—
Symbolic aspects—History—17th century.   6. Gardens—England
—Symbolic aspects—History—18th century.   7. Garden structures—
England—History—17th century.   8. Garden structures—England—
History—18th century.   I. Title.
SB457.6.C64   1994
712'.0942'09032—dc20   93-34998

This book has been composed in Caslon
by The Composing Room of Michigan, Inc.

Princeton University Press books are printed on acid-free paper
and meet the guidelines for permanence and durability of the
Committee on Production Guidelines for Book Longevity of
the Council on Library Resources

Printed in the United States of America

10 9 8 7 6 5 4 3 2 1

DESIGNED BY LAURY A. EGAN

CONTENTS

List of Illustrations

PREFACE

Scholars of English gardening will be aware that I have been particularly dependent for ideas and information on several earlier eminent studies, especially John Dixon Hunt, *The Figure in the Landscape*, 1976; Sir Roy Strong, *The Renaissance Garden in England*, 1979; and Sir Keith Thomas, *Man and the Natural World*, 1983. Among those scholars and students who have contributed to this work are Tracy Ehrlich, Lisa Maddox, Barbara Paca, and Vanessa Sellers to whom I am much indebted.

The last chapter on memorials is, of course, not a catalogue striving for any completeness, but a selection to give some idea of the variety and the relative quantity of some types. Certainly I shall be berated for not including some reader's favorite example, as I shall be chided for the boring repetition of examples.

My home during the research and writing of this work has been the Marquand Library of art at Princeton University with daily forays into nearby Firestone Library. The staff of both libraries have been of inestimable help in my work. I am also very grateful to the Department of Art and Archaeology of Princeton University for the assistance of its Spears Research Fund. Elizabeth Powers of the Princeton University Press has again offered her gracious encouragement and gentle guidance of the editing of the work and Tim Wardell has not only been exacting in his copyediting, often improving the literary expression, but has as production editor offered many helpful suggestions. Laury Egan as designer has again skillfully and artfully ordered the whole.

David R. Coffin

The English Garden

Introduction

M ORE THAN OTHER EUROPEANS the English sought contemplative consolation in their gardens or wooded "wildernesses."
Certainly they reveled in boisterous hunting parties ending with bounteous
picnics in temporary, rustic banqueting halls erected in their parks or
enjoyed gay soirees like that honoring Princess Amelia in the Elysian Fields
at Stowe in 1770 described by Horace Walpole or that where the masque
"Alfred" was performed in the gardens of the prince of Wales at Cliveden in
1740 when the anthem "Rule Britannia" was first heard.[1] Nevertheless,
there was at least from the Elizabethan age a regular tradition of solitary
contemplation in the artificial nature of a garden. Occasionally an individual like Thomas Bushell at Enstone in Oxfordshire or Henry Hereford on
Backbury Hill[2] might even have tried to emulate a medieval hermit. By the
eighteenth century, however, to lead the life of a hermit was no longer a
serious religious pursuit, but a mode of theatrics.

In seventeenth- and eighteenth-century France the garden was always a
center for social intercourse, whether it was merely conversational walks or
elaborate theatrical performances and spectacles. The fete that the king's ill-
fated superintendent of finances, Nicolas Fouquet, offered his sovereign at
the completion of the magnificent chateau and gardens of Vaux-le-Vicomte
in May 1661 set the standard for the social enjoyment of a garden.[3] After
supper in the chateau the noble company led by the king and queen repaired
to the gardens where theatrical settings had been erected by Torelli at "the
lower level of the fir alley" and Molière's company performed a comedy, *Les
Fâcheux*, written by him especially for the occasion. The entertainment,
including ballet interludes, terminated with a splendid fireworks display.
The king could confiscate the chateau and gardens, but to diminish the
acclaim of Fouquet's celebration the king had to present an even more lavish
festival in the gardens of his chateau at Versailles. So for five days in August
1664 a series of spectacles, *Les plaisirs de l'île enchantée*, featuring ballet,

jousting, parades, and a Molière comedy accompanied by Lully's musicians, all based on the epic poem *Orlando furioso* of the Italian writer Ariosto, were presented at different locations in the gardens.[4] Four years later Cardinal Flavio Chigi, who had just been the papal legate to the court of King Louis XIV at Versailles, emulated the king with a musical drama and feast in the garden at his Villa alle Quattro Fontane in Rome organized by the architect Carlo Fontana.[5] It is, however, the eighteenth-century French poet Carmontelle who offered in detail the most charming reflection of the French attitude toward the garden and landscaped park in the introduction to his account in 1779 of the Parc Monceau at Paris designed in the English mode of naturalistic gardening for the duc de Chartres.[6] Carmontelle cites as the charms of the countryside in France the "pure air" and "liberty," but then claims that these are insufficient "without those [pleasures] of society." "One Frenchman is not self-contented by himself; he wishes to please, to love and be loved, these are his needs; he never disassociates his existence from that of others, . . . In spite of the charms that nature can offer, we must find there good cheer, hunting, games, concerts, spectacles, . . . In place of shunning one another in order to go dream, we seek one another for conversation; we are far from wishing to nourish melancholy; . . . One is busy pleasing women, they are the ones who make for the charm of society, so far from leaving them to themselves, as the English do, we only do what suits them." And the delightful engravings in his book depicting the Parc Monceau are peopled with couples and groups of elegantly dressed men and women strolling through the gardens.

In the Catholic countries of France and Italy contemplation and meditation were the functions of the church and the confessional, not the garden, whereas nonconformists like Mary Rich, countess of Warwick, or much later John Wesley would turn to gardens or wildernesses as their confessional where they personally sought their deity without the intervention of a priest in a Catholic or Anglican confessional. Richard Burton in *The Anatomy of Melancholy*, first published in 1621, identified a "religious melancholy" (pt. 3, sect. 4) as a subsection of "love melancholy."[7] The religious and social tensions of the late Tudor and early Stuart ages that culminated in civil war created a despondent spirit that characterizes Burton's treatise.

During the late sixteenth century English literature and art were dominated by melancholic heroes, so that melancholy has been dubbed the "Elizabethan malady." The Elizabethan melancholic poseur was often viewed as a fad out of Italy, where Renaissance physiology had promoted the nature of the four humors, with "black bile" the source of human melancholy. The fifteenth-century Florentine philosopher Marsilio Ficino had popularized the idea, supposedly of Aristotelian origin, of the melancholic man of genius governed by the planet Saturn, as was Ficino himself.[8] This melancholy, however, could taint the human personality as any disease might. Several medical treatises of the Elizabethan period, such as Timothy Bright's *A Treatise of Melancholie* (1586) or Richard Surphlet's translation of the French work of André du Laurens, *A Discourse of the Preservation of the Sight* (1599), preceded Richard Burton's mammoth compendium of the subject. These chroniclers of melancholy constantly note how those imbued with melancholy are alienated from society and seek solitary retreats. Du Laurens labels the melancholic "a sauadge creature, haunting the shadowed places, suspicious, solitarie," and Thomas Walkington in 1607 likens him to "heremits and olde anchors" who "liue in grots, Caues, and other hidden celles of the earthe," as later Thomas Bushell would do at Enstone or Dr. Harvey at Combe.[9]

Melancholy, however, not only dominated the Elizabethan and early Stuart periods of England, but came into equal prominence during the eighteenth century, when it was also known as the "spleen" and was noted as being a particularly "English malady," which was the title of a dissertation on the spleen in 1733 by the popular Dr. George Cheyne. The English climate, therefore, was often identified as the cause of the prevalence of the malady or condition which by then was recognized as much a psychological as a physiological disorder. Burton had already identified thick, cloudy, misty air like that of England as conducive to melancholy, but it would be foreigners conscious of the particular quality of the English climate who would repeatedly recognize it as one of the causes of the "English malady."[10] So Abbé Le Blanc in his letters describing England, first published in 1745, claims: "It is to the fogs with which their Island is nearly always covered that the English owe both the richness of their pastures and the melancholic spirit of their temperament." Similarly Goldsmith in two of his letters published in the *Public Ledger* in 1760 has his Chinese visitor to England credit the prevalence of the spleen or melancholy "to the influence of the weather" for there is "no country where the influence of climate and soil is more visible." It was the same climate that affected so severely the national temperament that promoted the green grass and verdure where those afflicted sought solace. Three centuries earlier Ficino had suggested that one of the palliatives for the distress of melancholy was the green of nature sought by "the haunting of gardens and groves and pleasant walks along rivers and through lovely meadows."[11] Just so, about 1590, Nicholas Hilliard painted a miniature portrait of the ninth earl of Northumberland, now in Amsterdam (fig. 1), clothed in the black garb and open shirt of the melancholic reclining in a

1. Nicholas Hilliard, *Portrait of Henry Percy, ninth earl of Northumberland*, Rijksmuseum, Amsterdam

4

hedge-enclosed garden retreat under the shade of a file of trees.[12] The treed grove in which the melancholic youth seeks relaxation may be the "wilderness" outside of the paradisical garden where those inspired to meditation found refuge, as will be considered later. Burton in his *Anatomy of Melancholy* advocates the same surcease, recommending that the melancholic should "walk amongst orchards, gardens, bowers, mounts, and arbours, artificial wildernesses, green thickets, arches, groves, lawns, rivulets, fountains, and such-like pleasant places" (pt. 2, sect. 2, mem. 4).

John Evelyn, who in his passion for gardening wished to form a society of "Hortulan saints," commissioned Robert Walker in 1648 to paint his portrait, now at Christ Church, Oxford, in a melancholic guise, his head supported in one hand as his other hand rests on a skull as a *memento mori*.[13] At the top of the portrait is a Greek motto which has been translated as "Second thoughts are the beginning of philosophy." Already five years earlier, Evelyn, living at his brother's estate at Wotton, related in his autobiography having built in the garden "a little study over a Cascade, to passe my Malencholy houres shaded there with Trees, & silent Enough."

By the mid-seventeenth century the poet Andrew Marvell in his poem *The Garden* claims that the green verdure of the garden purges all the anxieties and particulars of the material world.

> Annihilating all that's made
> To a green Thought in a green Shade.

So when the youthful duke of Gloucester died in 1700 his mother Princess Anne, later to be Queen Anne, could not face the trial of his funeral. It was reported that "the Princess continues at Windsor and is daily carried in her chair to the garden, to divert her melancholy thoughts."[14]

Robert Burton also claims in his *Anatomy* that melancholy inflicts its sufferer with an enhanced sense of time. In the late sixteenth and early seventeenth century the gradual perfection of the mechanical clock inevitably altered everyone's experience of time. The inexorable passing of time, the transience of the material world, the certainty of death were all marked by the relentless pace of the clock. Shakespeare's sonnets are dominated by "devouring" time and death as in sonnet XII.

> When I do count the clock that tells the time,
> And see the brave day sunk in hideous night;
> . . . .
> And nothing 'gainst Time's scythe can make defence
> Save breed, to brave him when he takes thee hence.

5

The sermons of Bishop Andrewes and especially those of John Donne dwelt on the theme of human mortality. In his life of the poet, Isaac Walton claims that Donne rose from his deathbed and clad in his "winding sheet" posed for a life-size image in death on which he gazed during his last moments and which served as a model for the tomb carved by Nicholas Stone for St. Paul's.[15] Even the Lord Mayor's shows at London in 1611 and 1616 featured tombs from which past mayors rose to join the triumph honoring the new leader.[16]

For the English the garden was the locale where harmony with nature and with God could be achieved.[17] So in 1714 the clergyman John Laurence (1668–1732) published a small treatise on gardening written specifically for his reverend colleagues which reached six editions in the next twelve years. In the preface he claims that gardening "has tended very much to the ease and quiet of my own Mind, and the Retirement I find therein, by Walking and Meditation, has help'd to set forward many useful Thoughts upon more divine Subjects." Soon Laurence added another short treatise to *The Clergy-Man's Recreation* directed to the gentry where he considered "that all the best and noblest Entertainments are to be met with in a Garden. There a Man may converse with his God, by contemplating his Works of wonder in each Flower and in every Plant: And then the devout Admirer cannot but lift his Eyes and his Heart in praise of the great Creator of all Things."

It will be some of these subjects in relation specifically to the garden that I wish to explore. The meaning of a work of art to its owner or to spectators, along with its function in their lives, offers the ultimate reason for its existence. This study is based very much on their original comments as I believe that contemporary accounts offer more perceptive observations than later paraphrases or speculations. In addition, the mode of expression and the words with which different commentators at different times expressed their ideas are important, I believe, for a full understanding of their beliefs. So in the discussion of the "wilderness" in chapter II the words Sir Francis Bacon used in his essay on gardens when compared with those of Timothy Nourse much later elucidate the relationship between the two accounts. Similarly the words William Harison chose to portray the ruins in his poem *Woodstock Park* stand out dramatically in his otherwise dull, classically oriented composition. The naive raptures of young Catharine Battie in her account of the tea party at Gilbert White's hermitage on The Hanger at Selborne conveys delightfully the rustic pleasures of a middle-class family and friends.

CHAPTER I

Transience

G ARDENS have always confronted men and women with their mortality, with the transience of life, but perhaps most particularly in early seventeenth-century England. John Melton in his *Astrologaster* of 1620, after lauding the pleasures of a visit to a friend's garden, cautions:

> But as I was seriously looking ouer this AEden of delight, my eyes tooke notice of a withered banke of flowers, hanging donne their weather-beaten heads, that not seuen dayes before had flourished in their full prime; intimating vnto Man, that the beautie of all Mundane and Earthly pleasures haue no perpetuitie. Not farre from them grew a sweet companie of fresh and redolent flowers, that like so many young Gallants, thought the brightness of their glory would neuer vanish, but that their beautie and colour was dyed in such a deepe graine of perpetuitie, that neyther the violence of a Storme, the pruning North-winds, nor the heat of the Mid-day Sunne, could beat downe, nippe, or wither them. And these fading and flourishing Plants were not onely the Emblemes of Man's mortalitie, but the true Type of his Death and Resurrection; of his Death, in their decay; of his Resurrection in their growth and flourishing.[1]

Even the practical botanist and gardener John Parkinson in the preface to his famous treatise, *Paradisi in Sole Paradisus Terrestris* (1629) warned that "the frailty also of Mans life is learned by the soone fading of [flowers] before their flowring, or in their pride, or soone after, being either cropt by the hand of the spectator, or by a sudden blast withered and parched, or by the reuolution of time decaying of its owne nature."[2]

7

More poignant is George Herbert's poem, *Life*, written shortly before his death in 1633.

> I made a posie while the day ran by,
> Here will I smell my remnant out, and tie
> My life within this band,
> But time did beckon to the flowers, and they
> By noon most cunningly did steal away
> And wither'd in my hand,
>
> My hand was next to them, and then my heart,
> I took, without more thinking, in good part
> Time's gentle admonition;
> Who did so sweetly death's sad taste convey,
> Making my minde to smell my fat all day,
> Yet sugring the suspicion,
>
> Farewell deare flowers! Sweetly your time ye spent,
> Fit, while ye liv'd, for smell or ornament,
> And after death for cures,
> I follow straight without complaints or grief,
> Since if my sent be good, I care not if
> It be as short as yours.[3]

THE SUNDIAL

THE SUNDIAL, which was often the chief ornament of gardens in the sixteenth and early seventeenth centuries, enhanced the association of transience with the garden. For early seventeenth-century emblem writers and poets the sundial was one of the most common images employed to assert the brevity of life and the mortality of men and women. In the popular emblem book of Francis Quarles the depiction of a garden sundial (Book III, emblem xiii; fig. 2) illustrates the text from Job (X, xx): "Are not my dayes few? Cease then and let me alone that I may bewaile myselfe a little." This is accompanied by Quarles' poetic commentary.

> Read on this diall, how the shades devoure
> My short-liv'd winters day; How'e eats up howre;
> Alas, the total's but from eight to foure.

2. Francis Quarles, *Emblemes*, 1635, III, emblem xiii

Behold these Lillies (which thy hands have made
Faire copies of my life, and open laid
to view) how soone they droop, how soone they fade.[4]

The garden sundial itself spoke of the transitoriness of life, for many dials, since at least the mid-sixteenth century, were inscribed with pithy epigrams. So a dial at Stanwardine Hall dated 1560 was inscribed:

In the hours of death God be merciful unto me
For as tyme doth haste
So life doth waste.[5]

9

A four-sided sundial at Manington Hall in Shropshire dated 1595 has as its principal motto:

> These shades do fleet
> From day to day:
> And so this life
> Passeth Awaie.

On each of the four sides of the dial is one of the following Latin epigrams.

> Deus Mihi Lux
> [God is my light]

> Finis Itineris sepulchrum
> [The sepulcher is the end of the journey]

> Fui es, eris ut sum
> [I was as you are, you will be as I am]

> Ut hora, sit vita
> [Life is as an hour]

The popularity of sundials as the major ornament of Tudor gardens, often standing at the center of crossed alleys in a small *hortus conclusus*, may have been promoted by the fondness Henry VIII held for them. Described in 1520 as "deviser of the King's horologies," a Bavarian mathematician Nicholas Kratzer was at Corpus Christi College at Oxford in 1523 presumably to lecture on astronomy.[6] In honor of his appointment, Kratzer, whose portrait now in the Louvre was painted by Holbein in 1528, designed an elaborate sundial to ornament the orchard or garden of his college at Oxford and left a manuscript, still in the college library, on the manner of devising sundials. His sundial, which was extant about 1668 but is now lost, was depicted (fig. 3) and described about 1625 by a later Fellow of the college, Robert Hegge, in his manuscript, "A Treatise of Dials and Dialling," also in the college library. Hegge notes that the dial was provided with twelve gnomons to determine the time on several dials, including an "Aequinoctial" dial, a polar one, a "Convex dial elevated in triumph vpon 4 iron arches," and a concave dial.

Sundials had been the major device for measuring time since antiquity, but the invention of the mechanical clock in the late thirteenth century and its gradual perfection over the centuries transformed the human conception of time.[7] The mechanical composition of the clock imposed a rigid regularity on the intervals of time which it measured whether they were days,

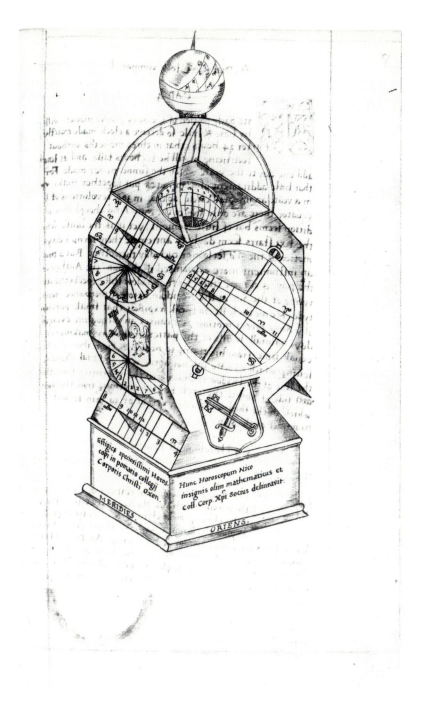

Effigies speciosissimi Horos
copi in pomario collegij
Corporis Christi Oxon.

Hunc Horoscopum Nico
insignis olim mathematicus et
coll. Corp. Xpi socius delineavit.

MERIDIES.

ORIENS.

3. Oxford, Corpus Christi College, sundial, drawing, MS 430, Corpus Christi
College Library, Oxford

hours, or minutes, contrary to the human experience of the passage of days and nights of uneven duration related to seasonal change. The sundial on the other hand directly reflected the variety of nature. Its time responded to the birth, maturation, and cessation of the light of the sun as the nature of the garden did. Over time clockmakers and scientists devoted their attention to attempting to perfect the precision of the clock which constantly had to be corrected against the sundial. At the same time mathematicians were devising formulas required to fashion a correct sundial in a variety of forms—concave, convex, or flat dials, horizontal, vertical, or declinate dials, or at a variety of geographical locations—for almost every sundial was uniquely governed by its form and position. To challenge the author of a sundial, the dials could reflect different systems of time measurement. Babylonian hours consisted of a day twenty-four hours in length beginning at sunrise; Jewish hours with two periods of twelve hours relative in length to the season of the year; or Italian hours with twenty-four equal hours commencing at sunset. As sundials developed during the sixteenth and seventeenth centuries they taxed the ingenuity of mathematicians to devise more intricate ones, as if they were mathematical games, for many of their intricacies were of no practical use. Meanwhile, as the mechanical time of the clock was gradually perfected it served as midwife to the new world of science, eventually reducing the sundial to a playful ornament of the garden, for even the churchyard sundial was replaced by the church clock tower.

Accounts commencing in 1533 record the creation for Henry VIII of a large, new Privy Garden at Hampton Court Palace which he had obtained from Cardinal Wolsey in 1528.[8] In June 1534 a Westminster "clokemaker," Brise Augustyn, was paid for making twenty bronze sundials for the king's new garden at the rate of four shillings fourpence a dial. The accounts and depictions of the garden reveal that the individual flower beds in the garden were enclosed by wooden railings painted the Tudor colors, green and white, and supporting gaily painted, carved heraldic beasts. Each of the twenty sundials may then have been set as a centerpiece in a flower bed or at the crossing of the alleys. Earlier, in 1530, another Westminster clockmaker, Anthony Transylyon, had furnished seven dials at the same price for the new Privy Orchard on the other side of the palace. The large quantity of dials furnished for Henry's gardens may suggest that their utilitarian function was less important than their decorative value in presiding over the heraldic ambience of his gardens.

Perhaps the most notable sundial in the history of English gardening was that erected in the Privy Garden of the royal Whitehall Palace at London.[9]

The so-called Great Garden at Whitehall, later known as the Privy Garden, was created for Henry VIII before 1545, but the earliest description of the garden was written by the German visitor Von Wedel, who recorded in 1584: "In the middle of the garden is a nice fountain with a remarkable sundial, showing the time in thirty different ways." This dial had replaced an earlier one, for in 1581–82 the surveyor Robert Adams and an instrument maker Humphrey Cole were paid for "new making the Dial in the Great Garden" at Whitehall. The earlier dial may have been designed by Henry VIII's astronomer Kratzer. A later German visitor, Paul Hentzner, reported that the sundial incorporated one of the trick waterworks so popular in the late sixteenth century, for it was a *"jet d'eau,* with a sun dial, which while strangers are looking at, a quantity of water, forced by a wheel, which the gardener turns at a distance, through a number of little pipes, plentifully sprinkles those that are standing round." The addition of the deceitful watertrick to the sundial cast a playful aura over what had been a utilitarian instrument.

In the early seventeenth century the records of the eminent scuptormason Nicholas Stone list numerous commissions for the carving of pillars for sundials.[10] Probably the earliest example was for a dial at St. James's Palace in London for James I for which Stone received almost seven pounds, the crown supplying the stone. Among other commissions was a sundial to accompany the statues of an old gardener and his wife for the garden of Sir John Danvers at Chelsea, London, from about 1623, for which Stone received seven pounds. Later the historian John Aubrey in his book on the natural history of Wiltshire identified the Danvers garden as the first Italianate garden in England, but the sundial suggests a persistence of the Tudor tradition. Among Stone's sundials was another replacement for the Tudor sundial in the Privy Garden at Whitehall Palace for which he claimed in his notebook that he received forty-six pounds in 1622. In 1624 Edmund Gunter, professor of astronomy at Gresham College, who had designed this dial, published a description of the sundial at the command of Charles, the prince of Wales, dedicated to his father, James I.[11] After Charles succeeded to the throne it was asserted that "His Majesty delighted much in the great concave dial at Whitehall." Gunter claims that the stone pillar fashioned by Stone was identical to the Tudor one except that it was carved from a single block of Purbeck stone rather than being composed of several pieces of Caen stone as was the older version. Weighing about five tons, the base was more than four and a half feet square and three and a quarter feet high. On the upper part were five dials, one on each of the four corners and the "great Horizontall Concaue" dial, some forty inches in diameter and twenty inches deep in the center. Numerous other dials—plane, concave, and cylindrical—were on the four sides of the block. Latin verses offered instruction on the use of the various dials based on the different colored lines inscribed on them.

A type of sundial that expressed the unmistakable transience of existence was the floral or horticultural sundial which was popular in the seventeenth century. English gardeners planted flowers and shrubs in the semblance of sundials, which, of course, are preserved only in occasional prints or literary accounts. Several of the colleges of Cambridge and Oxford, being traditional institutions often retaining old fashioned topiary work in their gardens, had such floral or boxwood sundials as ornament. David Loggan's engraved views of the colleges in his *Oxonia Illustrata* (1675) and *Cantabrigia Illustrata* (c. 1690) illustrate several horticultural dials. New College, Oxford, had four elaborate parterres of topiary work below the mount in its principal garden. One bed was cut in the form of the royal arms, another had the college arms, a third the founder's arms, and lastly a "*Dial* cut in *Box*" as Plot describes it in his book on the natural history of Oxfordshire.[12] The engraving in Williams' *Oxonia Depicta* of the 1730s indicates that the figural parterres were still maintained at that late date. Thomas Baskerville's account of the New College garden identifies the four displays and adds that on top of the mount was "a diall resembling a bundle of Books." At Cambridge in June 1689 the Bostonian Samuel Sewall recorded in his diary having seen at Queen's College "in the Garden a Dial on the Ground, Hours cut in Box" and at Pembroke College one in the Master's Garden. In 1672 William Hughes described in detail in an edition of his *Flower Garden* how such floral sundials may be made using rosemary, hyssop, thyme, or box.[13] Occasionally in the early eighteenth century some conservative private gardens might have continued the tradition of the horticultural sundial. In 1710 the German tourist Von Uffenbach recorded that a wealthy flax-merchant Cox had in his gardens at Epsom not only topiary of "beasts, men, ships," but also a "parterre of box, forming a sun-dial."[14]

The loveliest celebration of a floral sundial is the last stanza of Andrew Marvell's poem *The Garden*, from the middle of the seventeenth century, where he equates the passing of time with the nature of flowers and bees.

> How well the skilful gardener drew
> Of flowers and herbs this dial new!
> Where, from above, the milder sun
> Does through a fragrant zodiac run:

And, as it works, the industrious bee
Computes its time as well as we.
How could such sweet and wholesome hours
Be reckoned, but with herbs and flowers!

The royal accounts frequently list payments for refashioning the king's sundial in the Privy Garden at Whitehall which had been restored by Edmund Gunter and Nicholas Stone. In March 1666 the mathematician William Marre was paid two hundred pounds for "making the dial in the King's privy Garden at Whitehall" and again in 1688 Marre requested two hundred and fifty pounds in payment for "new lineating the Dyall in the Privy Garden," but was paid only one hundred and fifty pounds.[15] Such work would presumably have entailed only the redelineation of the dials.

The most dramatic step in perfecting the precision of the mechanical clock developed about 1656 when Christiaan Huygens adapted the pendulum to regulate the movement of clocks. Charles II, who was a keen patron of scientific endeavors, resolved, however, to have in the Privy Garden at Whitehall a new, even more intricate sundial. An elderly Jesuit mathematician, Father Francis Line, also known as Father Hall, was commissioned in 1669 to devise the new sundial.[16] Father Line had created dials at the College of the English Jesuits at Liege, which were known to Charles II during his earlier exile on the continent. The instrument having been completed in July 1669, Father Line published in 1673 a detailed description of it, occasioned in part by the damage caused to it by a severe winter, since, as he noted, its cover ordered by the king had never been made (fig. 4). A pyramid about ten feet tall surmounted by an orb and cross was formed by six so-called "tables" of diminishing diameter supported by a stone pedestal four feet in height. More than two hundred and fifty dials were attached to the several "tables," the lowest of which about forty inches in diameter had twenty vertical declining dials covered with glass giving "the hours according to the Jewish, Babylonian, Italian and astronomical ways of reckoning." Each gnomon was either a lion's paw or a unicorn's horn in the tradition of British heraldry. An upper level contained portraits on glass of the king, queen, queen mother, duke of York, and Prince Rupert. There was even a device by which a blind person could divine the time by the sun burning his hand. The description of the garden dial with royal symbols and portraits suggests that it retained the same heraldic significance associated with the Tudor sundials. The royal instrument would now help, however, to enunciate the king's interest in and support of scientific endeavors. So Father Line himself claims his goal was "of adorn-

15

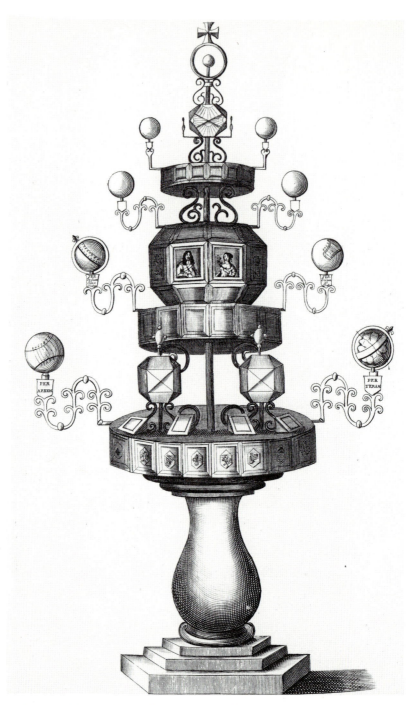

4. London, Whitehall Palace, Privy Garden, sundial

ing his Majesty's Garden with some curiosity that might in this kind surpasse what might elsewhere be found."

Although natural elements endangered the fragile device, courtiers were even more destructive. On June 16, 1676, one George Scott wrote to Edinburgh: "My Lord Rochester in a frolick after a rant did yesterday beat doune the dyill which stood in the middle of the Privie [—]ing, which was esteemed the rarest in Europ. I doe not know if upon that accompt he will be found impertinent, or if it is by the fall beat in peeces."[17] Later John Aubrey furnished more details, although under the wrong date, in his life of Father Line.

> He printed a discourse of dialling in quarto, Latin, and made the Jesuits College there the finest dialls in the world, which are described in that book. The like dialls he made (which resemble something candlesticks) in the garden at Whitehall, which were one night, *anno Dni.* 1674, as I take it, broken all to pieces (for they were of glass spheres) by the earl of Rochester, lord Buckhurst, Fleetwood Shephard, etc., comeing in from their revells. "What!" said the earl of Rochester, "dost thou stand heer to . . . time?" Dash they fell to worke. Ther was a watchman alwayes stood there to secure it.

Understandably the following autumn and winter were spent by Rochester in exile in Oxfordshire far from the king and court.

Andrew Marvell soon referred to the incident in the third stanza of his poem *The Statue at Charing Cross.*

> For a Diall the place is too insecure
> Since the privy garden could not it defend,
> And soe near to the Court they will never indure
> Any monument how their time they mispend.[18]

If Aubrey's quotation of Rochester's comment is accurate, the earl was concerned by the expression of the transience of time suggested by the sundial and at least subconsciously may have been disturbed by its commentary on his own mortality.

Epigrams on sundials during the second half of the seventeenth century constantly reminded their readers of the inevitability of death. A dial of Sir Francis Howard at Corby Castle dated 1658 bears reliefs illustrating the emblems of the Passion of Christ and the epigram:

> Deathe, judgment / heaven, hell /
> Upon this / moment depens / eternitie
> O Eternitie / o eternitie / o eternitie[19]

Chapter I

A dial of 1660 at Brougham Hall in Westmoreland cautions: "O wretched man remember thou must die. Sence all things passe and nothinge certain be," and also bears the Latin motto "*Ut hora sic vita*" [Life is as an hour], which is probably the most frequently encountered sundial inscription. A garden sundial at Penrhos in Wales dated 1683 notes in bad Latin:

> *Here mi, nescis hora*
> *Morieris, si quaeris, qua*
> [My master, thou knowest not, if thou askest, the hour
> in which thou shalt die]

Much later, in 1799, Philip Yorke recollected seeing in the "old gardens at Llanerch" in Wales "a sun-dial, which as you approached spouted water in your face"; on it was written:

> Alas! my friend, time soon will o'ertake you
> And if you do not cry, by G—d I'll make you!

The association of a garden sundial with the mortality of its owner was made explicit at the death of Sir William Temple in 1699 when his will instructed that his heart should be buried "six feet underground on the south-east side of the stone dial in the little garden at Moor Park."[20] The consequences of this action for Temple's reputation will be discussed later.

In the late eighteenth century, Edward Young, author of *Night Thoughts*, had in his garden at Welwyn a sundial admonishing the spectator of the swift passage of time. Boswell reports a diverting incident that Young himself related regarding his sundial.

> An instance at once of [Young's] pensive turn of mind and his cheerfulness of temper, appeared in a little story which he himself told to Mr. Langton, when they were walking in his garden: "Here (said he) I had put a handsome sun-dial, with this inscription, *Eheu fugaces!* which (speaking with a smile) was sadly verified, for by the next morning my dial had been carried off."[21]

These sundials were architectural forms, usually consisting of flat, bronze or stone, inscribed dials supported by columns, possibly twisted columns as at Corby, or stone pillars inscribed with dials. From the late seventeenth century on there would seem to have been less interest in the mathematical intricacies of the dials and more concern for the richness of the supports. A large sundial near the palace at Hampton Court from the time of William and Mary (c. 1689–94) illustrates this (fig. 5). The simple

5. Hampton Court (Middlesex), sundial

bronze dial plate is borne on a bulbous pedestal with a simple foliate capital and is engraved with the monogram of William and Mary.

John Worlidge in his horticultural treatise of 1677 decried the passion during the Restoration for statuary as garden ornament and preferred sundials:

Many Dials of various and curious workmanship are made and may be placed on Pedestals in the midst of the squares instead of Statues, which better become the shades.

Dials of Glass, were it not for the casualties they are subject unto, pre-excel any other for Beauty, especially the Globe with its Axis through the midst and duely elevated with small beads on it, placed at their due distance according to the lines of the Celestial Globe, painted on the superficies of your orbicular Glass, which will not only give you the true hour of the day, but all other variations that a Dial can direct.[22]

At least by the time of the Commonwealth, sculptural, figural supports for sundials began to appear. Joseph Moxon, later a member of the Royal Society, illustrated in his treatise on astronomy first published in 1659 a glass-globe sundial, such as Worlidge preferred, that Robert Titchborn, Lord Mayor of London in 1657, had in his garden supported by a figure of Atlas (fig. 6).[23] The ultimate source of the figure was probably the ancient Roman marble statue of a kneeling Atlas bearing on his shoulders a globe inscribed with the zodiac, formerly in the Farnese collection in Rome and now in the National Archaeological Museum in Naples. The Roman piece was not an actual sundial, but may have served as a garden fountain decoration. There had indeed been an earlier garden decoration of an Atlas shouldering a globe at Wadham College in Oxford. In 1650 the famous Dr. Wilkins, Warden of Wadham College and leading spirit in the founding of the Royal Society, had begun to lay out the Warden's garden, which had on top of the mount in the center of the garden, a large standing figure of Atlas supporting a globe, as depicted in Loggan's view of 1675. The statue remained until it was blown down and smashed in 1753. Contemporary accounts, however, never mention a sundial associated with the statue.

The importation from the Lowlands of the technique of lead-cast figures to decorate a garden encouraged figural sundials. John van Nost the Elder (d. 1729), who emigrated to England from Malines, had at the turn of the century a very popular workshop for the production of such lead garden statuary.[24] In 1701, Van Nost shipped to Hampton Court Palace two sundials, one supported by a kneeling youthful blackamoor, five foot high, costing thirty pounds, and the other by a kneeling Indian slave. The 1725 Inventory of Cannons in Middlesex records also "In the North Wilderness a Negro Slave kneeling on one Knee and bearing a Sun Dyall on his head wch: He supports wth: both hands." Such figures, of course, made no allusion to the transience of time and, therefore, could be used in situations other than as supports for sundials. Such figures had geographical rather than temporal allusions, thus expressing the universality of the sun and associating the garden and its plants with the wonders of the new worlds

6. London, Titchborn garden, sundial

explored by the plant collectors. In fact, contemporary with the Hampton Court sundials, Van Nost supplied Thomas Coke with numerous lead statues for his garden at Melbourne in Derbyshire, including kneeling figures of "an Indian and a blackmore," each supporting on his head a tray bearing an elaborate urn. The two pieces of sculpture still stand at Melbourne in the center of the grassed parterres below the house. Celia Fiennes on one of her tours between 1701 and 1703 mentions at Fetcham Park in Surrey "a brass figure of a Black Moore large very natural with a great dish on his head like a shield." Although she does not specify that the figure is kneeling and is perhaps in error about its material, mistaking painted lead for bronze, the statue was probably another of Van Nost's. A sundial with a lead blackamoor holding a brass dial at Dunham Massey in Cheshire may be by Andries Carpentière (fig. 7); another example is at Norton Conyers in Yorkshire.

About 1739 the young sculptor John Cheere bought the Van Nost yard with its moulds for lead statues. A much later account of his workshop claims that the figure "of an African, kneeling with a sundial on his head found the most extensive sale." In 1741 Cheere supplied a "blackmore" sundial for Okeover Hall, Staffordshire, probably from Van Nost's mould. Others, still extant, were probably supplied for Enfield Old Park, Middlesex; Guy's Cliff, Warwickshire; Hampton Court, Herefordshire; and West Green in Hampshire. A late example, inscribed on its dial with the date 1781, stood originally in the garden of Clement's Inn in London, but is now in the gardens of the Inner Temple.

A copy of the kneeling Indian figure seen at Melbourne Hall, but designed to bear a sundial like the blackamoor figures, probably was created by Van Nost the Elder for the gardens at Arley Hall in Cheshire.

Although the blackamoor and Indian sundials make no reference to time and its transience, other eighteenth-century dials did. A limestone sundial about five feet high carved by Caius Cibber is at Belton House in Lincolnshire, its bronze dial inscribed with the name Thomas Wright, "Instrument maker of his Royal Highness Prince of Wales, 1725."[25] The pedestal of the dial is supported on the knee of a winged Father Time sitting on a globe, who with an assisting, winged putto closely embraces the pedestal (fig. 8). With the inclusion of the globe both geographical and temporal aspects are expressed. On the terrace of Duncombe Park in Yorkshire on the central axis of the terrace in front of the house is a stone-pedestal sundial behind which stands a life-size image of a winged Father Time leaning over and watching the dial (fig. 9), which is inscribed *Non Tardius Appereor* [I tarry not for the slow].[26] The Rotunda at one end of the terrace has been ascribed to the architect Sir John Vanbrugh, because of its resemblance to his rotunda at Stowe, and the sundial possibly to Van Nost.

There are at least three examples of kneeling figures supporting sundials on their heads in which the blackamoor or Indian have been transformed into depictions of a winged Father Time. One by John Cheere is at Blair Atholl in Scotland, another by an unknown sculptor is at St. Paul's Walden Bury in Hertfordshire (fig. 10), and a third, which came on the art market,

7. Dunham Massey (Cheshire), sundial

8. Belton House
(Lincs), sundial

9. Duncombe Park
(Yorks), sundial

10. St. Paul's Walden Bury (Herts), sundial

is from the old Fonthill House in Wiltshire and is attributed to John Cheere from the middle of the century.[27]

By 1732 when Gilbert West published his poem honoring the extensive gardens of Lord Cobham at Stowe, he identified there the so-called Sun-Dial Parlour, a small circular area described more fully in an anonymous account of 1738:

> The entrance into the Sunn Dial Parlour, so calld from a Sun Dial in the middle of it; it is nothing more than [a] round Plot of about 54 feet in Diameter, encompassd with an Evergreen hedge cut into usual forms. Though this place enjoys the Title of the Sun Dial Parlour I

25

apprehend (from the Closeness of it, being so encircled with Plantations) that the Planet it is dedicated to seldom makes a longer Visit, than just peeping in at the Door.

Having taken Leave of it (which considering Phoebus seldom gives you leave to correct your Watch by his Interpreter here).[28]

A stone-pedestal sundial, behind which a statue of Father Time stands grasping the dial in his hands (fig. 11), somewhat like the sundial at Duncombe Park, is now at Anglesey Abbey in Cambridgeshire where it was moved from Stowe.

The poet William Shenstone, however, was somewhat disdainful of having sundials at his garden park of The Leasowes, writing his friend Graves in 1755:

> As to Sun-Dials, I never much affected the Things themselves, nor indeed any Mottos with which I have seen them inscribed. . . . However, I have often had Thoughts of placing a slight one somewhere upon my Premises, for the Sake of inscribing it with a couple of Lines from Virgil: Sed fugit interea fugit, irreparabile tempus. Singula dum capti circumvectamur amore.[29] [But time meanwhile is flying, flying beyond recall, while we, charmed with love of our theme, linger around each detail. Vergil, *Georgics*, III, 284–85]

During the seventeenth century the utilitarian value of the sundial diminished with the increasing popularity of clocks and watches, although it was noted that Charles II would stop in the Whitehall Privy Garden to check or set his watch by the sundial.[30] The anonymous account of Stowe in 1738 quoted above also mentions the habit of checking a watch against a sundial, a practice that survived into the nineteenth century. By the eighteenth century the primary purpose of sundials was to serve as garden ornaments, giving focus to a part of the garden or to the center of a small plot. The ornamental character of the garden sundial undoubtedly promoted the reliance on figural supports.

RUINS

AT THE SAME TIME the popularity of another garden ornament, a ruin or an artificial ruin, also enhanced the association of the garden with the element of transience.[31] Sundials, of a relatively modest scale, were suitable to small, formal gardens, whereas the architectural form of ruins

11. Anglesey Abbey (Cambridge), sundial

was of a scale more appropriate to the vast garden parks of the eighteenth century. The most astute critic of eighteenth-century gardening, Thomas Whately, dedicated a section of his book on gardening of 1770 to ruins, in which he characterized the associative value of ruins as well as their formal, aesthetic qualities.

All remains excite an inquiry into the former state of the edifice, and fix the mind in a contemplation on the use it was applied to; besides the characters expressed by their style and position, they suggest ideas which would not arise from the buildings, if entire. . . . Whatever building we see in decay, we naturally contrast its present to its former state, and delight to ruminate on the comparison. It is true that such effects properly belong to real ruins; but they are produced in a certain degree by those which are fictitious; the impressions are not so strong, but they are exactly similar; and the representation, though it does not present acts to the memory, yet suggests subjects to the imagination.[32]

Whately then called attention to those elements and qualities that may ensure the credibility of artificial ruins, and later recalled the series of associations a ruin may provoke.

At the sight of a ruin, reflections on change, the decay, and the desolation before us, naturally occur; and they introduce a long succession of others, all tinctured with that melancholy which these have inspired: or if the monument revive the memory of former times, we do not stop at the simple fact which it records, but recollect many more coaeval circumstances, which we see, not perhaps as they were, but as they are come down to us, venerable with age, and magnified by fame.[33]

British ruins, especially those of monasteries, had been of great interest to antiquarians at least since John Leland's tour of the island about 1535–43. The great ruins of Stonehenge and Avebury aroused questions regarding their origin and meaning in visitors such as King James I, questions the architect Inigo Jones or later the antiquarian John Aubrey would attempt to answer. Antiquarian accounts, however, were basically descriptive, arousing no associations. Bishop Joseph Hall in his *Occasional Meditations* of 1633, which also included a meditation on a sundial, featured one "Upon the Ruins of an Abbey" in which he viewed the dismal remains of the religious structure as a moral and religious warning regarding its former Roman Catholic inhabitants.[34] Anthony à Wood reveals an exceptional awareness in the seventeenth century of the transience evoked by ruins when he recorded his visit to the abbey at Eynsham in 1657, claiming that he "was there wonderfully stricken with a veneration of the stately, yet much lamented, ruins of the abbey there, built before the Norman Conquest. . . . He spent some time with a melancholy delight in taking a prospect of the ruins of that place. . . . The place hath yet some ruins to show and to instruct the pensive beholder with an exemplary frailty."[35] Even a poet such as John Dryden, who introduced a ruin, that of the Barbican in London, into his poem *Mac Flecknoe* of 1682, offers an image that is reserved and noncommittal, simply a setting for contemporary life.[36]

A more evocative image of an actual ruin appears in the poem *Woodstock Park* of 1706 by the Oxford scholar William Harison. The poem is to honor the great military hero, the duke of Marlborough, who had been given the royal manor of Woodstock in Oxfordshire a year previously as the site for the huge, new Blenheim Palace designed by Sir John Vanbrugh. Woodstock was the location where the romance of King Henry II and the "fair" Rosamond had transpired. Much of Harison's poem applauds the duke in rather trite classic terms, addressing the duke and duchess as "the God of War, and beauteous Queen of Love," but the story of Rosamond and the description of the ruins of the manor of Woodstock are rather pictorial.

> Did not the Maid, whose wond'rous Beauty seen,
> Inflamed great *Henry*, and incens'd his Queen,
> With pleasing Sorrow move me to survey
> A Neighb'ring Structure, awful in Decay,
> For ever sacred, and in ruin blest,
> Which heretofore contain'd that lovely Guest.
> Admiring Strangers, who attentive come
> To learn the Tale of this romantick Dome,
> By faithful Monuments instructed, view
> (Tho' Time should spare) what Civil Rage can do.
> Where Landskips once, in rich Apartment high,
> Through various Prospects led the wand'ring Eye:
> . . . .
>   Now Hemlock thrives, and Weeds of pow'rful Charms
> O'er ragged Walls extend their baleful Arms,
> Monsters obscene their pois'nous Roots invade,
> And bloated pant beneath the gloomy Shade,
>   Thus noblest Buildings are with ease effac'd,
> And what's well wrote alone, will always last.
>   Ev'n *Vanbrook*'s Fame, that does so brightly shine
> In Rules exact, and Greatness of Design,
> Would fall a Victim to devouring Age,
> Had not that Hand, which built, adorn'd the Stage.[37]

Inspired perhaps by Harison's poem, the architect and playwright Sir John Vanbrugh was the first to express clearly the eighteenth-century concern for both the associative and aesthetic qualities of a ruin in his tragic argument with the duchess of Marlborough over the remains of the medieval manor of Woodstock on the grounds of the new Blenheim Palace he was designing to celebrate the duke's victory at Blenheim. The ruins of the royal manor stood on the far bank of the chasm in front of the new palace and had been ordered razed by the duchess. In a letter of June 11, 1709 from Vanbrugh to the duchess he makes a last-minute plea to her, which would be in vain, to allow some of the historic ruins to remain and outlines his reasons.

> There is perhaps no one thing, which the most Polite part of Mankind have more universally agreed in; than the Vallue they have ever set upon the Remains of distant Times. Nor amongst the Severall kinds of those Antiquitys, are there any so much regarded, as those of Buildings; More for their Magnificence, or Curious Workmanship; And others; as they move more lively and pleasing Reflections (than History without their Aid can do) On the Persons who have Inhabited them; On the Remarkable things which have been transacted in them, Or the extraordinary Occasions of Erecting them.[38]

After presenting his historical, associative reasons for the retention of the remains, Vanbrugh offers an aesthetic, picturesque reason, thus encompassing both the values that the eighteenth century identified with ruins.

> But if the Historicall Argument Stands in need of Assistance; there is Still much to be said on Other Considerations.
>
> That Part of the Park in which is Seen from the North Front of the New Building, has Little Variety of Objects Nor does the Country beyond it Afford any of Vallue, It therefore Stands in Need of all the helps that can be given, which are only Five; Buildings, And Plantations. These rightly dispos'd will indeed Supply all the wants of Nature in that Place. And the most Agreable Dispositions is to Mix them: in which this Old Manour gives so happy an *Occasion* for; that were the inclosure filld with Trees (principally Fine Yews and Hollys) Promiscuously Set to grow up in a Wild Thicket. So that all the Building left, (which is only the Habitable Part and the Chapel) might Appear in Two Risings amongst 'em, it wou'd make One of the Most Agreable Objects that the best of Landskip Painters can invent.

The negative response of the duchess was the normal English reaction of the time. Vanbrugh's appreciation of the picturesque quality of the ruins of Woodstock was a premature anticipation of the later fervor for ruins.

An acquaintance of Vanbrugh, the politician John Aislabie, who was involved in the disastrous failure of the South Sea Company in 1720,

16. Hagley (Worcester), Gothic Ruin

Even the furnishings of the tearoom at the top of the tower were to be designed by Miller in the Gothic style.[57]

Miller's fame as a designer of Gothic ruins was apparent as noted by a letter of January 1749 of Lord Dacre to Miller: "You have got everlasting fame by this castle at Hagley, so that I hear talk of nothing else." Despite the slights of Shenstone and Lady Luxborough, the ultimate praise of Miller's ruin came from the difficult garden critic Horace Walpole, who uttered the most eloquent associative comment on it in a letter to Richard Bentley in 1753: "There is a ruined castle, built by Miller, that would get him his freedom even of Strawberry: it has the true rust of the Barons' Wars."[58] Later, in 1777, Joseph Heely was even more brutally pictorial in his associations.

> I make no doubt that an antiquarian like my friend, would sigh to know in what area it was founded, and by whom:—what sieges it had sustained;—what blood had been spilt upon its walls:—and would lament that hostile discord, or the iron hand of all-mouldering time, should so rapaciously destroy it.

The fame of the ruin at Hagley immediately motivated the Lord Chancellor, the first earl of Hardwicke, to have a similar folly built at his estate of Wimpole in Cambridgeshire.[59] So in 1749 George Lyttelton informed Sanderson Miller that Hardwicke had requested the plan of the Hagley ruin, but Lyttelton had deftly persuaded Hardwicke to consider another design by Miller.

> My Lord Chancellor [Hardwicke] told me in a conversation that I had with him lately that he wanted to see the plan of my castle, having a mind to build one at Wimple himself. Upon further inquiry I found it would be better for him not to copy mine, but have one upon something like the same idea, but differing in many respects, particularly in this, that he wants no house nor even room in it but mearly the walls and semblance of an old castle to make an object from his house. At most he only desires to have a staircase carried up one of the towers, and a leaded gallery half round it to stand on and view the prospect. It will have a fine wood of firrs for a backing behind it and will stand on an eminence at a proper distance from his house. . . . With regard to the dimensions of my Ld. Chancellor's castle, you are not confined, but may make it of just what height and breadth you think fitt. He desired me to make his compliments to you, and to say

he would take it as a great favour if you would sketch it for him as soon as you conveniently can.

Miller's response was prompt, for a few days later Lyttelton wrote Miller with more particulars.

> It is a hill about half a mile from the house to which the ground rises gently all the way. My Ld. agrees to your notion of having some firrs before part of the walls. As the back view will be immediately closed by the wood there is no regard to be had of it, nor to the left side, but only to the front and the right side as you look from the house. As my Lord designs it mearly as an object he would have no staircase nor leads many of the towers, but mearly the walls built as to have the appearance of a ruined castle. For materials he has freestone, or a mixture of flint pebbles and other stone, of which an old church in the parish is built, and also bricks in his neighborhood.

Miller prepared some drawings of distant views of a ruined tower, but for some reason, perhaps parsimony, for the Chancellor was renowned for frugality, Hardwicke did not pursue the project, informing Miller in March 1750 that "the building of this castle requires no great haste."

The second earl of Hardwicke, who succeeded in 1764, called on the popular landscapist Capability Brown in 1767 to "improve" Wimpole, including incorporating into the grounds Johnson's Hill which was the location planned for Miller's ruin. By April 1768 the steward at Wimpole wrote the Cambridge architect James Essex to inquire as to the progress on the Tower he had agreed to begin that month on Johnson's Hill, for Essex apparently had been commissioned to carry out the earlier project for a ruined castle on the hill. This ruined folly now stands at Wimpole, although with some minor changes (fig. 17). Built of limestone cramped to brick, the central portion of the structure is a four-story, round tower from which proceed at right angles two ruined walls, two feet thick, each ending in the remains of a tower. The walls and tower contain ruined Gothic windows and portals. The tall central tower, with crosslet loopholes, is raised high above the other remains to serve as an eyecatcher visible from the house about a half mile away. Although the original folly was not to contain any rooms, when Humphry Repton prepared one of his Red Books in 1801 illustrating further improvement in the landscaping, he recommended that the ruin be made more useful "by adding floors in the Tower . . . to form a Keeper's lodge," which was done.

17. Wimpole (Cambridge), Gothic Ruin

From about 1743 on, the poet William Shenstone transformed his modest farm, The Leasowes in Shropshire, a neighbor to the great Lyttelton estate of Hagley, into an ornamental park or farm, a *ferme ornée* as he described it.[60] With only modest means to improve his farm Shenstone constantly complained to his friend Lady Luxborough, as seen previously, that his ideas were being realized by the Lytteltons because of their greater wealth. Over the years Shenstone cut a circuitous walk around the periphery of his farm, along which he erected homely roothouses or benches and urns, from which particularly fine vistas could be enjoyed. In 1754 one of Shenstone's inexpensive structures was destroyed and he wrote Lady Luxborough on July 17: "Let me tell you, my little Pavilion in ye water is no more! I yesterday enjoy'd it in Ruins, but my Pleasure was mix'd with melancholy: as the case would be, were I to survey ye noblest Ruins upon earth." He wrote similarly in his essay "Unconnected Thoughts on Gardening":

> There seem however to be some objects, which afford a pleasure not
> reducible to either of the foregoing heads. A ruin, for instance, may

44

be neither new to us, nor majestic, nor beautiful, yet afford that pleasing melancholy which proceeds from a reflection on decayed magnificence.[61]

In 1757 Shenstone erected a ruined Gothic priory, utilizing stones from the nearby medieval abbey of Halesowen, some of whose window frames had already been incorporated into the Lyttelton's ruined castle at Hagley. Like the Hagley ruin, Shenstone's priory had a usable interior with appropriate, though modest, furnishings, as described in a contemporary account.

A pleasing Deception. It appears a Ruin of a Chapel built some hundred Years ago, whereas it has not yet been built two years.—It is reared in the Gothic taste, & notwithstanding the outward Face, has some comfortable Rooms in the Heart of it, particularly a Gothic Parlor, with antique Paper, finished in a most happy Taste. This Building is not merely ornamental, for the habitable part is let to an old Man & an old woman for the yearly rent of 4£.[62]

Along with Sanderson Miller, another leading exponent of the Gothic style of architecture in the mid-eighteenth century was the mathematician-astronomer-architect Thomas Wright.[63] Some rather unusual ruins at Shugborough in Staffordshire from about 1748–50 have been attributed to Wright. Behind the mansion on the bank of the small river or stream, the Sow, are the remnants of a built ruin which was originally much larger and included a Gothic pigeoncote, now gone (fig. 18). The ruin comprised fragments from the earlier seventeenth-century house left from the addition by Wright of bow windows, some remains of the medieval palace of the bishop of Lichfield, which according to tradition stood at the site of the ruin, and some new broken balustrades and pillars. A painting at Shugborough of the west front of the mansion of 1768 by Nicholas Dall depicts on the opposite side of the river Sow from the ruin and the mansion a ruined, hexastyle Doric colonnade, no longer extant.

In July 1750 a Dr. Sneyd Davies described the recently completed ruin.

Mr. Anson's—a beautiful house and river; grounds well disposed; Chinese buildings and bridges; a church-like pigeon house; excellent modern ruins.—He has erected a pile of broken arches, and of imperfect pillars, to counterfeit the remains of antiquity.—The architect could not perform his part satisfactoriy without finishing the whole. Then comes *Mr. Anson* with axes and chissels to demolish as much of it as taste and judgment claimed; and this without affectation, for he is very disciplined, grave and sensible.[64]

Probably about the same time Davies composed a poem honoring Admiral George Anson, younger brother of the owner Thomas Anson and also resident at Shugborough, in which the ruin figures.

> May not the broken pile's disorder'd state
> Express in emblem all-consuming fate

In 1772, on one of his tours, William Gilpin stopped at Shugborough to view the improvements. After Wright's work, the architect James "Athenian" Stuart, who had measured the antiquities of Athens, had added in the park at Shugborough in the 1760s reconstructions of several famous Athenian buildings such as the Tower of the Winds and the Lanthorn of Demosthenes. Gilpin was rather belittling of the Greek reconstructions, particularly in terms of their settings, but was even more critical of the ruin.

> The windows of the room, in which these pictures hang, look towards a pile of artificial ruins in the park. But Mr. Anson has been less happy in fabricating fictitious ruins; than in restoring such as are real.

18. Shugborough (Staffords), view with ruin, detail, drawing by Nicholas Dall, Shugborough

If a ruin be intended to take a station merely in some distant, inaccessible place; one or two points of view are all that need be provided for. The construction therefore of such a ruin is a matter of less nicety. It is a ruin in a picture.

But if it be presented on a spot, as this is, where the spectator may walk round it, and survey it on every side—perhaps enter it—the construction of it becomes then a matter of great difficulty.[65]

About 1750, certainly before an engraving dated 1755, the formal plantations of Mount Edgecumbe, on a headland on the Cornish side of the river Tamar with wonderful vistas of Plymouth and the Plymouth Sound, began to be naturalized in the eighteenth-century style.[66] At the edge of the park, with a magnificent view of the Sound, a tall, Gothic ruined folly visible to the sailors approaching the harbor was erected. Stairs led up to a viewing platform where a huge, dismantled Gothic window framed the expansive vista. Similarly, at another point, a seat disguised as a ruined Gothic chapel stood at the head of a little valley called the Picklecombe with a view across the lawn to the sea.

Occasionally the passion for ruins went to absurd lengths. Henry Fox, first Lord Holland, built just such a complex of buildings and memorials on the estate he rented from 1762 at Kingsgate on the Isle of Thanet in Kent.[67] The site had many historic associations, for according to tradition a battle between Danes and Saxons had taken place in 853 on the heights overlooking the bay. Its name Kingsgate came from a chance landing there of Charles II. A small house above the rocky beach was enlarged with a Doric colonnade supposedly in imitation of Cicero's villa at Baiae. From 1762 until at least 1768 Holland added around this villa a cluster of strange buildings and monuments, some as artificial ruins, designed by two amateur architects, J. L. Nicholl and Thomas Wynne, later Baron Newborough. On the heights southeast of the house the stables were housed in a ruined castle with a tall, cylindrical tower of which only the tower remains. Nearby was the so-called Countess Fort, meant to be the icehouse, consisting of a partially ruined tower supporting a tall flagstaff and ringed by earthworks. Lady Holland, who was an avid gardener with little opportunity for her interest at Kingsgate, was not particularly taken by her husband's passion, writing in 1764: "Lord Holland's works don't amuse me; building old ruins and gateways I can't care about; they amuse him tho', which gives me great satisfaction—'tis not fancy in him." William Gilpin, however, as a presumed impersonal observer was more outspoken: "Among all the crude conceptions of depraved taste, we scarce ever meet with anything more completely absurd than this collection of heterogenous ruins."

Not all artificial garden ruins in the mid-eighteenth century were Gothic in style. From 1738 on, for about thirty-five years, Charles Hamilton planted and decorated a magnificent garden park called Painshill at Cobham in Surrey.[68] In addition to such landscape features as a delightful grotto and a waterwheel, Hamilton had some six garden buildings, designed by Robert Adam and Henry Keene, erected between 1758 and 1762. These structures were of a broad variety of architectural styles, including Gothic, with a later artificial ruined abbey, Turkish, Greek, and Roman. The so-called Roman Mausoleum, completed by 1760 when it appeared in an engraving by Woollett, was conceived as a ruin (fig. 19). Set near the head of the lake the mausoleum was in the form of a ruined triumphal arch with niches containing funereal urns, a sarcophagus, and sepulchral inscriptions, many of which were ancient Roman remains brought from Italy. Both Horace Walpole and William Gilpin, who soon remarked on the ruin, were rather critical of its decoration. Walpole viewing it in 1761 wrote:

> The Ruin is much better imagined [than a Gothic building], but has great faults. It represents a Triumphal Arch and yet never could have had a column, which would certainly have accompanied so rich a soffit. Then this arch is made to have been a Columbarium. You may as well suppose an Alderman's family buried in Temple Bar. Had it been closed behind and there is no reason it should not, for it leads no where, one might imagine it a private burial place, though the fashion uncommon. The upper row of niches in the columbarium are too high and in proportion more gothic than Roman. The tesselated pavement unluckily resembles a painted oil cloth.

Presumably Hamilton had attempted to emphasize the melancholy aspect of death by the ruined condition of the structure. Gilpin in 1765, however, was even more succinct in his criticism: "The triumphal arch is a most beautiful piece of modern ruin. The antique sculpture it is adorned with is very poor. The modern urn in the middle is no ornament as it mixes disagreeably with the antique."

At the same time that Hamilton was presenting such a variety of architectural taste at Painshill, the architect Sir William Chambers, from 1757 to 1763, was building at Kew for the dowager princess of Wales a similar melange, including the Gothic, Chinese, Moslem, and classical styles.[69]

19. Painshill (Surrey), Mausoleum

As early as 1751, just after the death of the prince of Wales in March, Chambers, then in Rome, had revealed an interest in ruined architecture by depicting among his several projects for a mausoleum for the prince one version showing the section of a mausoleum in ruins, undoubtedly inspired by his Roman ambience (fig. 20). Of his works at Kew only one modest structure was built as a garden ruin. This was the so-called Roman arch which was a bridge to allow livestock to proceed from Kew Road into the pastures in the center of the park without disturbing the peripheral walk for visitors (fig. 21). The arch also served as a visual frame through which spectators on the walk could view the distant Temple of Victory. Some fragments of broken capitals and cornices lying near the arch helped to convey the idea of a ruin.

Such classical ruins, however, were becoming less frequent in the mid and late eighteenth century. In 1762, Lord Kames condemned ruins in the Greek style in his work, *Elements of Criticism*.

> Whether should a ruin be in the Gothic or Grecian form? In the former, I think; because it exhibits the triumph of time over strength; a melancholy, but not pleasant thought: a Grecian ruin suggests rather

49

20. Sir William Chambers, drawing of ruined mausoleum for prince of Wales, Victoria and Albert Museum, London

21. Kew (Surrey), Roman Arch, engraving

the triumph of barbarity over taste; a gloomy and discouraging thought.[70]

Later the poet-gardener William Mason in his famous poem *The English Garden* was more convincing by criticizing classic ruins as historically inappropriate for England.

> But Time's rude mace has here all Roman piles
> Levell'd so low, that who, on British ground
> Attempts the task, builds but a splendid lye
> Which mocks historical credence. Hence the cause
> Why Saxon piles or Norman here prevail:
> Form they a rude, 'tis yet an English whole.[71]

With the increasing taste for picturesque beauty even artificial Gothic ruins were suspect. Arthur Young in a letter of June 1768 on his tour through northern England summed up the picturesque attitude toward ruins, emphasizing the "religious melancholy" inspired by the deprecations of time.

> It may not here be impertinent to consider for a moment what is the just stile for a ruin to appear in. We generally find them in retired, neglected spots, half filled with rubbish, and the habitation rather of bats, owls, and wild beasts, than of man: The horrible wildness greatly strengthens the idea raised by falling walls, ruined columns, and imperfect arches, both are awful, and impress upon the mind a kind of religious melancholy! an effect so difficult to raise by art, that we scarcely ever find a modern ruin that, in causing such, has the least power.—Ruins generally appear best at a distance; if you approach them, the effect is weakened, unless the access is somewhat difficult: And, as to penetrating every part by means of artificial paths, it is a question . . . whether the more you see by such means does not proportionaly lessen the general idea of the whole. . . . These reasons appear to me of sufficient force to justify the leaving a ruin in the wildest and most melancholy state the ravaging hand of Time can have thrown it into.[72]

Young is particularly opposed to the creation of artificial ruins to serve as teahouses or places of entertainment, such as Sanderson Miller's follies at Radway and Hagley.

> The taste of an artificial ruin is decided in a moment; it should be an exact imitation of a real one: for this reason it should never serve a

double purpose, that of an object, and a banqueting or tea room; because the contrast between the out and inside, is apparently too great and dissonant. The one is an image of melancholy; the other a temple of festivity.

A few owners of estates were fortunate enough to have actual medieval ruins which they could employ as visual ornaments of their landscaped parks. In the late sixteenth century Queen Elizabeth gave Sir Walter Raleigh the ancient Norman castle of the former bishop of Sarum at Sherborne in Dorset and in 1594 Raleigh had built for himself a new mansion across the river valley south of the old castle.[73] During the Civil War in 1645, the castle, then a possession of the Digby family, was destroyed by the Parliamentary troops. Sometime in the seventeenth century a formal water garden, including a T-shaped canal, a triangular wilderness, terraces, and a bowling green, were devised on the north side of the house in the valley below the ruins of the castle, which served as a backdrop. Undoubtedly Lord Digby had not chosen the site for an appreciation of the ruins, but for the natural water source furnished by the river Yeo in the valley. The poet Alexander Pope, in an eighteenth-century spirit, valued the picturesque quality of these ruins in a long letter to Martha Blount of June 22, 1724. He suggested that the ruins be adapted to the gardens so that "The open Courts from building to building might be thrown into Circles or Octagons of Grass or flowers, and even in the gaming rooms, you have fine trees grown, that might be made a natural Tapistry to the walls, & arch you overhead where time has uncovered them to the Sky." Most important, foreshadowing Shenstone at The Leasowes, he advocated "Seats placed here and there, to enjoy those views, which are more romantick than Imagination can form them." In 1756 the landscapist Capability Brown was consulted, but work took place only in 1775–79 when he floated a large lake down the valley destroying the old, formal water garden.

Perhaps the most successful instance of incorporating ruins in an eighteenth-century garden was that of the ruins of the twelfth-century Cistercian abbey of Rievaulx set in a deep valley near Helmsley in Yorkshire.[74] By 1713 Thomas Duncombe had built a new mansion at Helmsley and he and his son Thomas II laid out and completed a magnificent terrace about a half mile long in front of the house, where the sundial with Father Time, discussed earlier, is located. From about 1758 a grandson, Thomas III, repeated the idea with a terrace about three miles away along the northern edge of Rievaulx valley overlooking the ruined abbey. The Rievaulx terrace, serpentine in form, has classical temples at each end, a circular, so-called Tuscan Temple at the east end complemented at the other end by the rectangular Ionic Temple, which held an elegant, small banqueting hall or tearoom with kitchen in its basement. The terrace was devised so that as one promenaded from one temple to the other, changing vistas were offered of the broad expanse of the valley and of the ruins of the abbey below (fig. 22). The ruins, therefore, satisfied Young's suggestion that they "appear best at a distance." In fact, Young awarded the terrace the ultimate accolade during his 1770 tour, noting: "It is a most bewitching spot," and continuing with an extensive pictorial description in which a view of the ruins "is a casual glance at a little paradise, which seems as it were in another region."[75]

The Rievaulx terrace was probably the inspiration for Richard Woods' plan to landscape the ruins of Wardour Castle in Wiltshire.[76] Old Wardour Castle had been built about 1393 as a hexagonal tower house with a hexagonal interior court. About 1578, the date inscribed over the entrance, the castle, then a possession of the Arundell family, received some classical modifications, such as a new entrance portal after the designs of the Elizabethan architect Robert Smythson. During the Civil War, however, the castle was severely damaged by sieges in both 1643 and 1644. The Arundell family made no attempt to restore the ruins of the old castle, building a small house nearby and making their principal residence elsewhere. An engraving dated 1735 depicts formal gardens planted around the ruins and payments in 1742 indicate the purchase of statues and potted plants presumably for the gardens. In 1763 the poet and amateur gardener Joseph Spence was consulted by the Arundells regarding the landscape and revealed, in a memorandum, a desire to have the ruins preserved in some form: "As both Lord and Lady Arundel seem most inclined to have their new house built on the site of the Old Castle, one could wish that an Imitation of the Ruins (as they now are) was to be built on Barker's Hill; or on some other eminence nearer the house."[77]

Soon the professional landscapist Richard Woods took charge and persuaded the Arundells to locate a new house about two and a half miles to the west of the ruins leaving them as a feature in his new landscape as depicted in his plan of 1765. A medieval fish pond to the west of the Old Castle was enlarged into Swan Pond with a cascade connecting it to a smaller, new pond. Part of Woods' plan comprised a densely wooded terrace curving along the crest of a slope overlooking the ruins of the Old Castle and the new Castle begun by James Paine in 1770. A drive winding along the terrace through the woods offered dramatic views of the Old Castle as the Dutch visitor, Spaen van Biljoen, recounted in 1791.

22. Rievaulx Terrace (Yorks), view of ruined abbey

Among other features, nothing can be more picturesque than the venerable ruins of the ancient castle, which by its majestic aspect and the traces of grandeur that linger among its remains, together with the imposing silence which reigns all around, the ancient trees witnesses of its former splendour, form a romantic and melancholy scene in the grandest manner.[78]

A less successful adaptation of a ruin to an improved landscape was that at Sandbeck Park in Yorkshire.[79] A new house designed by James Paine was built at Sandbeck in 1765 and the noted landscapist Capability Brown improved the grounds near the new house, including the addition of a lake close to the building. The ruins of the Cistercian Roche Abbey in a narrow valley about one and a half miles away were left untouched for almost a decade until in September 1774 Lord Scarborough and Capability Brown signed a contract, which specified, among other work, "To finish all the valley of Roach Abbey in all its Parts, according to the Ideas fixed on with Lord Scarbrough (with Poet's feeling and with Painter's eye)." The parenthetical reference to the poetic and pictorial expression was a line from William Mason's *The English Garden* (book I, line 21), the first three books of which had just been published in 1772. Brown, very conscious of the emphasis on the pictorial aspect of his improvement, raised the ground level around the architectural remains so as to cover the extensive network of foundations that survived, leaving visible only the tall, ruinous walls of the transept of the abbey church. The grounds were then sown with grass and Dutch clover to create a smooth greensward, or as Gilpin remarks "a neat bowling green," as a contrast to the tall ruins. The contract with Brown specified that the landscaping should be completed by December 1777, but already in 1776 the site was visited by William Gilpin on his tour to Scotland.[80] As might be expected, Gilpin was unhappy with the prettification of the ruins: "There is certainly little judgment shown in this mode of improvement." He claims "in a *ruin* the reigning ideas are *solitude, neglect,* and *desolation.* . . . If there is force in *this* reason, it surely holds true, that a ruin should be left in a state of wildness, and negligence." Brown's conception is now visible only in old views as the foundations of the abbey have again been exposed.

By the end of the eighteenth century the enthusiasm for ruins in gardens waned. One last important example was built at Frogmore for Queen Charlotte about a half mile from Windsor Castle.[81] In 1793 the Queen

23. Frogmore (Berks), Gothic Ruin

commissioned her Vice-Chamberlain Major William Price, brother of the famous exponent of the picturesque Sir Uvedale Price, to design her gardens in which a serpentine lake containing an island was opposite the main house. On the island the architect James Wyatt created the so-called Gothic Ruin, a small, one-story building with Gothic windows, buttresses, and crenelations, to serve as a breakfast room for the queen in summer (fig. 23). Some fragments of masonry attached to the structure suggested that it was the remains of a medieval monastery. Colonel Greville, who visited in August 1794, remarked on "the new Ruins erecting in the Gardens" and how Wyatt was using a recent "invention from Birmingham" of "Thin Sheets of Iron plated with lead" for a cheap roofing. Queen Charlotte's Gothic Ruin has none of the melancholic atmosphere associated with a ruin in the eighteenth century, but still confirms Arthur Young's earlier comment that artificial ruins should not serve as tearooms, or in this case a breakfast room, "a temple of festivity."

By the end of the century the domination of the Picturesque Movement left little enthusiasm for artificial ruins. Humphry Repton, the leading landscape theorist at the turn of the century, afforded artificial ruins no role in his principles of landscaping which were basically dependent on the characteristics of nature and a particular site. At the same time, the Industrial Revolution in nineteenth-century England, whose product of iron coated with lead had been used earlier by Wyatt at Frogmore, emphasized the idea of progress, lessening any melancholic pleasure in the contemplation of the passage of time and the destruction it wrought.

During the sixteenth and seventeenth centuries the sundial epigrams had urged spectators to accept their own mortality. By the eighteenth century not only had individuals accepted the challenge, but found a "pleasurable melancholy," as Thomas Warton described it in his poem of 1745, in the mortality of their own creations overturned by time and the elements. Ever since Anthony à Wood in 1657 expressed "melancholic delight" at viewing the ruins of the abbey at Eynsham almost every poet or tourist saw mouldering ruins or even their artificial models as "images of melancholy." Rather than the "Elizabethan malady" that found surcease in the green shades of nature, eighteenth-century melancholy was enhanced by the ravages of nature.

CHAPTER II

Meditation

O N A PRIL 19, 1549, Hugh Latimer, renowned preacher and former
bishop of Worcester, mounted the stairs to the outdoor pulpit in a
garden in the royal Whitehall Palace at London to preach the Good Friday
sermon to the king and the court (fig. 24). The young King Edward VI
with the Council sat in a gallery opposite Latimer and the court nobility
crowded into the garden around the pulpit. Appropriate to the time and
setting Latimer preached on Christ in the garden of Gethsemane.

> Our Saviour Christ had a garden, but he had little pleasure in it. You
> have many goodly gardens: I would you would in the midest of them
> consider what agony our Saviour Christ suffered in his garden. A
> goodly meditation to have in your gardens! It shall occasion you to
> delight no farther in vanities, but to remember what he suffered for
> you. It may draw you from sin. It is a good monument, a good sign, a
> good mention, to consider how he behaved himself in this gar-
> den. . . . Let your gardens monish you, your pleasant gardens, what
> Christ suffered for you in the garden, and what commodity you have
> by his sufferings. [1]

Latimer's admonitions were apparently not acquiesced to by the English
Protestants of the Elizabethan age. At least the Protestant divines at the turn
of the century, such as Richard Greenham and Richard Rogers, lamented
the lack of interest in meditation as a popular devotion among the Protestants. In fact, Rogers claims in the preface to his *Seven Treatises* of 1603
that he undertook to write the book because "the Papists cast in our teeth,
that we have nothing set out for the certaine and daily direction of a
Christian, when yet they haue published (they say) many treatises of that

24. London, Whitehall Palace, Privy Garden, Hugh Latimer preaching

argument."[2] Rogers then devoted the sixth chapter of the third treatise to meditation, defining the nature of meditation as self-examination and bible reading, pointing out "that when we meditate, we ought to separate our selues from all company and troublesome occasions, as our Sauiour commandeth vs to doe, *when we pray privately* (these two being companions) as in our chamber privately, or in the field, or some commodious place, that we may the better performe it."

The Reverend Joseph Hall, later bishop, first of Exeter and then of Norwich, began in 1605 publishing his three volumes of *Meditations and Vowes, Diuine and Morall* and, in 1607, his popular *The Arte of Divine Meditation,* which would soon vigorously encourage the Protestant devotion of meditation.[3] References to gardens and to flowers occur repeatedly through his meditative writings.

Solitude was seen as a prime requisite for meditation, as Richard Rogers noted, so that gardens became in fair weather, due to their tradition of privacy in the Tudor and Stuart periods, the principal location for meditation. Until the eighteenth century English houses were not planned to promote privacy. Corridors or hallways were scarce, as they were considered wasted spaces, so that communication proceeded directly from one room into another. At the same time houses were peopled with armies of servants; even a modest household supported several servants. Hence, anyone in private conversation might be unexpectedly overheard or interrupted by a passing servant or a rival courtier. In William Roper's biography of his father-in-law, Sir Thomas More, the account of Henry VIII suddenly stopping at More's house at Chelsea and "in a faire garden of his, walked with him by the space of an houre, holding his arme about his necke" is not merely a portrayal of an act of friendship. Undoubtedly the king was desirous of discussing in privacy affairs of state whether domestic or international.[4] Shakespeare in several of his plays found dramatic possibilities in the Tudor habit to choose gardens for private conversations, which might then be overheard either deliberately or by accident. Such scenes occur, for example, in *Much Ado About Nothing* (act II, scene iii and act III, scene i), *Twelfth Night* (act II, scene v), and *King Richard II* (act III, scene iv). Later the habit to seek the privacy of a garden for personal or business affairs is repeatedly demonstrated throughout the diary of Samuel Pepys.

Lady Margaret Hoby at the end of the sixteenth century recorded in her diary her constant visits to her garden at Hackness in Yorkshire for recreation, work, and meditation. On September 24, 1599, after church, she "cam in and walked in the garden, medeitatinge of the pointes of the sarmon and prainge tell hard before I went to supper," and in April 1600, "walked to Garden and there medetated: after dined."[5]

The diary of the indomitable Lady Anne Clifford, particularly in her younger days when she was resisting her successive husbands' threatening importunities supported by the king, constantly chronicles her seeking relief in meditation in the garden or park.[6] In April 1616 at Knole in Kent she notes her routine there: "About this time I used to rise early in the Morning & go to the Standing in the garden, & taking my Prayer Book with me beseech God to be merciful to me in this and to help me as He always hath done." This is also the pattern during the following year, except that on October 25 she remarks that she and several friends "walked . . . all the Wilderness over." Lady Clifford's usual term "Standing," meaning a hunting location, is presumably her designation for the wooded area beyond the garden, the wilderness, which will be considered later.

Not only was the garden a desirable retreat for meditation, but also for mental relaxation from the so-called "Elizabethen malady" of melancholy. Already in 1586 Timothy Bright in his *A Treatise of Melancholie* alleged: "If the melancholie be of abilitie, . . . a pleasant garden and hortyard: with a liuelie springe, is aboue all domesticall delight & meetest for the melancholy heart and brayne."[7] In the Jacobean period, in 1621, Robert Burton published his masterly analysis of the "Elizabethan malady," *The Anatomy of Melancholy*, in which he found the ultimate remedy in walking abroad in "gardens" and "artificial wildernesses," as well as in natural locales. So John Evelyn, the great horticulturist, relates in his autobiography that as a young man in 1643 living at his brother's estate at Wotton he built in the garden "a little study over a Cascade, to passe my Melancholia houres shaded there with Trees, & silent Enough."

Frequently the religious tradition of solitary meditation in a garden was misunderstood for melancholy. In 1617 Anne Slingsby corrected any misconception that her father might have: "I here that sum should say that I growe mallincoly, but in truth they are deceived in mee for I am not, nether have they any coues to say so: the moste of my time I spend ether in my closet reading, or in the garden walkeing and meditateing what I have read."[8]

Much later the Viscountess Conway, who suffered severe headaches throughout her life, was warned by her friend Henry More, her brother's tutor at Christ Church College, Oxford, "that you encrease your disease by over much meditation. . . . For unless you favour your self when you are well, study and meditation will so heat your spirits and increase melancholy, that you will necessarily bring the distemper upon you againe. Wherefore, Madam, walk into the cool fresh air, mornings and evenings, play at any trifling and easy games, pass away the time merrily with your Associates and Companions, and give your minde abundance of ease from curious meditations."[9] In 1664 Anne Conway was still importuning her husband to have his gardener "not forgett to have your garden in order to be walked in, some one walk with out doores being absolutely necessary to make me delight in any place, though there be a gallery with in."

Many of the men involved in the early stages of the English sciences seem to have pursued occasional periods of meditation in nature. The Yorkshire botanist and doctor Richard Shane, whose principal occupation was planting gardens and orchards, "avoyded companie as much as he could and took much pleasure to walke in woods and to be solitarie."[10] It was noted that he regularly read the English translation of a Spanish book of meditation and that late in life, in 1620, he composed his own book of prayers and meditations culled from religious writings. John Aubrey in his *Lives* recounts how Sir Francis Bacon was accustomed to walk in the coppice wood in his garden at Gorhambury, "where are walkes cutt-out as straight as a line," presumably a Wilderness.[11] There Bacon, accompanied by the future philosopher Thomas Hobbes, would meditate "and when a notion darted into his mind, Mr. Hobbs was presently to write it downe." The doctor and anatomist William Harvey, according to Aubrey, sought his solitude at his house at Combe in Surrey "where he had caves made in the earth in which in summer time he delighted to meditate." Harvey's patron Thomas Howard, earl of Arundell, also had grottoes or caves in his favorite gardens at Albury in Surrey "wherein he delighted to sit and discourse." Arundell and his friend William Oughtred, an eminent mathematician and rector at Albury, barely escaped from the collapse of a grotto presumably after such a "discourse."

For a Catholic such as the Jesuit Henry Hawkins a garden was not only a location for meditation, but a subject for meditation. In 1633 Hawkins published an emblem book entitled *Partheneia Sacra*, elucidating symbols for the Virgin Mary inspired solely by the *hortus conclusus*, the "enclosed garden" of the *Song of Solomon* (fig. 25). In "The Discourse" to the first symbol of the garden he informs his reader that he is not concerned with the actual gardens of Covent Garden, the Temple, or Gray's Inn, nor the botanical gardens of Padua or Montpellier nor with the mythical gardens of the Hesperides or the Elysian Fields nor even with the Biblical gardens of Eden or of Gethsemane.[12] "But I speake of Thee that Garden so knowne by the name of Hortus Conclusus; wherein are al things mysteriously and spiritually to be found." The garden "being so mysterious and delicious an Object, requires not to be rashly lookt upon, or perfunctoriously to be slighted over, but, as the manner is of such as enter into a Garden, to glance at first thereon with a light regard, then to reflect upon it with a better heed, to find some gentle mysterie or concept upon it, to some use or other: and then liking it better, to review the same againe, and so to make a Survey therupon to the same use."[13]

Ralph Josselin, vicar and schoolmaster at Earls Colne in Essex, inscribed in his diary the gardening activities of both him and his wife in their flower garden and orchard, accompanied by frequent requests for the blessing of god for their labors. In July 1659 he noted: "I began to raise my little house in the orchard, I intend it (if god please) for a retiring, meditating place to contemplate and view my god with delight in his word and works and doings in the world, other uses will fall in."[14]

A garden was often the only place an individual desiring a moment of meditation could find for his devotions. This was particularly remarked on in the brief, contemporary biography of Susanna Perwich, who lived at her father's school at Hackney, died young in 1661, and was renowned for her piety.

25. Henry Hawkins, *Partheneia Sacra*, 1633, *hortus conclusus*

Indeed that was one of the matters of her *complaint*, that she wanted conveniency for *retirement*, where she might *fully* vent her *Soul* to God, without disturbance or observation; and therefore because the house was alwayes *full* of company, having well nigh an *hundred,* and sometimes more of *Gentlewomen* with their attendants; and the *Servants* and *Children* of the house every where going up and down, in *every* Room, so that she could get no place of *privacy;* her manner was in the daytime to get into the *Garden*, at such hours when *others* might not so freely come in to it, and there with her *Bible*, or some other *choice* Book, spent an *hour* or *more* in Reading, Meditation, and such *ejaculations* as she could send up to *Heaven* in walking at which *seasons,* she hath sometimes said to *such* as she was wont to tell her *mind* to, her *heart* hath been as much *warmed* and refreshed in converse with God, as when she hath been *most affected* upon her knees elsewhere. [15]

John Evelyn, the distinguished horticulturist, was convinced that gardens could benefit humanity not only physically through their produce, but more particularly morally and spiritually. He began about 1653 to write and accumulate material for a huge work on every aspect of gardening, including the history of gardens, which was to be entitled *Elysium Britannicum*. After more than forty years consideration of the subject he abandoned the project apparently overwhelmed by its magnitude. At the beginning of the project in January 1660 Evelyn wrote Sir Thomas Browne an extended outline of his proposal preceded by his explanation for writing it.

We will endeavour to shew how the aire and genious of Gardens operat vpon humane spirits towards virtue and sanctitie. I meane in a remote, preparatory, and instrumentall working. How Caues, Grotts, Mounts, and irregular ornaments of Gardens do contribute to contemplative and philosophicall Enthusiasm; how *Elysium, Antrum, Nemus, Paradysus, Hortus, Lucus,* &c., signifie all of them *rem sacram et diviunam;* for these expedients to influence the soule and spirits of man, and prepare them for converse with good Angells; besides which, they contribute to the lesse abstracted pleasures, phylosophy naturall and longevitie. [16]

The constant entries in the diary of Mary Rich, countess of Warwick and pietistic daughter of the wealthy Richard Boyle, earl of Cork, are a complete confirmation of Evelyn's beliefs in the nature and power of gardens. [17] The invariable routine of the countess was to rise about 6 a.m. and immediately, after dressing, retire for two hours of meditation in her garden, either at London, at Beddington, or in the wilderness when she was at the country estate at Leighs Priory in Essex. After the period of meditation she then went to breakfast. In 1663 the countess had begun to compose her own "Occasional Meditations," often inspired by observations in her garden or parks, as demonstrated by some of their titles.

> Upon a flower that opened itself towards the sun.
> Upon the phyllerea hedge that grew before the great parlour door.
> Upon walking and being much delighted with doing so in a very
>   glorious morning in which the birds sing very sweetly.
> Upon observing a mower to go sometimes to a whetstone to whet
>   his scythe; and then presently return again to his mowing.
> Upon seeing when the sun shined upon a Dial, great crowds run to
>   it, but as soon as the sun was withdrawn, all the former
>   company go from it, and take not more notice of it.

This meditation on a sundial was inspired by one of Bishop Joseph Hall's meditations of 1630.

> Upon the sight of a dial.
> If the sun did not shine upon this dial, nobody would look at it:
> in a cloudy day it stands like an useless post, unheeded,
>   unregarded;
> but when once those beams break forth, every passenger runs to
> it, and gazes on it. [18]

The women who served as weeders in the gardens and wilderness were of particular concern to her. In addition to writing a meditation "Upon the Weeders," she recorded in her diary that on September 6, 1671, "I spent some part of this morning in catechizing some of the poor weeders, and in stirring them up to look after their souls."

There was a long tradition of such private devotions in the Puritanical atmosphere at Leighs Priory. Already in July 1644 the Reverend John Beadle of Banston had insisted in a sermon that "every Christian ought to keep a record of his owne actions & wayes." [19] On July 25, 1666, the countess of Warwick began her own devotional diary, noting that "in the evening, went alone into the park, and begged again of God for mercy, and to give me assurance of my everlasting condition." After that almost every entry reads: "In the morning, as soon as I awoke, I blessed God, then went out alone into the wilderness to meditate." On July 30 she continues: "And there God was pleased to give me sweet communion with him, and to fixing thoughts much upon my death, and to make me pray with strong cries and abundance of tears that I might be prepared for that great change. . . . I came away much refreshed, and with my heart exceedingly cheered." On September 4, she observed: "I retired into the wilderness to think of the sad miseries of poor London," the Great Fire of London having commenced on September 2 and still raging.

In London at Warwick House in Chelsea, Lady Warwick would meditate in the garden. On May 16, 1667, she undertook a very painful, personal meditation: "I kept a private fast, being the day three years upon which my son died. As soon as up, I retired into the garden to meditate; had there large meditations upon the sickness and death of my only child." In August she visited Beddington in Surrey.

> In the afternoon, I went to see Beddington, and as I walked in the garden in the retired walks, where I used to meditate. I blessed God for the sweet refreshing hours I had in those walks, where formerly I had often enjoyed communion with God.

The garden at Beddington offered at least one object conducive to meditation on death. John Aubrey mentioned in 1673 that Sir Francis Carew had a red and white table from the late sixteenth century in his summer house in the garden at Beddington, "formerly a Grave-Stone, I conjecture." Its inscription in Dutch read: "Hier leghet myn wrowe Margriete de Medewe" (Here lies my wife Margriete de Medewe).[20] The table was probably to serve as a memento mori in the ambience of a garden, where nature constantly recalled the mortality of men and women.

In 1673, to the dismay of the countess, her husband ordered the wilderness to be cut down in order to renew the woods. This drastic measure awakened the countess again to the tragic loss of her son as recounted in her meditation entitled "Upon ye cutting down of ye wilderness."

> This sweet place that I have sen ye first sprouting, growth, and flourishing of for above twenty years together, and almost daily taken delight in, I have also now to my trouble seen by my Lord's command ye cutting down of, in order to its after growing again thicker and better, tho' I have often interceded with him to have it longer spared.
> This brought to my remembrance afresh ye death of my only son, whom I had also seen ye first growth of in his childhood and ye flourishing of to my unspeakable satisfaction for almost twenty-one years; and on a short space of time, to my inspeakable grief, by my

great Lord's command cut down by death that he might rise again in a better and more flourishing condition; though I often implored, if it were agreeable to the Divine will, he might be longer continued to me.

Lady Warwick continued her diary until late in November 1677, not long before her death in April of the following year.

Just before Lady Warwick ceased to make entries in her diary, John Thoresby, a well-to-do merchant of Leeds, wrote his youthful son Ralph on August 15, 1677, advising him "to be always employed in some lawful employment," including listening to good sermons, and to keep "a little journal of any thing remarkable every day, principally as to yourself."[21] The dutiful son began his diary on September 2 and would continue it throughout his life. Ralph Thoresby continued his father's mercantile affairs but was obviously more interested in gathering material on English antiquities and topography, writing a topography of the city of Leeds. A non-conformist until 1699, Thoresby, particularly during his youthful days, noted in his diary reading or meditating in his garden. On April 6, 1682, he "was the whole day entirely at the new garden, by the water, overseeing work-folk, and reading Sir William Waller's Divine Meditations" and on July 30: "Morning, and much of the forenoon, walking in the garden, reading, or meditating; was sometimes much affected, especially with Dr. Wilkins' incomparable treatise of prayer."

At the end of the century the Reverend William Turner claimed that Adam's sons and daughters planted gardens, modern gardens of Eden, for retirement. In a practical spirit, however, Turner discussed the plants suitable for such gardens in a chapter entitled "Strange Vegetables, Trees, Plants, &c."

> Adam, when he was innocent, was placed in a Garden and after he had sinned, was turned out into the wide and wild World; most of his wiser Posterity, after they have sinned away a great part of their Life, and ramble about through the Bustle and Cares of the World, desire to make a Garden the place of their Retreat, as suitable for Retirement, Meditation and Devotion. For such Purposes this chapter will be serviceable, wherein I take not upon me to mention every Vegetable, and, as Solomon, to give the Natural History of all Plants, from the tall Cedars of Lebanon, to the Hysop upon the Wall.[22]

Timothy Nourse when at Oxford had been renowned for his preaching, but by converting to Roman Catholicism in 1673 he lost his fellowship and,

in a typical English gesture, retired to the country to write and philoso-
phize. His book *Campania Foelix*, published in 1700, just after his death,
describes in detail a country gentleman's life and activities. The essay "Of a
Country House" at the end of the book associates the garden with its
reminder of man's immortality.

> And if he be a Man of Contemplative Genius, the Seat of his House
> cannot but suggest manlike Thoughts. The same Eminence of
> Ground which displays the Beauties of the Earth by day entertains
> him with a much larger and more beautiful Prospect of the heavens by
> night, which may direct his desires towards a more lasting Mansion.
> The Variety of Flowers beautiful and fragrant, with which his Gar-
> dens are adorn'd, opening themselves and dying one after another,
> must admonish him of the fading state of Earthly Pleasures, of the
> frailty of life, and of the succeeding Generations to which he must
> give place. The constant Current of a Fountain or Rivolet must mind
> him of the Flux of Time which never returns, nor causes to run on, till
> it ends in Immensity. But if he find Fastidiousness amidst Fruition, as
> it happens usually in the greatest Pleasures (those excepted of the
> Mind) he may then recollect himself and think, that since such Plea-
> sures are unsatisfactory and transitory, the Mind is yet capable of
> farther Enjoyments more durable and sincere, which since it cannot
> meet with amidst earthly Divirtisements, it must look for a plentiful
> Entertainment in another Region.[23]

Such reflections did not need a country setting. The duke of Buckingham
in 1709 responded similarly to his urban garden attached to Buckingham
House in London.

> For though my garden is such as by not pretending to rarities or
> curiosities, has nothing in it to inveagle one's thoughts, yet by the
> advantage of situation and prospect, it is able to suggest the noblest
> that can be; in presenting at once to view a vast town, a Palace, and a
> magnificent Cathedral, I confess the last with all its splendour, has less
> share in exciting my devotion, than the most common shrub in my
> garden: For though I am apt to be sincerely devout in any sort of
> religious assemblies, from the very best (that of our own church) even
> to those of *Jews*, *Turks*, and *Indians:* Yet the works of nature appear
> to me the better sort of sermons; and every flower contains in it the
> most edifying rhetorick, to fill us with admiration of its omnipotent
> Creator."[24]

Jonathan Tyers, the proprietor of the public Vauxhall Gardens in London, created at his country estate of Denbies near Dorking in Surrey perhaps the ultimate garden setting for meditation, particularly on death.[25] Tyers lived regularly at his home at Vauxhall Gardens, but after having purchased Denbies in 1734 he would visit his country estate on weekends, where from the mid-1740s he developed his own version of a garden of Christian morality. Whereas the public garden at Vauxhall reflected Milton's *L'Allegro* with Handel's statue and music, and Hayman's lively paintings of country sports, so Denbies mirrored *Il Penseroso*. The entrance at Denbies, inscribed "Procul este profani" (Away unhallowed ones) from Vergil's *Aeneid* (VI, 258), suggested to visitors that they were about to enter a sacred area. Immediately within was a dense wood of some eight acres, called "Il Penseroso" by Tyers. A labyrinth of walks wound through the woods in which was a thatched hermitage known as the Temple of Death, housing appropriate morbid memorials. A desk in the center of the room, "for reading and meditation," bore volumes bound in black, such as Edward Young's *Night Thoughts* and Robert Blair's *The Grave*, and a clock striking every minute reminded the visitor of the inexorable passage of time. On the end wall of the hermitage was a stucco monument by the sculptor Roubiliac to Tyer's friend Robert Lord Petre, an ardent botanist and tree collector who had died in 1742 at the age of twenty-nine. The monument depicted an angel blowing a trumpet to announce the Last Judgment as the corpse, tearing apart his shroud, was about to rise from the sepulcher. Everywhere inscriptions and poems warned visitors of the inevitability of death. Over the door, verses by Mr. Robson, tutor to Tyers' boys, exhorted:

> What place is this? An universal school,
> The master Death, the scholar is the Soul,
> Confess thy faults, and mend, My fault is pride
> . . . .
> Whoe'er thou art, whatever thy degree,
> Here may'st thou sit and read, reflect and see,
> And what thou art, and what thou soon wilt be.

Beyond the temple was a gate supported by stone coffins bearing human skulls that opened into the "Valley of the Shadow of Death" where two large paintings by Francis Hayman with life-size figures were set in compartments in the wall of a stone alcove. One painting portrayed the serene *Death of a Christian* accompanied by the Bible and sermons of Clarke and Tillotson, in contrast to the other of the tortured death of an unbeliever surrounded by books of Hobbes, Tyndale, Spinoza, and Lord Rochester. As the description of Denbies in *The Gentleman's Magazine* of 1763 remarked: "The whole, with the entrance to the place, which has something in it very particular, is truly striking to a contemplative mind." The death of Tyers himself in 1767 brought destruction of his garden and its admonitions. While early seventeenth-century emblem books depended upon garden imagery to convey morality and religious beliefs, in the early eighteenth century an actual garden itself could present such ideas.

In 1755 Edward Young, author of the *Night Thoughts* that was exhibited at Jonathan Tyers's Denbies, in one of his later letters on pleasure, claimed that a garden was a picture of "a goodman's Happiness."

> A garden has ever had the praise and affection of the wise. What is requisite to make a wise and happy man, but reflection and peace and both are the natural growth of a garden. Nor is a garden only a promoter of a good man's happiness, but a picture of it; and in some sort, shows him to himself. Its culture, order, fruitfulness, and seclusion from the world compared to the weeds, wildness, and exposure of a common field, is no bad emblem of a good man, compared to the multitude. A garden weeds the mind; it weeds it of worldly thoughts, and sows celestial seed in their stead. For what see we there, but what awakens in us our gratitude to Heaven? A garden to the virtuous is a paradise still extant; a paradise unlost.[26]

For Young a garden was a sacred area, a duplicate church, the equivalent of the Garden of Eden. The outside wall of the summerhouse in his garden at Welwyn in Hertfordshire bore the biblical inscription, "Ambulantes in horto audiebant vocem Dei" (Walking in the garden they heard the voice of the Lord God, Genesis, iii, 8).[27]

The leaders of the Methodist movement in England and America turned to gardens as a locus for their meditations. George Whitefield, who would later fall out with John Wesley and go his own way promoting Methodism, particularly in America, came to Methodism in 1735, while at Oxford. In his journal he recounts his attempt to emulate Christ's retreat into the wilderness.

> Being willing, as I thought to imitate Jesus Christ, after supper I went into Christ Church walk, near our college, and continued in silent prayer under one of the trees for nearly two hours, sometimes lying flat on my face, sometimes kneeling upon my knees, all the while filled with fear and concern lest some of my brethren should be over-

whelmed with pride. The night being stormy, it gave me awful thoughts of the Day of Judgment till the great bell rung for retirement to the college, not without finding some reluctance in the natural man against staying so long in the cold.

The next night I repeated the same exercise at the same place. But the hour of extremity being now come, God was pleased to make an open show of those diabolical devices by which I had been deceived.[28]

John Wesley filled his journals for about fifty years with almost daily references to gardens, where he would meditate and work. His typical journal entries are very brief. During his visit to Oglethorpe's new colony of Georgia in America from 1736 to 1737 he spent forty minutes in the German Moravian garden at Savannah on March 12, 1737, in prayer and meditation, reading the Greek Testament and singing as he meditated.[29] On Sunday, March 14, in preparation for his preaching, he meditated in the garden on the writings of the mystic Thomas à Kempis. The following Sunday, already dressed in his surplice, Wesley walked in the garden singing and reading his Greek testament, while meditating on the sermon he was to preach. On his return to England, after he began to make his tours preaching to the people, he took advantage of his excursions to visit all the famous eighteenth-century gardens, obviously enjoying their beauties of which he could also be very critical, but almost always qualifying his remarks with some religious or moral reflection. When he explored the extensive gardens at Wrest Park in Bedfordshire on June 20, 1754, he recorded that he preferred them to the gardens at Stowe. He added, however, with a pun on the name: "But how little did the place answer its name! How little rest did its miserable master enjoy! Thou, O God, hast made our heart for Thyself, and it cannot rest till it resteth in Thee." At Alnwick on May 21, 1766, he noted that the duke of Northumberland was improving the gardens and creating "a little paradise. What pity that he must leave all these and die like a common man!" Wesley's passionate fondness for the gardens he toured obviously disquieted him. At the picturesque woods of Piercefield in Wales on August 25, 1769, after describing their attractions, he appended the comment: "And must all these be burned up? What will become of us, then if we set our hearts upon them?"

Wesley was particularly fond of Hamilton's garden-park at Painshill in Surrey, visiting it alone or in company at least three times.[30] At the first visit in 1771, Wesley commented on the fact that after a lifetime of work by Hamilton he was advertising it for sale. "Is there anything under the sun that can satisfy a spirit made for God?" At the last tour in 1790, Wesley noted that after an hour of walking over the landscape, "still the eye was not satisfied with seeing. An immortal spirit can be satisfied with nothing but seeing God." To Wesley, the personal loss of an owner was reflected in his garden. On October 11, 1775, at Lord Shelburne's house at Wycombe, Wesley praised the landscaping and then reflected: "But can the owner rejoice in this paradise? No, for his wife is snatched away in the bloom of youth!"

At the time of Wesley's trip to Painshill in 1779, when he also viewed Stourhead, which he even preferred to Painshill, he surveyed again the gardens at Stowe and was even more severe in his criticism of many of its features than before. The architecture of some of the garden buildings was characterized as "ugly" and "clumsy." The interior decoration of the Temple of Venus from Spenser's *Faerie Queene*, now lost, was described as a "lewd story." Not only were some of the paintings "dirty," but so was the water. "The river on which it [a grotto] stands is a black, filthy puddle, exactly resembling a common sewer."[31] No matter where he was Wesley continued his habit of visiting a garden for meditation. In London when he was eighty years old Wesley could still jot down in his journal on June 6, 1783: "8 [p.m.] garden meditated, conversed."

The Wilderness

THE WORD "wilderness" which Lady Warwick used to identify her place of meditation at Leighs Priory can be very misleading to nature lovers brought up in the picturesque tradition and familiar with the American public park system for whom the wilderness is an untouched nature of irregularity and disorder. Even the author of one of the earliest accounts of a wilderness recognized the ambiguity of the term. Anthony Watson, rector of Cheam and later bishop of Chichester, penned a record of the gardens of the former royal palace of Nonsuch in Surrey. The description, which is undated, has been identified as being composed after 1582, but probably before 1592.

> Leaving the garden, we enter the wilderness which is, in fact, neither wild nor deserted. The land, which is naturally somewhat hilly and is plentifully watered, is set out with lofty and magnificent tree-lined walks to the south and west. At the end of the path to the south, the trees have been trimmed to form canopies. Through the heart of the wilderness there are three paths, the middle one worn and sandy and

the others turfed. There are trees for shade and for fruit: almost countless young apple trees, shrubs, evergreens, ferns, vines.[32]

All documents indicate that the area called a wilderness in the seventeenth century was a carefully planted and maintained part of the landscaping of a country house. In the summer of 1605, when the gardens and orchards at Ashley House in Surrey were being laid out and planted, a financial account listed the purchase of "Settes for the wilderness," amounting to almost eleven pounds.[33] Robert Burton in his account of the pleasure of walking of 1621 speaks of strolling among "artificial wildernesses," implying that they were planted by men.

The wilderness was probably related to the traditional garden labyrinth or maze, although it was actually the English descendant of the Italian *bosco* and the French *bosquet*. Lieutenant Hammond, when he visited Lady Wotton's garden at St. Augustine's Abbey in Canterbury, spoke of the "Labirinthlike wildernesses and Groues," and the Parliamentarian survey of the royal gardens of Wimbledon in Surrey in 1649 described a great maze and a wilderness paired together on the south side of the turfed terrace above the house and gardens.

> The maze to lie towards the east, and the wilderness the west; the maze consists of young trees, wood, and sprayes of a good growth and height, cut out into severall meanders, circles, semicircles, wyndings, and intricat turnings, the walkes or intervalls whereof are all grass plotts; this maze, as it is now ordered, adds very much to the worth of the upper level; the wilderness (a work of a vast expence to the maker thereof) consists of many young trees, woods, and sprayes of a good growth and height, cut out and formed into severall ovals, squares, and angles, very well ordered, in most of the angular points whereof, as allsoe in the center of every ovall, stands a lyme tree or elme; all the allies of this wilderness, being in number eighteene, are of gravelled earth, very well ordered and maynteyned.[34]

It is interesting to observe that the Parliamentarian writer used almost identical words and phrases to describe the two horticultural features. Visualization of the similarity between mazes and wildernesses is offered in 1670 in Leonard Meager's treatise *The English Gardener*, where he includes a selection of designs for parterres and wildernesses. Some of those labelled wildernesses could very readily be confused with mazes, having entry points and twisting interior alleys.

A wilderness required constant maintenance. In one of Lady Warwick's meditations at Leighs Priory her solitude in the wilderness was disturbed by the activity and noise of two laborers who were "employed in rowling a gravel walk in ye wilderness, which though at a very remote distance from the arbor where I was set, yet their rude loud mode of speaking had made their voices approach my ears."[35] At about the same time a servant at Knole was fined the rather severe penalty of threepence a week out of his weekly wage of five shillings for forty-two weeks "for not burning the brakes out of the Wilderness." The clearance of underbrush and the rolling of gravel walks suggest a picture of careful, orderly gardening. This is confirmed by the few depictions of wildernesses in contemporary plans of gardens and landscapes. In 1653 John Evelyn drew a plan of his large garden at Sayes Court in Kent (fig. 26).[36] In the center of the garden is a large rectangular area planted with shrubbery and trees. Long radiating alleys cut through the plantation and cross a circular alley toward the center. The design slightly resembles the plan of a wilderness devised at Hampton Court to be discussed later. Other parts of the garden at Sayes Court were extensively treed, with the trees carefully organized on the ancient Roman quincuncial pattern. Evelyn does not seem to use the term wilderness for his plantations, but much later, in 1684 and 1686, his friend Robert Berkeley refers to Evelyn's "wilderness" at Sayes Court.

From 1672 to 1675 the duke and duchess of Lauderdale, just married, expanded and revised their residence of Ham House in Surrey, which had been recently inherited by the duchess.[37] A plan of the house and grounds by the German engineer John Slezer, usually dated about 1671, preserves the layout of the gardens and wilderness behind the building. On the south side of the house was a long terrace with steps down into a garden composed of eight square plots which Batty Langley described much later as grassed. Beyond the grassed parterres was the rectangular wilderness, somewhat similar to the design at Sayes Court. Eight avenues radiated out from a central circular opening, the alley on axis with the house being wider than the others. An oval alley encircled the center. The principal difference from Evelyn's plan was the irregular, serpentine paths meandering through the treed triangles suggestive of Batty Langley's much later designs. A slightly later prospect of the south front of the house, attributed to Slezer about 1675–76, after the garden gateway piers had been erected, shows the wilderness composed of dense groves of evergreens, and a contemporary painting by Hendrik Danckerts records life-size statues on pedestals at the ends of the files of trees and tall hedges outlining some of the alleys. More

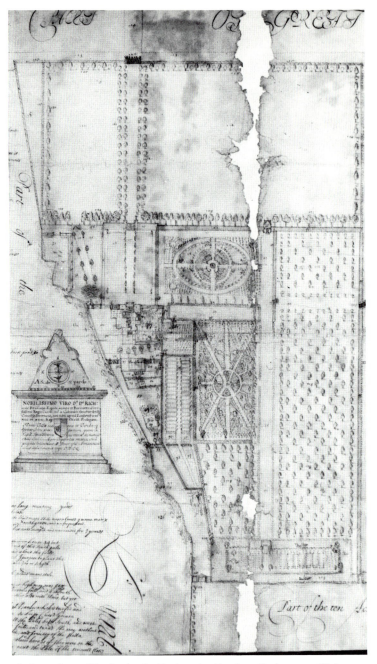

26. Sayes Court (Kent), plan by Evelyn, detail, 1653, Evelyn MSS, Christ
Church College, Oxford

than a half century later the basic layout of the garden and wilderness was preserved in the fourth volume of *Vitruvius Britannicus* of 1739 (fig. 27). The engraving, however, omits the serpentine walks in the treed wilderness and suggests a circular alley rather than an oval one around the central opening, both probably representing changes in execution from Slezer's original project.

Such formal, geometric gardening was a long tradition at Ham House, for a plan of the grounds drawn by the architect Robert Smythson in 1609 during his visit to London depicts a geometrically planted orchard directly behind the house in the location of the later grass parterres, but there is no evidence that it might have been considered a wilderness. It has been suggested that the plan of the orchard at Ham House was of French derivation and in particular from Claude Mollet's gardening at S. Germain-en-Laye.[38] Certainly the wilderness designs in most English gardens were inspired by plans for bosquets in the French horticultural treatises of Jacques Boyceau (1638) and of André Mollet (1651). Not all wildernesses, however, were laid out with complicated geometrical patterns. A drawing of about 1676 by Henry Winstanley of the royal house and gardens at Audley End in Essex has the Privy or Mount Garden on the south side of the house.[39] On the north side was the smaller Cellar Garden with the wilderness behind it toward the east (fig. 28). Here the trees are planted in a simple checkerboard pattern, not even the quincunx that Evelyn used for large groves.

At Hampton Court during the expansion of the palace by Sir Christopher Wren for William III, new gardens were laid out, including the wilderness probably begun in 1689 on the northern side of the palace (fig. 29).[40] Alleys bordered by tall, clipped hedges formed a St. Andrew's cross radiating from a central, circular opening emphasized by a single, tall pine tree. An outer path assumed a figure-eight pattern. A large, triangular maze and several semicircular or circular labyrinths were planted in the various compartments. Single trees and shrubs were then scattered throughout the design.

About the same time as the creation of the wilderness at Hampton Court the avid gardener Sir Christopher Hatton IV laid out a wilderness at his country estate at Kirby in Northamptonshire.[41] Having inherited the house in 1670, it wasn't until 1685 that Hatton had the opportunity to begin work on the new Great Garden on the western side of the building, including the traditional feature of a mount at the south end mounded over the foundations of a demolished church. In 1689 Hatton began to enlarge the layout

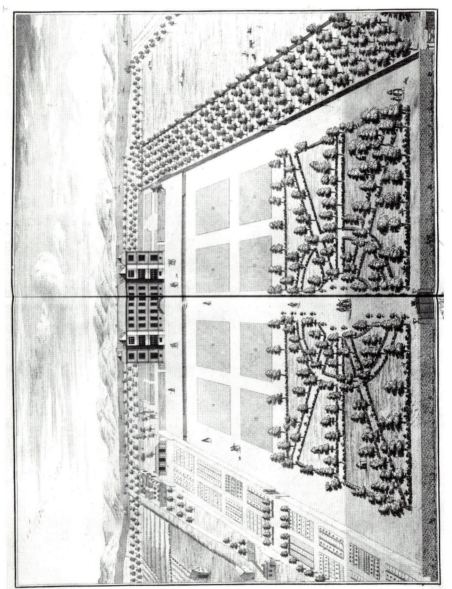

27. Ham House (Surrey), view, 1739

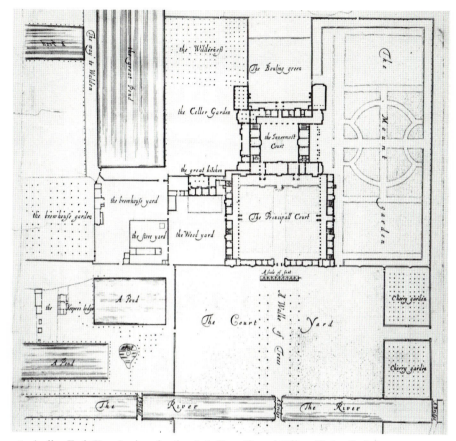

28. Audley End (Essex), plan, detail, 1676, Essex Record Office, Chelmsford

toward the south with a wilderness beyond the orchard. At this time the Kirby accounts reveal an interest in a great variety of trees presumably for the wilderness, which was completed in 1692. Two years later the southern wall and gateway of the garden were leveled in order to allow an unimpeded view from the garden into the wilderness.

One of the most fervent gardeners and botanical collectors at the turn of the century was the duchess of Beaufort, at Beaufort House at Chelsea in London but more particularly at her country residence at Badminton in Gloucestershire.[42] Cassandra Willoughby, the duchess of Chandos, during her visit to Badminton in 1697 was obviously charmed by the gardens, remarking that:

29. Hampton Court (Middlesex), plan by Wren, detail of wilderness, 1689, Sir John Soane's Museum, London

The Wilderness is very fine, y^e trees so large as to make it very shadowy; they are all Ash and Elm except shrubs to thicken in ye bottom. Y^e earth is covered with variety of plants and primroses, periwinkle etc. I observed there that Barberries grew as well under ye droppings of ye trees as any shrub.

The description by the duchess conveys the impression of a rather informal plantation of trees, shrubs, and flowers in the manner of a medieval pleasance, but an anonymous drawing at Badminton labelled "Draught of a wilderness garden" depicts a very formal planting with evergreens trimmed in the forms of obelisks and globes around a circular basin with a jet of water. Another example of a formal type of wilderness is drawn on the eighteenth-century copy of an estate plan of Holland House at Kensington in London dating from 1694–95.[43] Beyond the garden was a large French bosquet of eight treed avenues radiating out from a circular central opening. The planting is labelled "Wilderness."

Contemporary with the work at Kirby Hall and Badminton were the great gardens laid out at Boughton House in Northamptonshire for the first duke of Montagu who had served previously as ambassador to France. His architectural additions and gardens were, therefore, inspired by French taste, although the chief gardener from 1685 until at least Montagu's death in 1709 was a Dutchman, Van der Meulen.[44] John Morton in his book on the natural history of Northamptonshire gives an account of two wildernesses at Boughton, as a drawn survey of the layout in 1715 preserves a plan of the whole, both of which support the origin of the wildernesses in French bosquets.

On the North Side of the *Parterre*-Garden is a small Wilderness which is call'd the *Wilderness* of *Apartments*, an exceeding delightful Place, and nobly adorned with Basins, Jet d'Eaus, Statues, with the *Platanus*, Lime-Tree, Beech, Bayes, &c. all in exquisite Form and Order. To the Southward of the lower part of the Parterre-Garden, is a larger *Wilderness* of a different Figure, having Ten equidistant Walks concentring in a round Area, and adorn'd also with Statues. In one of the Quarters is a fine Pheasantry. The larger Trees upon the Sides of the Walks have Eglantine and Woodbind climbing up and clasping about the Bodies of them.

Already at the beginning of the century William Blathwayt in laying out his gardens and orchard at Dyrham Park in Gloucestershire made provision in his wilderness for meditative reading in comfort.[45] In 1704 Blathwayt wrote his agent at Dyrham: "If Mr. Oliver can shew how the Stand for Books in ye Arbors are to be made as at my Lord Fauconberg's I would have one made forthwith for that Seat Arbor which stands in ye corner of ye Wilderness to ye N.E. looking towards Bristoll." The engraving by Johannes Kip of Dyrham published in Sir Robert Atkyns, *The Ancient and Present State of Gloucestershire* (1712) depicts the wilderness above the terraced hillside at the north (fig. 30). Later, the professional gardener Stephen Switzer published in his treatise *Ichnographia Rustica* a detailed description of the wilderness.

> From this Seat you descend again to a flourishing Wilderness, on an easy Slope, cut out into the utmost Variety of Walkes, especially solitary Walks, and beautify'd with Statues: In the Middle there is a delightful square Garden, having four large Seats at the Corners, and a Seat round an aspiring Fir-Tree in the Center, from whence your Prospect terminates in a large old Church, at a very great Distance. I never in my whole Life did see so agreeable a Place for the sublimest Studies, as this is in the Summer, and here are small Desks erected in Seats for that Purpose. On one Side you ascend several Grass-Steps, and come to an artificial Mount, whereon is a large spreading Tree, with a Vane at the Top, and a Seat enclosing it, commanding a most agreeable and entire Prospect of the Vale below; from hence you come down to a very magnificent Arbour, with the Convenience of Water-Works to play round it.[46]

The poet Alexander Pope in his letter of 1724 to Martha Blount describing the landscaping of Sherborne in Dorset offers a brief picture of a charming, small wilderness there.

> Thence into a little triangular wilderness, from whose Centre you see the town of Sherborne in a valley, interspersed with trees. From the corner of this you issue at once upon a high green Terras the whole breadth of the Garden, which has five more green Terras's hanging under each other, without hedges, only a few pyramid yews & large round Honisuckles between them. The Honisuckles hereabouts are the largest & finest I ever saw. You'd be pleasd when I tell you the Quarters of the above mentioned little Wilderness are filld with these & with Cherry trees of the best kinds all within reach of the hand.[47]

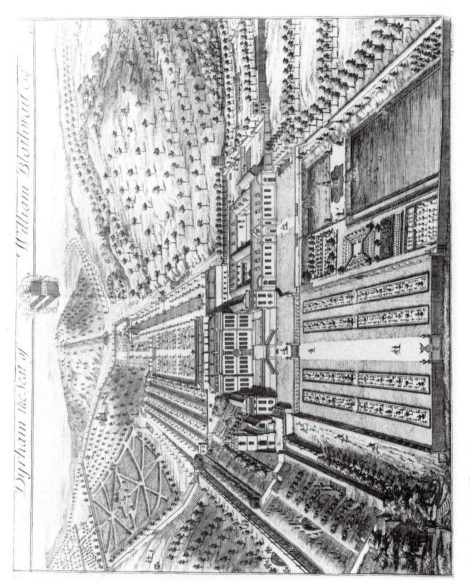

Dyrham the Seat of Willham Blathwait Esq.

30. Dyrham Park (Glos), view, 1712

Switzer's and Pope's descriptions are concerned with specific sites, but Timothy Nourse already in 1700 in his essay "Of a Country House" offered an extensive and generalized account of the character of a wilderness.

The Third or last Region of our Pleasure-Garden I would have wholly to be design'd for Boscage: Only three long Alleys running to the farther end by way of continuance of those which traverse to the Lower Gardens. Let there be likewise up and down little private Alleys or Walks of Beech, for this is a delicate Green: here likewise let there be Tufts of Cypress-Trees, planted in the Form of a Theater, with a Fountain at the bottom, and Statues round about; likewise Fir-Trees in some negligent Order, as also Lawrels, Philyrea's, Bays, Tumarist, the Silac Tree, *Althea* Fruits, Pyracanthe, Yew, Juniper, Holly, Cork Tree, and in a word, with all sorts of Winter Greens which may be made to grow, together with wild Vines, Bean-Trefoile, *Spanish Ash*, Horse-Chesnut, Sweet-Brier, Honey-Suckles, Roses, Almond-Trees, Mulberries, &c. Also up and down let there be little Banks of Hillocks, planted with wild Thyme, Violets, Primroses, Cowslips Daffadille, Lillies of the Valley, Blew-Bottles, Daisies, with all kinds of Flowers which grow wild in the Fields and Woods; as also amongst the Shades Strawberries, and up and down the Green-Walks let there be good store of Camomile, Water-Mint, Organy, and the like; for these being trod upon, yield a pleasant Smell; and let the Walls be planted with Hedera Canadensis, and Philyrea's, &c. So that this Third Garden, Grove or Wilderness, should be made to represent a perpetual Spring: To which end and purpose let there be large Aviaries in convenient places, which should have Ever-Green Trees growing in them, especially such as bear Berries, together with little Receptacles for Fresh Water. Likewise for Variety's sake, let there be here and there a Fruit-Tree as Plumbs and Cherries, Haw-thorn, with such like as will not run to Timber; for, these Trees also have their Beauties in their several Seasons. In a word, let this Third Region or Wilderness be Natural-Artificial; that is, let all things be dispos'd with that cunning, as to deceive us into a belief of a real Wilderness or Thicket, and yet to be furnished with all the Varieties of nature: And at the upper end of this Wilderness, let there be a Grate-Gate, answering the Entrance to the Garden; beyond which, and without the Territory of our Garden, let there be planted Walks of Trees to adorn the Landskip; Likewise a Bowling-Green and Poddock would be suitable to this higher Ground; and thus at length the Prospect may terminate on Mountains, Woods, or such Views as the Scituation will admit of.[48]

Nourse's image of a wilderness is perhaps pivotal in the consideration of the form and meaning of the wilderness in English gardening. On one hand it would seem possible that Blathwayt, as he proceeded with his work at Dyrham, had read Nourse's account. Both had a variety of walks and statues, but more particularly Nourse emphasized that beyond the wilderness there must be a distant prospect focusing on some feature of the landscape. Blathwayt himself had insisted that from his wilderness he should be able to enjoy a vista of Bristol, and Switzer records that from the "aspiring Fir-Tree in the Center" of the wilderness was a view terminated by a "Church, at a very great Distance." On the other hand there can be no question that Nourse has adapted much of his characterization of the wilderness from Sir Francis Bacon's essay "Of Gardens," first published in 1625. Bacon also divided his description of a garden into three parts of which the third part, beyond the garden, was called the "heath" or in one instance a "natural wildness." Bacon insisted that his garden must be a garden for all seasons, a *ver perpetuum* or eternal spring, likening it thus to the Garden of Eden, and similarly Nourse said that the "Third Garden, Grove or Wilderness, should be made to represent a perpetual Spring." Both Bacon and Nourse provide large aviaries, Bacon's turfed and with living plants, Nourse's with evergreens, but Bacon's aviaries were to be in his garden, while those of Nourse are in the wilderness. The major difference is that Bacon's heath does not have trees. Bacon's heath, however, is to have "molehills growing thyme, violets, strawberries, cowslips, and daisies," while Nourse's wilderness has hillocks of similar herbs and flowers. For scent Bacon had three herbs, burnet, thyme, and watermint, planted underfoot where they may be "trodden upon and crushed," while Nourse would plant in his walks camomile, watermint, and oregano, "for these being trod upon yield a pleasant Smell."

It was Michael Jermin, chaplain to Charles I, who first clearly identified the relationship of the horticultural wilderness to the pleasure garden in his *A Commentary upon Ecclesiastes* (1639) when he mentions "the invention of a *wildernesse* which often is adjoyned to great gardens belonging to great houses, and by a multitude of thick bushes and trees affecting an ostentation of solitarinesse in the midst of worldly pleasure."[49] Already more than a century previously, among the poetic proverbs that decorated the walls and ceiling of the castles of the fifth earl of Northumberland at Leconfield and

Wressel in Yorkshire, a similar differentiation between the garden and the wilderness was expressed.[50] In a manuscript, also containing poetry of c. 1520 by William Peeris, a priest, poet, and secretary of the earl, an anonymous dialogue between the sensual and intellectual pleasures that embellished the castle at Leconfield is preservd.

> The parte sensatyue
> To walke in gardynge all garnyshede w^t floures
> What pleasure is it / bycause of the swete odowres.
> And in the arburis to here the byrdis synge.
> Which to mane hart grete conforth brynge.
> The part intellectyue
> For the soule thou shall fynde more quyetnes.
> Of repentaunce to walk in the wildernes.
> Amonge thrones of aduersitie yf thou take payne,
> To swete flowres of paciens thou maist attayne.
> Vanitas vanitatū All other is but vayne.

The garden was the place of pleasure and entertainment made attractive by its colors and fragrances. Beyond it was the solitary wilderness, in the words of Nicholas Breton's poem *The Pilgrimage to Paradise* of 1592:

> A forrest, ful of wild, and cruell beastes:
> The earth vntile, the fruit vnhappines,
> The trees all hollow, full of howletes nests.[51]

It was from the Garden of Eden that Adam and Eve were banished into the untilled wilderness. The Israelites would wander in the wilderness for forty years of testing as they sought the Promised Land. In turn, after His baptism, Christ would retreat into the wilderness for forty days and nights of trial, or as related in the Pseudo-Bonaventura life of Christ:

When our Lorde Jesus was baptised as is aforesaid, presently he departed and went into the deserte: And ther vpon a highe hille which was from the place of his baptisme some foure myle, and is called *Quarenta,* he fasted fortie dayes and fortie nightes, not eatinge any kind of sustenance, as the Evangelist saint Marke testifieth who farther sayeth that his dwellinge was there amongst the brute beastes. . . . And here we are to consider four pointes which specially appertaine to all spiritual persons, to wit: solitarines; fastings, prayer, and bodily penance, as the meanes wherby they may obtaine that cleanes of soule and harte which they ought so principally to seek and desier.[52]

In 1725 the philosopher Francis Hutcheson commented on the appropriateness of groves of trees as a "Retreat to those who love *Solitude*," and, as was observed earlier, the youthful George Whitefield in his religious ardor to partake of Christ's trials in the wilderness sought the treed walks of Christ Church at Oxford.[53] About the same time the more practical Batty Langley, who looked to treed groves only for physical refreshment, complained that in the previous gardening of the period of London and Wise: "Their Wildernesses and Groves (when they planted any) were always placed at the most remote Parts of the Garden: so that before we can enter them, in the *Heat of Summer*, when they are most useful, we are obliged to pass thro' the *Scorching Heat of the Sun*."[54]

Philip Miller's *The Gardeners Dictionary*, the bible of eighteenth-century gardeners, had in its sixth edition of 1752 an extensive article on wildernesses, specifying a few basic principles. Evergreens must never be intermixed with deciduous trees, but should be in "a separate Part of the Wilderness by themselves." The plants should always be adapted to the size of the plantation as the walks should be proportioned to the size of the grounds.[55] Miller points out that the "usual Method of contriving Wildernesses is, to divide the whole Compass of Ground, either into Squares, Angles, Circles, or other Figures, making the walks correspondent to them; planting the Sides of the Walks with Hedges of Lime, Elm, Hornbeam, &c. and the Quarters within are planted with various Kinds of Trees promiscuously without Order." He, however, disapproves of this method, citing the expense of maintaining the hedges and their unnatural appearance. He also recommends that the walks should meander, "and the more these Walks are turn'd, the greater Pleasure they will afford." Within the wilderness will be circular, turfed openings decorated with "either an Obelisk, Statue, or Fountain." The *Dictionary*'s principal strength was the horticultural and botanical knowledge it conveyed. In terms of garden design it was very conservative, ensuring its appeal to the average gardener. After the mid-eighteenth century the "wilderness" gradually disappeared from English gardening and was replaced by the "Shrubbery." No artificial wilderness would have been able to satisfy the aesthetic desires of the picturesque age. Already in 1742 Samuel Richardson, in his edition of Defoe's *Tour*, regretted the regularity of the wilderness of Peckham which was planted in the seventeenth century during the reign of James II: "The

Wilderness indeed was planted too regular, having diagonal Walks inter-
secting each other, with hedges on each Side; but this was the Taste which
prevailed, when those Gardens were laid out."[56]

The wilderness was basically a seventeenth-century English garden feature, although the dialogue contrasting the garden and the wilderness at
Leconfield dates to at least the early sixteenth century. Ralph Treswell's
estate maps of 1580 and 1587 of Holdenby in Northamptonshire portray
several treed areas around the gardens planted in simple checkerboard or
quincunx patterns, which in the seventeenth century, as at Audley End,
might have been described as wildernesses. At Holdenby, however, one is
labeled "The Spinney," the other "the Grove," on both plans.[57] The popularity of the wilderness as a horticultural attribute would seem, therefore,
to correspond to the importation to England of the French bosquet. At the
same time it accompanied the prevalence of the wilderness image in religion. G. H. Williams claims that "the wilderness impulse appeared everywhere" among the seventeenth-century British, "whether they were Irish
Catholics or Presbyterians. Caroline divines or Quakers."[58] He identifies
as one source of this impulse the formulation of the Book of Common
Prayer by Archbishop Cranmer in the mid-sixteenth century in which the
wilderness theme was expounded daily in the Morning Prayer.

> Harden not your hearts: as in the provocation, as in the day of tempta-
> tion in the wilderness . . . forty years long was I grieved with this
> generation, and said: it is a people that do err in their hearts, for they
> have not known my ways.

Hermits, Goths, and Druids

HERMITS AND HERMITAGES

THROUGHOUT the Tudor period knightly pageants featured hermits and hermitages.[1] In fact, as early as 1477 at the marriage of the duke of York, the marquis of Dorset appeared as a hermit riding in a hermitage. The guise was to honor his name saint, Anthony the hermit, but also to reflect that after this his last tournament Dorset was to retire from the active world of the court. Similarly in May 1591 when Queen Elizabeth came to visit Theobalds, the country residence of her treasurer Lord Burghley, she was greeted by his son Robert Cecil dressed as a hermit, who in a poem written by George Peele apologized for Burghley not personally welcoming the queen.[2] The hermit explained that since the death of Burghley's wife and daughter during the past two years, Burghley had retired from public life. In fact, it has been suggested that the queen's visit may have been to urge Burghley to return to a more active role at court. Although such hermits were playacting and offering entertainment, they were also commenting on a very important personal situation.

About 1630 Thomas Bushell, who had been a secretary to Sir Francis Bacon, ordered a servant, according to John Aubrey, to clear some woods on a hillside near Enstone in Oxfordshire and to dig there a cave where he might sit and read in contemplation.[3] The laborer, however, soon uncovered a huge, unusual rock "with pendants like icicles." Over the rock Bushell built a small dwelling with an adjoining garden. The ground floor of the structure was a grotto with waterworks playing over the rock (fig. 31), while in the garden nearby were also unusual waterworks and watertricks. Over the grotto was a banqueting hall flanked by two smaller cham-

TAB.XI
chap:g.
§52.

ad pag. 243

To the right Honorable
Edward Henry Earle of
Lichfield Viscount QUARRENDON
and Baron of Spelsbury, &c
This Eleventh Table
Shewing the exterior Prospect of ENSTON
Waterworks, in part erected, all restored
by his LORDP with all imaginable
respect is justly dedicated
by R.P. LL.D.

31. Enstone (Oxon), grotto, A: (*left*) exterior and B: (*right*) interior, engravings

88

bers, one a bedroom, the other a study "hung with blacke Cloth, representing a mancholly retyr'd life like a Hermits," according to the account of Lieutenant Hammond during his visit in 1635. Hammond continues the hermitical analogy by mentioning that he "tasted of the Hermits diet drinke, the cleare rocke water." On August 23, 1636, Charles I and Henrietta Maria, staying at Oxford, visited Enstone to view the wonders of the waterworks in the garden and grotto. Robert Plot in his book on Oxfordshire natural history remarks that at their arrival "there arose a *Hermite*," portrayed by Bushell himself, "out of the ground, and entertain'd them with a *Speech;* returning again in the close down to his peaceful *Urn*." Aubrey's brief life of Bushell depicts a man given to a solitary life overcast with melancholy, who at night "walkt in the garden and orchard." Forced to hide during the Civil War, "his hermitage over the rocks at Enstone were hung with black-bayes," and Bushell himself hid in a gallery in Lambeth marsh "hung all with black, and had some death's heads and bones painted."

About the same time, the young John Milton composed his famous twin poems, *L'Allegro* and *Il Penseroso*, of which the latter celebrates the pleasures of melancholy, those pleasures apparently sought by Bushell at this hermitage. The poet dwelt on the beauty of black (lines 15–21), the black of melancholy, the humor of black bile. Like Bushell, Il Penseroso walks abroad at night (lines 65–72).

> And may at last my weary age
> Find out the peaceful hermitage,
> The hairy gown and mossy cell,
> Where I may sit and rightly spell
> Of every star that heav'n doth shew,
> And every herb that sips the dew;
> Till old experience do attain
> To something like prophetic strain
> These pleasures, melancholy, give,
> And I with thee will choose to live (lines 167–76).

The rage for hermitages as features in a garden or park was characteristic of the eighteenth century.[4] The Irish Poet Thomas Parnell, who died young in 1717, introduced the subject to eighteenth-century England in his poem *The Hermit*, first published posthumously in 1722, but with numerous later editions.[5] The image presented is a traditional one.

Far in a Wild, unknown to publick View,
From Youth to Age a rev'rend *Hermit* grew;
The Moss his Bed, the Cave his humble Cell,
His Food the Fruits, his Drink the chrystal Well:
Remote from Man, with God he pass'd the Day,
Pray'r all his Bus'ness, all his Pleasure Praise.

The theme of the poem, however, is concerned with religious moralizing on evil, far from the romantic rusticity of most eighteenth-century hermitages. So in 1724 the poet Alexander Pope identified a "Hermits Seat" in his account of the landscape of Sherborne in Dorset, "a Rustick Seat of Stone, flagged and rough, with two Urns in the same rude taste upon pedestals, on each side: from whence you lose your eyes upon the glimmering of the Waters under the wood, & your ears in the constant clashing of the waves."[6]

It was royal patronage, however, that ensured the creation of a garden hermitage that, by its renown, established the idea that such a feature is an important element of English gardening. In 1730 the architect and landscapist William Kent began a hermitage for Queen Caroline in her gardens at Richmond.[7] To suggest the idea of an old, rustic hermitage, the exterior of the building was built roughly with some traces of ruin. On the interior, an octagonal, domed chamber was flanked by rectangular rooms, one serving as a library, the other as a bedroom. Although destroyed in the nineteenth century, a contemporary view of the interior shows an elegant set of chambers with stucco stalactites encircling the oculus of the dome and along its ribs to suggest a grotto (fig. 32). Five portrait busts set in niches in the central salon expressed the queen's belief that science and religion could be reconciled and buttress one another. At two corners were busts of the scientist Sir Isaac Newton and the natural philosopher John Locke. Opposite them were busts of two theologians, Dr. Samuel Clarke and William Wollaston. Clarke, who died in 1729, had been a student of Newton and the leader of weekly theological discussions encouraged by the queen. Clarke believed that the existence of God could be proven by a mathematical method and that moral laws were as certain as mathematical propositions. Wollaston held that human reason could discover religious truths without divine revelation. Newton, on the other hand, believed that his discoveries in physics proved the existence of God. Overseeing this pantheon of scientists and theologians in the exedra at the rear of the chamber was a bust of the scientist Robert Boyle surrounded by golden rays. In addition to his scien-

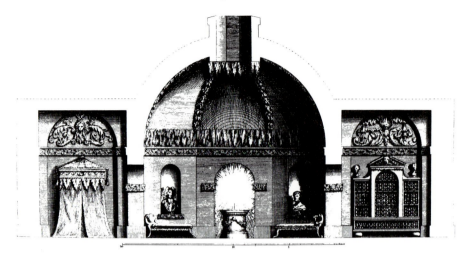

32. Richmond Gardens, Hermitage, interior, engraving

tific discoveries Boyle had published in 1665 his *Occasional Reflections upon Several Subjects* in which he jotted down the meditations he had formulated from observing small incidents on his customary long walks. The hermitage at Richmond, therefore, was an exposition celebrating Natural Religion.

The hermitage even had a "hermit," for its caretaker was the so-called "thresher-poet," Stephen Duck, an untutored, naive poet supported by the queen. Soon the poet wrote works honoring the hermitage and the Richmond gardens. By 1733 *The Gentleman's Magazine* offered a prize for the best poem on the hermitage and published dozens of poems praising it.

Soon Kent built in the gardens of Stowe a hermitage modelled on the queen's hermitage at Richmond and described by Gilbert West in his poem of 1732 as a ruin (fig. 14).[8] By the time of Milles' account in 1735, it was identified as "a little hermitage, (formerly designed for the ruins)," which is its designation in all later descriptions. By 1742, however, Richardson's version of Defoe's *Tour* lists not only the hermitage, but adds at another location "St. Augustine's Cave, which is a Building of Roots of Trees and Moss; and in it a Straw Couch with Three Inscriptions in *Monkish Latin*."

Meanwhile, the antiquarian William Stukeley, having graduated from Cambridge in medicine in 1719, had begun to investigate the early history of England, gradually concentrating his attention on the Druids.[9] During his inquiries he explored the caves of hermits in the Peak District, which he recorded in his *Itinerarium Curiosum* of 1724. His studies eventually led him to enter the Anglican church with a living at Stamford. Later, undoubtedly as a result of his earlier discoveries, Stukeley built in the garden of his house at Barnhill in Stamford a rockwork hermitage depicted in one of his drawings dated 1738 (fig. 33). The image portrays several very crude, rustic arched niches and a gothic window set in the garden. One arch frames a small cascade; another precariously supports a column and a globe.

From about 1740 until the end of the century hermitages or root houses proliferated in gardens throughout all of England and Ireland. The literary interest in the hermit continued with Francis Tolson's publication about 1740 of his *Hermathenae* or poetic emblems in which Emblem XLVII is devoted to the hermit depicted kneeling in prayer in a small, arched hermitage accompanied by a traditional poetic commentary that commences:

> Within thie lonely melancholy Cell
> Shou'd no vain thoughts, no Pride nor Envy dwell;
> The soul within herself serene, shou'd here
> Like nature's Golden Infancy appear,
> Religious, unambitious, and sincere.[10]

Much later the Reverend Thomas Percy, who in 1765 had issued an extremely popular anthology of medieval English poetry, *Reliques of Ancient English Poetry*, wrote from 1767 to 1770 his own ballad, *The Hermit of Warkworth*, which, published first in May 1771, required three editions during its first year and numerous further editions or reprintings.[11] His rather trite, sentimental offering to popular or hermitage poetry was inspired by an actual ruined, rockcut hermitage on the edge of the river Coquet near Warkworth Castle.

In December 1743 the poet William Shenstone mentioned in a letter that his neighbor George Lyttelton had built in his park at Hagley an alcove, "inscribed Sedes contemplationis, near his hermitage."[12] This is the earliest reference to the hermitage at Hagley, which is more fully described by Dr. Pococke in 1751 and Joseph Heely in 1777. Horace Walpole during his visit in 1753 when he enthused about the ruined castle there with "the true rust of the Barons' Wars" saw the hermitage as a reincarnation of a Sadeler print, presumably from the collection of engravings portraying hermits in their solitary retreat by the brothers Johann and Raphael Sadeler published in 1594 under the title *Solitudo, sive vitae Patrum Eremicolarum*. Heely, however, seems a little hesitant about the idea of a rude hermitage in a carefully nurtured park.

The Hermitage Stamford 1738.

W. S. f.

33. Stamford (Lincs), Barn Hill, Hermitage, drawing by Stukeley, Gough Maps 230, f. 411, The Bodleian Library, Oxford

One knows not how to reconcile an hermitage, or a cottage, standing within the polished park of a nobleman: there is an incongruity in both; and neither, in my opinion, should be countenanced in such places.

However, this hermitage, or call it what you will, is well enough adapted to the scenery about it, being rudely formed with chumps of wood, and jagged old roots, jambed together, and its interstices simply filled with moss: the floor is neatly paved with small pebbles, and a matted couch goes round it.

A door from this leads into another apartment much in the same dress; every thing within, and immediately about it, carries the face of poverty, and a contempt of the vain superfluities of the world, fit for the imaginary inhabitant, whom we are to suppose despises the follies and luxuries of life, and who devotes his melancholy hours, to meditation and rigid abstinence.

Heely continues by noting that inscribed in the first room are the lines from Milton's *Il Penseroso* quoted at the beginning of this chapter.

It has been observed that there was an unusual revival of interest in Milton's poems *L'Allegro* and *Il Penseroso* at this time.[13] During the first century of the existence of the two poems there had been some fourteen imitations of them, but in the decade 1736 to 1746 there appeared a total of forty-three versions. *Il Penseroso* particularly appealed at this time. In 1755 when Dodsley was issuing his anthology of contemporary poetry, the poet William Shenstone wrote: "I cannot help remarking that Milton's Il Penseroso has drove half our Poets crazy."[14] In the same letter Shenstone asserted: "There is nothing I am more pleas'd with than Father Francis's Prayer. Mᵣ Berkley repeated it to me in my Root-house this last summer, & I think said it was Mᵣ Wests." The poem entitled *Father Francis's Prayer to St. Agnes in Imitation of Chaucer* was first published anonymously in *The Gentleman's Magazine* in December 1746.[15] Written by Gilbert West, the poem praises Father Francis for abandoning the world of corruption, pride, and fashionable French fancies to dwell in a hermitage. Later when the prayer was published in Dodsley's anthology it bore the subtitle "Written in Lord Westmoreland's Hermitage" (at Mereworth in Kent).

As Shenstone wrote, he had a hermitage or roothouse in his ferme ornée at The Leasowes. Early in June 1749 he sent Lady Luxborough a plan for a Hermit's Seat to stand on a bank above his hermitage, of which apparently Lord Lyttelton disapproved.[16] Shenstone also included a draft of a poem for a roothouse, beginning:

Here in cool grott, & mossy Cell
We Fauns & playfull Fairies dwell.

Later Robert Dodsley printed an expanded and revised version of the poem, entitled "On a Root-House," in his 1758 edition of a collection of poems. In his 1764 description of The Leasowes he records that the poem was inscribed on a tablet in a small roothouse in the valley near the entrance to the park. Similarly, Lady Luxborough had a hermitage at her estate at Barrels in Warwickshire for which her friend Shenstone, in 1748–49, was constantly giving advice for planting and laying out an approach.[17] Apparently Shenstone was recognized as an authority on roothouses for in 1758 the poet Joseph Spence, who was a great garden enthusiast and garden designer, wrote Shenstone to ask: "Could you send me a Receipt how to build a Root House? In my wild Abbey-Grounds [Finchdale Priory at Durham], I have a Place that asks for one loudly; but we have neither any Gentlemen or Artist here, who understands any thing of that Stile of Architecture."

The Reverend William Cole, friend and unremitting correspondent of Horace Walpole, was considered an authority on several of the new exotic styles of garden architecture. In 1753 he had designed and built a Chinese-Gothic hexagonal garden seat at one end of the terrace walk on the north side of his garden at the parsonage at Blecheley, now Bletchley, in Buckinghamshire, which was soon followed by a hermitage at the other end of the terrace walk. Later, in 1765, Cole wrote a description of the two garden buildings accompanied by crude sketches of them.

> The Hermitage I built soon after the other was completed: the Back is all of Brick & the front Part wholly of rough & rude Stones, & black rough Bricks which had run together in various odd Forms at the Brickhill. I only plaistered it in the inside with Common Clay & paved it with Pebbles: it is of an octagon Form & will hold about 6 or 8 Persons & being at the South End of the Terras Walk is not fit to be sat in the Summer; but in an Evening & some warm Days in Winter it is a most comfortable Seat: it has the Temple or Chinese Gothic Seat in full view, & on the Side View a Prospect of Great Brickhill, Leighton-Bozard Steeple & Stukeley Church.[18]

Cole's sketch depicts the octagonal building with an arched entrance framed by rough stones opening on the front side and flanked on the receding sides by Gothic, pointed arched windows glazed with fragments of old stained glass collected by Cole. A thatched roof was surmounted by a crude cross of wood. By the time of Cole's description in 1765 the brickwork was cracked, as he admitted "by Reason the Foundations were not laid deep enough."

Tyers' Vauxhall Gardens in London had to have its version of a hermitage, so the narrow alley on the north side of the garden was called the Hermit's Walk because of a transparency toward the end of the walk depicting a hermit seated before his retreat studying by the light of the moon.[19] There may also have been a reference to Milton's *Il Penseroso* along the Hermit's Walk, for in John Lockman's description of the gardens in 1752 he notes that there "is a Statue representing our great Poet *Milton*, as drawn by himself in his *Il Penseroso*, seated on a Rock; and in an Attitude listening to soft music." The lead statue, attributed much later to Roubiliac without any authority, is now lost.

There are only brief literary accounts to offer any image of the ephemeral hermitages or roothouses at Hagley, Mereworth, The Leasowes, or Barrels. At Badminton in Gloucestershire, however, there is still preserved a hermitage designed by the architect-mathematician Thomas Wright, who, as discussed previously, was an early exponent of the Gothic style (fig. 34). Succeeding William Kent as architect and landscapist at Badminton for the duke of Beaufort, Wright began the hermitage in October 1747 and continued working there, adding other secondary buildings and follies.[20] The hermitage, a room about twenty feet by twenty-four, was originally set in a rather dense grove of trees now gone. Large, knotty tree trunks comprise the corner posts of the structure, as well as lintels and gable ends. The door frame is the fork of a large tree, the walls composed of tree roots, branches, and sticks, and the roof thatched. The interior room has the form of classical architecture expressed in rough wood covered with moss.

Thomas Wright was a fertile propagator of the designs of garden buildings. A large album of sketches by him at the Avery Library of Columbia University has many drawings of roothouses, arbors, and grottoes, some of which were built while others remained projects. In 1755 he published *Six Original Designs of Arbours*, which was to be book I of his treatise *Universal Architecture*, followed in 1758 by *Six Original Designs for Grottoes*. While working at Badminton Wright was also involved with the landscaping and design of garden buildings for Stoke Park in Gloucestershire.[21] Among the buildings erected there was one whose plan in the Avery sketchbook is labelled "Bladud's Temple." Later the duchess of Beaufort, sister of the owner Lord Botetourt, stated that an inscription over the entrance indicated that the rustic hermitage set in a dark grove of yews was meant to be the cell of the enchantress Urganda from the sixteenth-century Spanish romance *Amadis de Gaul*. This hermitage too has disappeared. Probably the only

34. Badminton (Glos), Hermitage

other eighteenth-century hermitages or roothouses that are preserved are those at Brocklesby in Lincolnshire and at Spetchley in Worcestershire, the former being very much an ornamental feature as only the front is fashioned as a roothouse with tree trunks and rock walls, the main body of the structure being a brick octagon with slate roof.[22]

At the same time that roothouses or hermitages were beginning to populate the English garden parks, architectural critics in France, such as Abbé Laugier, and then in England in the person of Sir William Chambers began to write about the origins of domestic architecture in terms of primitive huts composed of rough tree trunks.[23] In the second edition of Abbé Laugier's treatise, *Essai sur l'architecture,* in 1755, he included an illustration of a primitive hut with untrimmed tree trunks as columns; four years later Chambers in *A Treatise on Civil Architecture* depicted an early structure, "which gave birth to the Doric Order," with primitive columns bearing simple, square block capitals, supported on square blocks as bases. In 1761–62 the young architect Robert Adam built at Kedleston Hall in

Derbyshire for Lord Scarsdale a hermitage with a peripteral colonnade of eleven columns with large, block capitals and bases somewhat like those of Chambers, and a conical, thatched roof associated with primitive huts. Remains of the cella of the hut exist in a ruinous state about half a mile west of the house, but a drawing of the hermitage attributed to Adam from about 1760 is preserved at Kedleston.

Occasionally a hermitage might have served as a residence for a family member. It seems rather incongruous that the wealthy earl of Cork and Orrery erected at Marston in Somerset a crude hermitage for a younger son. Bishop Pococke during his visit in 1754 described it.

> At the other end of the garden in a corner is a little Hermitage near finished for my Lord's youngest son; there is a deep way cut down to it with wood on each side, a seat or two in it—one is made in the hollow of a tree; it leads to a little irregular court, with a fence of horses' heads and bones. It is a cabin, poorly thatch'd, and a bedstead covered with straw at one end, a chimney at the other, and some beginning made of very poor furniture.[24]

The popularization of the garden hermitage was furthered by the appearance in 1767 of the book *Grotesque Architecture* by William Wrighte. Twenty-eight engravings illustrated hermitages and grottoes. The publication also reflected the contemporary discussion regarding the origin of the classical orders in primitive wooden architecture, the first plate depicting a small, inexpensive hut in "the primitive state of the Dorick Order." Later, William Mason, in his poem *The English Garden*, invoked simplicity as a characteristic of beautiful gardening, and that the architecture that decorates a garden should participate in that rustic simplicity. In book IV his hero Alexander erects a shrine to his beloved Nerina.

> A shed of twisting roots and living moss,
> With rushes thatch'd, with wattled oziers lin'd.
> He bids them raise: It seem'd a Hermit's cell;
> Yet void of hour-glass, scull and maple dish;[25]

William Burgh in his commentary on this passage in the 1783 edition of Mason's poem notes:

> As it seems to have been our Author's intention to select from the variety of buildings, which have usually found a place in our modern Gardens, as were capable of being introduced with the greatest congruity, and, when so introduced, capable of producing the best effect,

he could not well overlook the most common of them all, the Hermitage; he has therefore allotted to it a situation retired and solitary; but, as the melancholy circumstances of his tale led him to do, he has also made it a kind of monumental structure; here as elsewhere, both by example and precept, conveying to us these important lessons, that such melancholy memorials should only be raised where a real interest, in their object gives them propriety, and that where the circumstance recorded is near the heart, simplicity should be most studiously consulted, as emblems and unappropriated ornaments must necessarily prove contemptible to a mind which is too much in earnest to derive any pleasure from fiction.

Unlike the earl of Cork and Orrery's hermitage at Marston, most hermitages of roothouses were built to convey the idea that they were secluded retreats for hermits weary with the sins and luxuries of the world. Throughout the second half of the eighteenth century owners of parks advertised to find resident hermits for their hermitages. Perhaps the most well-known example was at Charles Hamilton's landscape park at Painshill. Between 1758 and 1761 he erected several garden buildings including a hermitage which Sir John Parnell mentioned in the account of his 1763 visit as constructed of trunks of fir trees retaining their bark and with Gothic windows made of branches. He also included a very crude sketch of the structure with pointed windows and door, and a gabled roof.[26] During a later visit in 1769 Parnell was particularly appreciative of the planting around the hermitage. "The part it's in, though a mere plantation of Scots fir, larch, cedar and pines mixed with birch on the wildest part of the heath which comes into the improvement on that corner, has really the air of a wild forest, the ground amidst the trees so rough not a little contributing."

Even the wealthy banker Henry Hoare, who created at Stourhead in Wiltshire a remarkable garden park featuring classical allusions to Vergil and Ovid, succumbed to the hermitic rage, perhaps under the influence of his friend Charles Hamilton. In November 1771 Hoare wrote his granddaughter:

> I am building a Hermitage above the Rock. It is to be lined inside and out with old Gouty nobbly oakes, the Bark on, which Mr. Groves & my neighbours are so kind to give me & Mr. Chapman a clergyman showed me one yesterday called Judge Wyndham's seat which I take to be of the Year of Our Lord 1000 & I am not quite sure it is not Anti Diluvian. I believe I shall put it in to be myself the Hermit.[27]

Destroyed in 1814, the hermitage originally stood astride the zig-zag path suggested by Charles Hamilton to mount the hill to the classical Temple of Apollo perched high above the landscape lake. Soon after the completion of the hermitage, Maria Rishton in a letter of April 1773 to Fanny Burney described it as "a Prodigious fine root-house with Several Cells intended as a hermitage, a lamp Always Burning, hour glass, human bones, and several inscriptions." Later, when Druidic mythology dominated the British landscape, the Swedish landscape artist Frederik Magnus Piper included among his 1779 watercolors of Stourhead a plan and section of the hermitage (fig. 35), as well as several views of it, with an accompanying notation that it was called "The Druid's Cell."

Although Henry Hoare had facetiously told his granddaughter that he himself might serve as the hermit dweller of his roothouse, his friend Charles Hamilton desired a resident hermit for his refuge. Soon after the completion at Painshill of its hermitage, Hamilton is reported to have advertised for someone to serve as a hermit in his retreat. An applicant was to agree to remain in the hermitage for seven years where he was to be provided with a Bible, glasses, a mat for his bed, a hassock for a pillow, an hour-glass for his timepiece, water to drink, food from the house, but he was never to exchange words with the servants. He was to wear a "camlet robe," and was not to cut his beard or his nails, nor leave the grounds. For successful completion of the duty he was to be paid seven hundred guineas. For any failure of any condition the whole sum was to be forfeited.

Other examples of advertisements for hermits were at Marcham in Lancashire and much later at Derwent Water in the Lake Country.[28] At Marcham the hermit would receive fifty pounds a year for life with similar conditions as those at Painshill. At Derwent Water Joseph Pocklington had a Gothic hermitage built in 1795 on the grounds of his Barrow Cascade House on the eastern shore of the lake and when the young William Gell stopped to visit the site in 1797 he was amused to note in his diary that Pocklington was offering half-a-crown daily to any hermit prospect with the usual qualifications of not washing or cutting his hair or nails.

As resident hermits seem to have been difficult to find, an inexpensive solution was to have a wax image or even a mechanical robot to serve as the hermit. In 1753 Philip Thicknesse bought a thatched cottage near Harwich in Suffolk and soon decorated its garden with several statues and bits of garden architecture, including references to Milton's poems *L'Allegro* and *Il Penseroso*.[29] The latter was represented by the Hermit's Cave with the figure of a hermit seated at a table in front of the cave. A later account described the hermit.

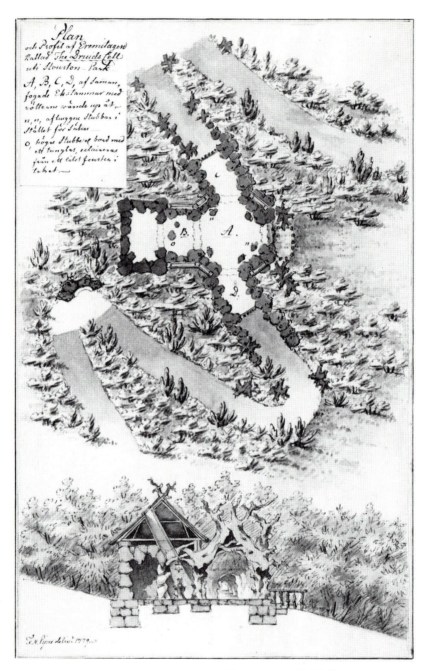

35. Stourhead (Wilts), roothouse or Druid's Cell, drawing by F. M. Piper, 1779, Kungl. Akademien för de fria Konsterna, Stockholm

The head and hands are finely modeled in wax. It was dressed in a long brown cloth habit tied around the waist with a cord, from which hung his chaplet. His hoary beard was of a most venerable length. The table was covered with a green cloth, and upon it the best edition of Milton, which opened at the following passage, to which the figure pointed with his fingers:

> A look that's fasten'd to the ground,
> A tongue chain'd up without a sound
> O sweetest, sweetest Melancholy!

In 1774 Thicknesse bought a cottage, S. Catherine's Hermitage, at Bathampton just outside Bath where, in a letter of November 1773, he had said that he planned to "divide the garden into Il Penseroso and L'Allegro." That same year Richard Graves described the garden of Mr. and Mrs. Rivers in his satirical novel *The Spiritual Quixote* as "laid out in a romantic taste, with a proper mixture of the allegro and the penseroso, the cheerful and the gloomy." At Bathampton *Il Penseroso* was denoted by a Hermit's Hut set in a small wood with meandering serpentine walks, near which in 1785 Thicknesse buried Anna, his young daughter of eighteen.

Lines from Milton's *Il Penseroso* were, of course, most suitable for hermitage inscriptions and the rage for garden hermitages in the eighteenth century helped spark the revival of Milton's two poems. The painter Thomas Robins the Elder noted the lines from *Il Penseroso* at the entrance of the hermitage of Dr. Jeremiah Pierce in Lansdown Wood at Bath.[30]

> And may not at last my weary age
> Find out the peaceful hermitage

The drawing by Robins of the hermitage portrays a crude stone cell with a thatched and gabled roof. A Gothic window and door are on the facade and the roof is topped by a thatched, open belfry. At Brougham Hall near Penrith in Wales a tour guide of 1800 records:

A *hermit's cell*, a small circular building covered with thatch, and lined with mosses of various kinds: the seats around are matted, and the windows of painted glass, with the usual characteristic of a hermit in his retirement, viz, the *hour-glass*, *cross*, and *beads*, and a *skull*. On the table some appropriate lines are painted from *Il Penseroso* of *Milton;* and in another part of the building is a scroll, with these lines:

Beneath this moss grown roof, this rustic cell
Truth, Liberty, Content, sequester'd dwell:
Say, you who dare our hermitage disdain,
What drawing-room can boast so fair a train?[31]

At Priestlands near Lymington in Hampshire John Newton, in 1784, shared his study with a hermit, writing in his diary:

> At Mr. Etty's I had a pretty retirement, a summer house, which was appropriated to me for a study. Underneath there is a grotto, lined with moss and shellwork, and a hermit in it; he is dressed in a friar's habit, and would almost make me ask his pardon for disturbing him; he looks so grave and so much alive, as if he was reading a paper that lies before him among several books upon a table.[32]

In several cases these dummy hermits could be animated. Sir Samuel Hellier had in his hermitage at Wodehouse Wombourn in Staffordshire a life-size model of a hermit called Father Francis after Gilbert West's poem.[33] John Loveday of Caversham claimed in 1765 that "by springs the hermit, formed very naturally, had motions that surprise his visitants who suppose him inanimate." An even more active dummy hermit, also called Francis, was in the hermitage in the awesome park at Hawkstone in Shropshire.[34] Sir Richard Hill inherited the property in 1783 and almost immediately added numerous features to the natural landscape, including a deep grotto or rockcut tunnel and a large, red sandstone Doric column. By 1787 there was a thatched hermitage where Sir Richard at first employed a local pauper to play the hermit, but as this arrangement apparently was not successful he substituted a dummy seated at a table. As visitors approached, the dummy hermit would rise to greet them, the visitors' guide having meanwhile crept stealthly around to a secret back door by which he entered to move the levers manipulating the robot. The figure would then mouth words, including poetry, spoken by the guide.

John Byng Viscount Torrington had a simple solution for a missing hermit for the hermitage in the garden of the Reverend Wolley Jolland at Louth in Lincolnshire.[35] Byng proposed to Jolland that in his moss-covered roothouse he should "have his gardener, at grand showings, properly attired as an hermit, and to be found in some other of the recesses, at his studies."

The role of a hermitage in the life of a large family and their neighbors is amply demonstrated in the diary or garden calendar and in the letters of the famous naturalist the Reverend Gilbert White of Selborne.[36] Presumably early in 1758 Harry White, a younger brother of Gilbert, erected a hermitage on the wooded hill called The Hanger beyond The Wakes, Gilbert White's house in Selborne. In April 1758, five shillings were subscribed toward the building of the hermitage and by June their friend John Mulso wrote that he wished that he was "in your Grotto," his name for the hermitage. In a later letter in February 1759 Mulso recorded that over the door to the retreat were lines from Milton's *Il Penseroso*. At this same time Gilbert White was passionately devoted to growing melons, being frequently in contact with the famous garden authority Philip Miller, curator of the Chelsea Apothecaries Garden in London, regarding their care. In the heat of summer White turned to the hermitage as a setting to taste his products. On August 25, 1758, he wrote in his garden-calendar: "Send a brace of the Cantaleupes to Lord Keen [the Lord Chancellor]: eat the Third at Home, which turned-out perfectly delicate; rather superior to ye first, eaten at the Hermitage." Another "brace of Cantaleupes" were savoured there on September 5 and on September 12: "Held a Cantaleupe-feast at ye Harmitage: cut-up a brace & an half of fruit among 14 people."[37]

In 1763 a young woman, Catharine Battie, and her sisters came for an extended stay at Selborne. Catharine faithfully kept a journal of the visit in which she noted almost daily that she and her sisters with the family and friends went to the hermitage to dine or to have tea. An evocative entry occurs on June 24 when:

> At two we ascended the zigzag [the path up The Hanger], to the enchanting spot [the hermitage], where we dined after dinner we went to the Tent here we sat still 6 when we went back to the Hermitage to tea in the middle of tea we had a visit from the old Hermit his appearance made me start he sat some time with us & then went away after tea we went into the Woods return'd to the Hermitage to see it by Lamp light it look'd sweetly indeed. Never shall I forget the happiness of this day which exceeded any I ever had in all my Life, sweet Hermitage agreeable Company fine day good spirits all combin'd to make it of all days the most agreeable.[38]

On July 20 and 21 Thomas Mulso appropriately read to them in the hermitage James Thomson's poem *The Seasons*. On July 28 there was another special celebration.

> After dinner we went up to the Dr. [Dear] Hermitage we drank tea afterwards the old Hermit came to us he told Nannie and H. Baker their fortunes after the old man had sat some time with us he retired &

we adjoined to the tent where we Shepherdesses danced; at nine the lamp was lighted, enchanting scene oh never did I see anything like 'tis 'tis Arcadia Happy Happy Vale when shall I see thee again.

Of the same gathering Gilbert White noted in his calendar:

July 28; Drank tea 20 of us at the hermitage: The Miss Batties & the Mulso family contributed much to our pleasure by their singing, & being dress'd as shepherds, & shepherdesses. It was a most elegant evening, & all the parties appear'd highly satisfy'd. The Hermit appear'd to great advantage.[39]

The mysterious "old Hermit" was actually Harry White, Gilbert's younger brother, who would quietly appear in hermit's garb and false beard, as he was depicted much later in a watercolor by S. H. Grimm in 1776 standing in front of the thatched hermitage (fig. 36). Harry White had first built the rustic retreat.

Later the poet William Cowper and friends found pleasure dining in a roothouse. In July 1781 he wrote William Unwin:

Yesterday sev'night we all dined together in the Spinney, a most delightfull retirement belonging to Mrs. Throgmorton [Anna Maria Throckmorton] of Weston. Lady Austen's laquey and a lad that waits on me in the garden, drove a wheel-barrow full of eatables and drinkables to the scene of our fete champetre. A board laid over the top of the barrow served us for a table, our dining room was a root:house lined with moss and Ivy. At Six o'clock the Servants who had dined under a great Elm upon the ground at a little distance, boiled the Kettle, and the said Wheel:barrow served us again for a tea table. We then took a walk from thence to the wilderness about half a mile off, and were at home again soon after eight.[40]

Cowper himself decided in 1793 that he wanted a rustic hermitage at his house at Weston Underwood and bid his servant Sam Roberts to build one making it "rude and rough," but to Cowper's dismay Roberts and a fellow carpenter built "a thing for Stowe Gardens."[41] Their creation not only irritated Cowper for its unnecessary cost, but perhaps even more for being inappropriate to a poem he had composed. "I had written one which I designed for a hermitage, and it will by no means suit the fine and pompous affair which they have made instead of one."

Samuel Johnson, who was not particularly a garden enthusiast, once asserting that garden grottoes were only fit for toads, held a rather jaun-

36. Selborne (Hants), Hermitage with Harry White as hermit, watercolor by S. H. Grimm, 1776, pfMS Eng 731.11, Houghton Library, Harvard University

diced point of view toward hermits and hermitages.[42] In his novel *Rasselas*, first published in 1759, his hermit abandons his solitary refuge saying: "I have been long comparing the evils with the advantages of society, and resolve to return into the world to morrow. The life of a solitary man will be certainly miserable, but not certainly devout." Much later Johnson composed a parody of the hermitage poetry proliferating in the eighteenth century.

> Hermit hoar, in solemn cell.
> Wearing out life's evening gray;
> Smite thy bosom, sage, and tell,
> Where is the bliss? and which the way?
> Thus I spoke; and speaking sigh'd;
> —Scarce repress'd the starting tear;—
> When the smiling sage reply'd—
> —Come, my lad, and drink some beer.[43]

As the convivial meetings in the White hermitage at Selborne demonstrated, hermitages in the eighteenth century had lost for the most part any grave, meditative aspect such as at Thomas Bushell's hermitage at Enstone in the seventeenth century, and had become ornamental playthings often with mock or dummy hermits. The Reverend Richard Graves, a close friend of Shenstone, who, as we have seen, was considered an authority on the fashion of roothouses, mocked the change in his poem *The Hermitage* published in 1776, long after Shenstone's death.

> "Friend Simon, where's your Hermitage?
> "Have you no temple, seat, or grotto?
> "Or root-house, deck'd with classic motto?
> "A place is now not worth a fardin,
> "With out some gimcrack in your garden,
> "Come! make this hut a little fine;
> "Plant roses, woodbine, eglantine:
> "Nail o'er the door two sticks across,
> "Then dish it out with shells and moss,
> "With pictur'd saint in vesture sable,
> "And place an hour-glass on the table:
> "And here you have an hermit's cell,
> "Where Austin's self might wish to dwell."
>   Lo thus our honest country mouse
> Has made his useful, little house

A place—for holy meditation.
For solitude, and contemplation;
Yet what himself will rarely use.
Unless to conn his weekly news;
Or with some jovial friends to sit in,
To take his glass, and smoke, and *spit* it.[44]

Horace Walpole in his history of modern gardening, first published in 1780, administered the coup de grace to the hermitage as garden decoration.

The Doric portico, the Palladian bridge, the Gothic ruin, the Chinese pagoda, that surprize the stranger, soon lose their charms to their surfeited master. . . . But the ornament whose merit soonest fades is the hermitage, or scene adapted to contemplation. It is almost comic to set aside a quarter of one's garden to be melancholy in.[45]

ANCIENT BRITAIN

THE POTPOURRI of cultural images that Walpole mentions as decorating eighteenth-century English gardens was augmented by a fascination for the inhabitants of ancient Britain, the Saxons, the Goths, the Druids, who were often confused historically.[46] About 1728 the sculptor Rysbrack was commissioned by Lord Cobham to carve from Portland stone seven figures of the Saxon gods after whom the English days of the week are named. The statues, almost life-size, were originally set in a grove of trees around a large circular altar with seven corresponding niches where priests might officiate as depicted in George Bickham's *The Beauties of Stow* (fig. 37). The meaning of the sylvan temple is explained by its description in 1732 in Gilbert West's poem on Stowe, which suggests that the concept was West's contribution to his uncle's garden.

Hail! Gods of our renown'd Forefathers, hail!
Ador'd Protectors once of *England's* Weal.
Gods, of a Nation, valiant, wise, and free,
Who conquer'd to establish Liberty!
To whose auspicious Care *Britannia* owes
Those Laws, on which she stands, by which she rose.[47]

The meaning of the statues was enhanced about 1743 when they were moved from their secluded retreat and were placed in a formal circle around

37. Stowe (Bucks), The Saxon Temple, engraving

the new Gothic building designed by James Gibbs and identified in Bick-ham's guide as the Temple of Liberty (fig. 63). In 1921 the statues were sold at auction and scattered throughout Britain. Recently all the figures, except that of Sunna, have been located and identified. Most of the deities, Thuner being an exception, are standing figures with their names inscribed in runes on their bases (fig. 38). The names and imagery of the seven deities were undoubtedly derived from the book by Richard Rowlands, under his pseudonym Verstegan, entitled *A Restitution of Decayed Intelligence: In Antiquities*, Antwerp, 1605. A drawing dated about 1735 identified as the plan of the garden at Boringdon House in Devonshire records there "The Altar of the Saxon Gods," as well as several other features derived from Stowe. There is, however, no evidence that the plan was ever realized.

The revival of the Gothic style of architecture in eighteenth-century England was due in part to the idea of ancient Gothic liberty as a foundation for English constitutional liberty, so Jonathan Swift repeatedly identified

38. J. M. Rysbrack, statue of *Thuner* from Stowe, Victoria and Albert
Museum, London

Parliament as a "Gothick institution" and John Oldmixon in 1724 in his history of England asserted that "No nation has preserv'd their Gothic Constitution better than the English."[48] The Gothic temple in the gardens at Shotover in Oxfordshire, dating about 1718, is often identified as the first constructed example of a Gothic revival building (fig. 39). The owner, Sir James Tyrrell, was an Oxford scholar of political history and promoted the idea that the Saxon Witan, or royal council, was the source of the British parliament. He had also been an ardent supporter of William III, so that it would seem most likely that he had authorized the use of the Gothic style in his garden building as an expression of his political beliefs.[49]

Anglo-Saxon mythology, however, was chameleon-like, adaptable to many political positions. Lord Bathurst, a Tory and firm backer of Queen Anne, named the ruined Gothic house in his park at Cirencester, probably the earliest example of a Gothic ruin, Alfred's Hall (fig. 13). After the completion of the hermitage in Richmond Park, in the summer of 1735, Queen Caroline again commissioned William Kent to build a garden retreat which was to be known as Merlin's Cave.[50] Three unusual, beehive-shaped, thatched roofs covering the building conveyed a primitive aspect to the structure, while the entrance was an ogival arch with tracery. The combination of primitivism with the native Gothic style created an appropriate architectural setting for the tableau within (fig. 40). Six life-size waxen figures were posed around a table in the interior. At the center was the ancient wizard Merlin, who in Spenser's *Faerie Queene* had prophesied the return of King Arthur, and who here proclaims the rightful inheritance of Arthur's throne by the new Hanoverian rulers. At the same time, the prince of Wales, who was politically and personally in opposition to his royal parents, ordered that a statue of King Alfred, the chief representative of Saxon liberties, be set up in his garden at St. James's Palace in London, thus associating himself and his supporters with ancient British values.[51] Later the wealthy London banker Henry Hoare took advantage of a local tradition at his country estate of Stourhead in Wiltshire to erect, from 1765 to 1772, a Gothic, brick, triangular tower designed by Henry Flitcroft on Kingsettle Hill north of his pleasure park where King Alfred was reputed to have repulsed the Danes in the ninth century (fig. 41).[52] An inscription on the tower praises Alfred as the protector of English liberty by the introduction of the jury system and the establishment of a militia and navy.

Poets and even religious writers discoursed at length on the association of political freedom with the ancient Britons. The outstanding example was James Thomson's poem *Liberty* dedicated to the prince of Wales and published in parts from 1734 to 1736, with a new revised edition in 1738. In

39. Shotover (Oxon), Gothic Temple, c. 1718.

40. Richmond Gardens, Merlin's Cave, interior, engraving

the poem the "yellow-haired, blue-eyed Saxon . . . brought a happy government along; / Formed by that freedom, which, with secret voice, / Impartial Nature teaches all her sons."[53] Later, in 1748, Bishop William Warburton preached a sermon celebrating the suppression of the Jacobite rebellion and honoring the ancient British liberties.

> When the fierce and free nations of the North dismembered and tore in pieces the Roman Empire, they established themselves in their new conquests, on one common principle of policy; in which, the Liberty of the People made, as it ought to do, the Base, and operating Power.[54]

Five years later the bishop in his commentary on Alexander Pope's *Epistle IV*, dedicated to Lord Burlington, expounded at length his theory of the origin of Gothic architecture in the semblance of groves of trees in which the ancient Britons were accustomed to worship. The bishop, however, was only amplifying a much earlier suggestion of his friend the antiquarian William Stukeley who in his book *Itinerarium Curiosum* of 1724 had asserted that Gothic architecture "'tis the best manner of building, because the idea of it is taken from a walk of trees, whose touching heads are curiously imitated by the roof." Both James Thomson in his poem and Bishop Warburton in his sermon of 1746 allude to the Druids, who accord-

41. Stourhead (Wilts), Alfred's Tower

ing to Thomson "had care and direction of all religious matters" for the ancient Britons. And when Thomson died in 1749 his friend William Collins composed an ode honoring him as a Druid.[55]

The poet Michael Drayton in the late sixteenth century and early seventeenth century was the first writer to devote some attention to the Druids. Drayton's poetic references were expanded by John Selden in his so-called "illustrations" or annotations to Drayton's poem *Poly-Olbion* of 1612 where Selden identified the Druids as "Philosophers, Priests, and Lawyers," and suggested that, while the Gauls were polytheists, the Druids were probably monotheists whose "invocation was to one *All-healing* and *All-saving* power," thus promoting the idea that would have a long history.[56] By the 1660s the historian John Aubrey had conceived an idea that the great primitive stone rings at Stonehenge and at Avebury were Druidic temples, but his hypothesis remained unpublished in manuscript. Earlier the eminent architect Inigo Jones had been requested by James I to study Stonehenge which he, and later his relative John Webb, identified as remains of Roman origin. This attribution was sharply questioned by Walter Charleton in his book *Chorea Gigantum* published at London in 1663 where he credited the Danes as creators of the circles. In 1695 Aubrey's conjecture appeared briefly in print in the notes of Edmund Gibson to his translation of Camden's *Britannia*, and there only as a tentative supposition.[57]

Poets, of course, cherished Druidic mythology. When the magnificent oak woods at Nunappleton in Yorkshire were cut down after General Fairfax's death in 1671, his cousin Brian Fairfax composed the poem *The Vocal Oak* which asserts that "learned Druids taught, / Then it was sacrilege to cut a tree; / To wound an oak,—to offend a deity."[58] The poem then goes on to commemorate the general who maintained the oaks and was accustomed to come and to read in their shade.

> He read diviner things than Druids knew,
> Such mysteries were then revealed to few;
> For his chief study was God's sacred law,
> And all his life did comments on it draw.

Later, in 1715, when the house and estate of the architect Vanbrugh, bought in 1711 by the earl of Clare, was renamed Claremont, reflecting the lord's new title, his friend Dr. Samuel Garth composed a poem observing the event. Garth praises the simplicity of the house and of Clare's mode of life, free from foreign fashions, by comparing them to that of the ancient Britons under the guidance of the Druids.[59] The poem ends with the Druid priests prophesying the reign of George I, who had come to the throne in

1714. The poem contains so many references to ancient Britons and Druids that Garth noted in the preface of the poem that readers "who would be more informed of what relates to the ancient Britons, and the Druids their priests, may be directed by the quotations to the authors that have mentioned them."

Probably the first association of Druidic mythology to actual gardening was made by the antiquarian William Stukeley at his home at Grantham in Lincolnshire. Stukeley had been trained in medicine, but was a keen investigator of the history of the Druids, and from 1719 to 1724 spent much time exploring the prehistoric ruins at Stonehenge. In 1726 he left London to live at Grantham where he became an avid gardener. In October 1728 he wrote his friend Samuel Gale:

> I am making a temple of the druids as I call it, 'tis thus; there is a circle of tall filberd trees in the nature of a hedg, which is 70 foot diameter, round it is a walk 15 foot broad, circular too, so that the whole is 100 foot diameter. This walk from one high point slopes each way so gradually, till you come to the lowest which is the opposite point, & ther is the entrance to the temple, to which the walk may be esteemed as the portico. When you enter the innermost circle or temple, you see in the center an ancient apple tree overgrown with sacred mistletoe; round it is another concentraic circle of 50 foot diameter made of pyramidal greens, at equal intervals, that may appear verdant, when the fruit trees have dropt their leaves. These pyramidals are in imitation of the inner circle at Stonehenge. The whole is included within a square wall on all sides, except that where is the grand avenue to the porticoe, which is a broad walk of old trees.[60]

During the following year Stukeley wrote to the archbishop of Canterbury to suggest that he would like to be ordained, his religious "inclinations" having been promoted in part by the contemplative mood inspired by gardening and in part through his studies of the Druids. In fact, he believed "that those religious philosophers had a perfect notion of the Trinity." By February 1730 Stukeley, an ordained priest, moved to hold the living of All Saints at Stamford. Continuing his Druidical studies, he published in 1740 his earlier investigations of Stonehenge and in 1743 of Avebury, both being identified as Druid temples. The two books were meant to be only two parts of a seven-part study devoted to Patriarchal Christianity, but the remaining works were never published. In the book on Avebury, dedicated to the earl of Pembroke, Stukeley claimed that the earl was building a "fine and costly model of Stonehenge" in his recently revised gardens at Wilton in Wiltshire.[61] The idea, however, seems not to have been pursued, as in 1759 Mrs. Lybbe Powys simply noted that "The late Lord Pembroke had thought, it seems, of erecting in his garden a Stonehenge in miniature, as 'twas suppose'd to have been in its first glory." Her comment presumably was made from reading Stukeley. It may have been about this same time that Francis Wise, appointed Radcliffe librarian at Oxford in 1748, was building in his small garden and nearby plot of land at Ellesfield "ponds, cascades, seats, a triumphal arch, the tower of Babel, a Druid temple, and an Egyptian pyramid. These buildings which were designed to resemble the structures of antiquity, were erected in exact scale and measure, to give, as far as miniature would permit, an exact idea of the edifices they were intended to represent."[62]

By the mid-century the passion for Druidic lore began to become a universal interest pervading in particular literature and gardening. The poets Thomas Gray and William Mason published works with Druidic themes. Gray's "Pindaric Ode" entitled *The Bard* was first published in 1757, its completion spurred on by listening to John Parry in May 1757 "play on the Welch Harp at a concert at Cambridge," and Mason, who had already in 1751 brought out *Elfrida*, a play on a Saxon theme, presented in 1759 his poetic drama *Caractacus* with a chorus of Druids.[63] Their mutual correspondence from 1756 to 1759 is littered with Druidic references or Welsh place names. Soon Gray was fascinated by the supposed translations of ancient Celtic poems fabricated by the Scotch poet James Macpherson. In letters to Thomas Wharton and Horace Walpole in 1760 Gray, despite many doubts, persisted in hoping that the translations were authentic since David Hume, the Scotch philosopher and historian, informed him that Adam Smith the economist had assured him that they were genuine. Regardless of the condemnation by critics such as Samuel Johnson, the Macpherson forgeries became the rage of a public already attuned to the mysterious ceremonies of the Druids.

The imitation Druid structure set up in gardens and English, eighteenth-century landscapes were not always stone circles. Bishop Pococke in his travel account of 1754 mentions at Mr. St. John's estate of Dogmansfield near Odiham in Hampshire that "there is an imitation of a British or Druid avenue to it [a Gothick arch] of large stones set up on end for half a mile, which are found on the sandy heath."[64] At Halswell in Somerset the so-called "Druid's Temple in the Wood" was a bark and thatched house in Mill Wood.[65] Built in 1756 by the surveyor-architect John-Jacob de Wilstar, the structure, destroyed in the 1950s but recorded in an earlier photograph (fig. 42), was modeled on a building depicted on

42. Halswell (Somerset), Druid's Temple

the title page of Thomas Wright's *Book of Arbours* published in 1755 to which Sir Charles Tynte, owner of Halswell, had been a subscriber.

When Bishop Pococke visited Piercefield Park in Wales in 1756 he noticed that "where there are large stones, they are making a small Doric Temple."[66] Three years later the poet Joseph Spence in his description of Piercefield wrote that "you come to a circlet of pieces of the rock (some left when they made the walks and others added to them) somewhat in imitation of Stonehenge," while at the same time Robert Dodsley only listed "A Druid's Throne and Temple *in a parterre*." The suggestion of a Druid's temple standing in a parterre sounds rather incongruous, but Dodsley was undoubtedly using the term parterre to describe merely a grassed opening in the woods. The picturesque, moody atmosphere must have offered an appropriate setting for the Druid's temple. Soon the Scotch poet James Macpherson issued his supposed translations of ancient Celtic poems such as *Fingal* (1762).

As hermits and hermitages became part of English social life, so did Druids. *The Gentleman's Magazine* in 1774 published an extended account of the fete to celebrate the engagement of Lady Betty Hamilton to Lord

Stanley held at his home, The Oaks, in Surrey.[67] In addition to a magnificent dining pavilion designed by the architect Robert Adam, the entertainment featured a musical play written by General "Gentleman Johnny" Burgoyne, uncle of Stanley, entitled "The Maid of the Oaks," for an oak tree was the main device of the Hamilton arms. In the masque, songs and dances alternated with complimentary verse declaimed by Captain Pigott in the guise of a Druid. The conclusion at dawn found the Druid at a hymneal altar and an oak proclaiming:

> Raise the trophy, place it high
> Sounds of triumph pierce the sky!
> Badge of honours nobly won
> Borne in the shield of Hamilton.

In 1796 when George Cumberland described Hafod Park in the narrow Welsh valley of the river Ystwyth he spoke "in the language of Ossian, 'When the blast has entered the womb of the mountain-cloud and scattered its curling gloom around,' for here, on this globose promontory, a bard might indeed sit, and draw all his fine images from nature!"[68] Cumberland's quotation of Ossian immediately follows his observation on his tour of a location appropriate for a Druid temple.

> in front, the woody valley, with the Ystwyth, in its bottom, opens before us, crowned on the left with sloping, lofty hills; while, in the midst, a smooth mound, half concealed with oaks, rises among the shades and seems designed by nature as a centre; whence, nor too high, nor too low, the whole expanse around, of intermingled beauties, may continually feed the eye: where, if a druid's temple never stood, a druid's temple is unquestionably called for; and, I cannot halp expressing hope, that a rude imitation will one day there be placed.

This comment is accompanied by a note: "Such I find since is the intention of Mr. Johnes." There is no evidence, however, that the artificial Druid memorial was ever erected, although Cumberland depicted on his map of Hafod a circle of stones labelled "Druid Temple." Commencing in the late 1780s the owner Thomas Johnes had fashioned a magnificent park with extensive walks and dramatic vistas. As a friend of Sir Uvedale Price and cousin of Richard Payne Knight, the advocates of the Picturesque Movement, Johnes "improved" the picturesque effect of his estate by planting at least two million trees in the last half decade of the century.

Often the owners of parks decorated with hermitages were not satisfied with just hermitages, but added Druids' remains. So at Wodehouse Wombourn where earlier Sir Samuel Hellier had created a hermitage with a robot hermit Father Francis, he added in 1773 a small Druid's temple, probably prompted by his visit to Stonehenge in 1768.[69] A contemporary watercolor depicts a miniature circle of upright stones with a capstone. Similarly, Joseph Pocklington, who had built a hermitage near his home on Derwent Water, had earlier discovered a large stone when excavating the foundations for his villa on an island in the lake. According to William Gell, the discovery inspired Pocklington to erect the stone as the first pillar of a Druid's circle.[70] In 1781 the Reverend Henry White recorded in his diary how he had a huge "druidical" stone discovered at Soper's Bottom brought, after one discouraging failure, to a grove at Fyfield in Hampshire.

> 1781, Mar. 21—Team brought home ye great stone and went to plough for Jno. Smith p.m. Borrowed Nash of Sarsons rope, and by putting it double took ye stone up safe and bot it safe to ye grove without injuring ye waggon in ye least, tho supposed to weigh near 4 tones. Gave Farmer Fuller 3 s. for it.
>
> 1781, April 12—Druidical Column or Kist Vaen erected in ye grove very successfully p.m. will make an excellent gnomon for a meridian line when settled firm.[71]

Previous Druidic monuments decorating gardens had been manufactured by their owners, but in one example an actual prehistoric stone circle was used to grace an English park. On August 12, 1785, a small stone circle was uncovered near the town of St. Helier on the island of Jersey.[72] The town then voted to present the remains to General Henry Conway, who was governor of the island. Conway had the circle disassembled, blocks marked and sent to the mainland where they were erected in his landscape of Park Place in Berkshire with other garden monuments, particularly a bridge decorated with sculpture by his daughter Mrs. Damer. With the arrival of the stones in 1787 a controversy arose about their new location, which can be followed in Horace Walpole's correspondence.[73] Walpole, a cousin of the general, and Mrs. Damer favored a site near the house, but the general erected the circle on the ridge of a hill some distance away which Walpole later admitted was the superior location. In Walpole's letter to Conway on November 11, 1781, the circle is called "little Master Stonehenge" and Walpole amusingly comments that "Dr. Stukeley will burst his crements to offer mistletoe in your Temple; and Mason [William Mason, author of the poem *The English Garden* and the play *Caractacus*], on the contrary, will die of vexation and spite that he cannot have *Caractacus* acted on the spot."

The stone circle, consisting of stones seven to ten feet high, is now twenty-seven feet in diameter, widened slightly from its original twenty-one feet (fig. 43). On the east side is a stone entrance ten feet long, but only four feet high. On the outside of one of the vertical monoliths is a long inscription in French memorializing the gift to the general.

The earl of Uxbridge had a natural Druidical monument in his park at Plas Newydd on the isle of Angelesy in Wales.[74] So when Humphry Repton arrived to survey the estate in November 1798 for landscape improvement, he devoted a section of his Red Book, the written and illustrated account of his project dated January 1799, to preserving the remains as a feature of the park.

The Cromlech

This rare Druidical remain is too curious to be passed in silence, in a plan which professes to show every object at Plas Newydd to the greatest advantage. I am sorry to remark that one of the supporters has been forced by violence from its bearing, & a large piece of the great stone has been broken off, yet to insert a new stone, or drive in a common wedge, might mislead future antiquaries, therefore I shd rather advise, that the necessary repair be made with a wedge of marble, on which the date & circumstance may be explained in something like these words

To preserve
A Druidical Monument
which is of a date before the Christian Era
(Tho' lately endangered
by wanton mischief)
this support is added
by order of the Earl of Uxbridge
in the year of Christ
1799.

There is no evidence that the work was carried out, but Repton's insistence that any repairs should be clearly apparent marks a distinct break with the Renaissance mode of renovating ancient monuments.

The fashion for Druidical garden ornament corresponded in time with the technological innovation of a successful artificial stone, usually known

43. Henley (Berks), Park Place, Druids' Circle, engraving

as Coade stone from the leading factory founded in 1769 by Mrs. Coade.[75] In 1775 Mrs. Coade bought up the stock of another manufacturer, a Mr. Bridges in Knightsbridge, and among the pieces, according to Christie's sales catalogue, was "a remarkably fine figure of a Druid." This was probably the model for a later series of images of a contemplative, bearded, and seated Druid swathed in a heavy garment and holding a tall staff in his right hand, while cradling his chin in his left hand. A version was erected at The Vyne in Hampshire, the home of John Chute, Walpole's friend and consultant on Gothic architecture, sometime before Chute's death in 1776 according to Walpole. The sculpture, now partially damaged, is still preserved standing in front of the so-called Garden Room at The Vyne. Another fairly complete figure, now in Priory Park at Chichester in Sussex, was originally not a garden decoration, but was erected as early as 1777 over a conduit in South Street in Chichester. The remaining statues of Druids seem to date later in the century. In August 1795 the earl of Coventry paid more than twenty-six pounds for a version crowned with an oak leaf wreath, now preserved in good condition in the gardens at Croome Court in Worcestershire. A badly damaged figure dating about the same time is at Erddig in Wales and another was added to the earlier artificial ruin at Shugborough in Staffordshire (fig. 44).

44. Shugborough (Staffords), *Druid*

The Picturesque Movement in landscaping and travel was an enthusiastic supporter of the interest in Druidical culture. The combination is
dramatically seen in the landscaping at Swinton in Yorkshire.[76] In 1795
William Danby of Swinton travelled to the picturesque Lake Country
probably inspired by reading Richard Payne Knight's poem *The Landscape*,
whose second edition of 1795 Danby had just purchased. The landscape of
Swinton, which Danby's father had improved in the 1760s, was a typical
Brownian landscape of rolling, wooded hills and chains of lakes and gentle
cascades, the type of landscape vigorously denounced by Payne Knight in
his poem. Commencing in 1796 and continuing well into the nineteenth
century, Danby undertook to transform the landscape into a seemingly
untouched, naturalistic setting with all the picturesque qualities of rough-
ness and strong contrasts of light and shadow. The soft outlines of the earlier
lakes were roughened with inlets and promontories. Great boulders were
moved to increase the irregularities of the topography and thousands of
evergreens, larch, and Scots pine were planted. Sometime before 1803
Danby incorporated into this milieu a most intricate Druid's circle (fig.
45). A very involved symbolism must be embodied in the layout with its

45. Swinton (Yorks), Druids' Circle

trilithons, cells, tables, and symbols of the elements and zodiac. The Druid's circle was to enhance the drama of the landscaped site.

The eighteenth-century English interest in British antiquity and the eremetical way of life must in part have resulted from the incipient nationalism occasioned by Marlborough's victory at Blenheim at the beginning of the century. By the middle of the century a well-to-do middle class might not be able to afford the time and cost of the Grand Tour of the continent, but would find an attractive substitute in exploring the more uncivilized periphery of the island as eulogized in William Gilpin's several guidebooks to the picturesque areas of Wales and the northern counties, a suitable setting for hermits and Druids. Even that arch urbanite Dr. Samuel Johnson made his way to the Hebrides and the painter Richard Wilson abandoned the gentle nature of the *campagna* around Rome for the rugged vastness of the mountains of Wales. Inevitably these new fads impinged upon the *furor hortensis* of the period and eventually resulted in a new landscape aesthetic.

CHAPTER IV

Burial in the Garden

JOHN EVELYN, the horticulturist and garden buff, planned to write a section entitled "Of Garden Burial" in his unrealized treatise *Elysium Britannicum* on which he toiled some forty years, but which, as a result of its scope and detail, remained an undigested mass of notes and drafts. Seventeenth-century English gentlemen like Evelyn, bred on the classics and often with personal experience of classical Italy, were familiar with the classical tradition of burial in the natural landscape or in a garden. They read in the life of the Greek philosopher Theophrastus by Diogenes Laertius that Theophrastus lived in a garden at Athens and that at his death he willed the garden to his friends as a study and as his burial ground.[1] Such Englishmen travelled to Italy to pay homage to the Roman poet Vergil at his supposed tomb near Naples which they found hidden in a garden covered in part by laurel trees, the poet's emblem. So Evelyn recorded in his travel diary going in February 1645 to visit the tomb "almost over growne with bushes, & wild bay trees."[2]

Later Evelyn discussed at length burial in a garden in his treatise on trees, *Sylva*, pointing out that Christ chose a garden for the location of His sepulcher.[3] The religious writers earlier in the century had frequently dwelt on the subject. Francis Quarles had termed one of his religious poems "Buried in a Garden."

> After his spirituall death, first *Adam's* cast
> Out of the Garden, where he had been plac'd.
> After his Corporall, second *Adam's* put
> Into a Garden, and there closely shut.

The first had not gone out but for his sin,
And but for ours, the second not come in.[4]

Similarly, Michael Jermin, chaplain to Charles I, in his commentary on *Ecclesiastes,* published in 1639, cautioned "as *Josephs* Sepulcher in his Garden was made the Sepulcher of Christ, so it were good also, that such in their Gardens would thinke of Christ's Sepulcher, that is, in their delights would thinke of the misery which he suffered for them." Evelyn condemned the practice of burial in or near a church as "being both a novel Presumption, undecent, sordid, and very prejudiced to health." His attack on church burial for health reasons became a vigorously argued controversy in early eighteenth-century England and later in France. Evelyn ended his discussion by recounting the burial of the heart of Sir William Temple in his garden, "and if my Executors will gratify me in what I have desir'd, I wish my *Corps* may be *Interr'd* as I have bespoke them: Not at all out of singularity, or for want of a *Dormitory,* (of which there is an ample one annext to the *Parish-Church*) but for other Reasons, not here necessary to trouble the Reader with; what I have said in General, being sufficient: However, let them order it as they think fit, so it be not in the *Church* or *Chancel.*" At his death in 1706, however, Evelyn's expressed wishes were ignored and he was buried in the chancel of the parish church at Wotton.

The religious fiats of the Anglican and Catholic churches regarding burial in consecrated ground were too strong to be defied by most members of those churches. The example of Sir William Temple mentioned by Evelyn offers a crucial instance. Temple, who died in January 1699, was buried with his wife in Westminster Abbey, but his "heart according to his own express desire, was interred 'six feet underground' on the southeast side of the stone diall in the little garden at Moor Park.'"[5] Much later William Gilpin remarked "A singularity of this kind, in preferring a garden to a church-yard, rather favours the opinion which Bishop Burnet gives us, of Temple's religious sentiments." Bishop Gilbert Burnet, who was a contemporary of Temple, implied that Temple was an atheist in his *History of His Own Time.*

> He [Temple] seemed to think that things were as they are from all eternity; at least he thought religion was fit only for the mob. He was a great admirer of the sect of Confucius in China, who were atheists themselves, but left religion to the rabble. He was a corrupter of all that came near him: and he delivered himself up wholly to study ease and pleasure.

Temple had published in 1690 an essay "Of Heroic Virtue" in which he discoursed at length on four great empires: China, Peru, Scythia, and Arabia. In the essay he was interested not only in their singular characteristics, but their common modalities that might give insight into human nature. He claimed that the intellectuals among both the Chinese and the Incas had no need for houses of worship, idols, or priests, but rather that a natural religion determined morality. The advocacy of natural religion and even of deism by some clerics such as William Wollaston, *The Religion of Nature Delineated* (1725), and Matthew Tindall, *Christianity as Old as Creation* (1730), threatened the orthodoxy of men such as Bishop Burnet and explain his attack on Temple, which he may have thought was confirmed by Temple's instructions for his burial. To men such as Evelyn and Temple, burial in a garden was not a matter of religious faith or lack thereof, but a reinstitution of a classical tradition that corresponded to their passionate love of gardens.

For other Englishmen burial in a garden might have been the only solution in a religious controversy. Evelyn in his commentary on garden burial in his *Sylva* mentions the instance of Edward Burton of Longnor in Shropshire.[6] Burton's great-grandson, William Burton, in his commentary on the travels of the Emperor Antoninus relates the account of his ancestor's death and burial. Edward Burton was a zealous Protestant who led a fearful existence during the reign of Queen Mary. In 1558 when all the church bells of nearby Shrewsbury began tolling, Burton divined that they marked the death of the queen, but in the joy of his relief of having the news confirmed he suddenly died. His body was then taken to the parish church of St. Chad for burial in the family vault. The priest, however, a strong adherent of the Roman church, refused him burial there, so his friends took his body back to his home where he was buried under a table tomb near the fishpond of his garden. In 1803 when the landscapist Humphry Repton was asked to advise on the house and the grounds he recommended that the house be rebuilt in a Tudor style befitting the tomb.

In October 1623 when some three hundred Catholics convened to hear mass at Hunsdown House, the French ambassador's residence in Blackfriars at London, the collapse of a floor of the structure caused the death of some one hundred of the assembly. Of these forty-seven were buried in the garden of the house for lack of proper burial grounds.[7] The reverse of the coin was experienced by the English ambassador in Paris in 1685 and 1686. On December 5, 1685, Sir William Turnbull, the English ambassador, wrote home to his superiors that with the death of an Englishman and an Englishwoman at Paris he had approached the police lieutenant of Paris regarding their place of burial. "He sent word, That there was no Publick Place appointed. And that all Strangers might bury their dead friends in ye Fields or Gardins."[8] Sir William, therefore, asked permission to join with the Dutch ambassador in pressing the French government for an official burial place for foreigners not adhering to the Catholic faith. Turnbull continued to importune the French in the name of James II pointing out "not onely ye Lawes and Practise of all nations and ye Common Sentiments of Humanity in ye same Case, But allso ye Libertie all wayes allow'd to ye French in England and ye great Inconveniencies and barbarous usage that had lately happned for want of this Permission." The latter is a reference to an incident early in January 1686 when the body of one of Lady Montagu's women was buried in a garden and a mob dragged the body through the streets until Lord Montagu rescued the corpse. Turnbull's pleas were in vain. The French government, having revoked the Edict of Nantes in October 1685, was determined to deny any religious rights to non-Catholics. Later in 1686 the ambassador had to bury one of his pages in the garden of his residence at Paris and the French owner of the house demanded that the ambassador leave a brief declaration of the action in the event that the body was discovered later.

The advent of Quakerism, or the Society of Friends, in the second half of the seventeenth century introduced a large group of religious adherents who were not only not acceptable for burial in established consecrated grounds, but in whose belief there should be no notoriety in burial. Burial in their own garden was a natural resolution of the problem, as took place in 1680 with Edward Champion at Chilton Polden in Somerset.[9] Other such burials are recorded without any specification of the reason, as in the case of one Thomas Matthew "buried the 14th day of November 1658 in his garden late taken out of his orchard" at Toddington in Berkshire, or the eminent physician Dr. William Bentley at Northwich in Cheshire where he was "interred in a vault at the summit of the garden, where his tomb was discovered (in taking down a summer-house over it)" with an inscription dated 1680.[10]

MAUSOLEA

IN THE EARLY eighteenth century the problem of church burial came to the fore in England, particularly with the plan for building the new, so-called Commissioners Churches in the suburbs of London. In 1711 Parliament decreed the building of fifty new churches in the growing suburbs of

London. The architects Sir Christopher Wren, as Surveyor of the Queen's Works, and Sir John Vanbrugh, as Comptroller, being members of the commission in charge of the building, wrote memoranda advising on the character of the new churches.[11] Both architects condemned the old tradition of church burial. Wren: "I could wish that all Burials in churches might be disallowed, which is not only unwholesom, but the Pavement can never be kept even, nor Pews upright." Vanbrugh listed as his eighth proposal: "That they [churches] may be free'd from that Inhumane Custome of being made Burial Places for the Dead." Both advocated new cemeteries planted with trees on the outskirts of the city. The wealthy could then erect freestanding mausolea in the sylvan enclosures of the new cemeteries. Vanbrugh referred in his proposal to the practice at the British colony at Surat in India and in the margin of the letter drew several such mausolea, including some with domes.

Sometime before June 1722 Vanbrugh must have proposed to the earl of Carlisle that he should build in the park at his new country estate of Castle Howard in Yorkshire a separate family mausoleum. Originally the little village of Henderskelfe and its parish church had been located very close to the earl's old manor house which was rebuilt after the design of Vanbrugh and renamed Castle Howard. With the rebuilding of the residence the village and church were destroyed so as to permit the broad landscaping the earl promoted around his new mansion. Since a new parish church would be some distance away, the mausoleum, presumably proposed by Vanbrugh, would substitute for burial of members of the Howard family. In a letter of June 19, 1722, to Carlisle, Vanbrugh recalled the idea in reference to the death of the duke of Marlborough.

> It having been referr'd to my Ld Godolphin with the other Executors, Clayton & Guidot, to consider about the Duke's funeral [Marlborough] and place of burying I have taken the liberty, to mention to my Lord what your Ldship designs at Castle Howard, and has been practic'd by the most polite peoples before Priestcraft got poor Carcasses into their keeping, to make a little money of. . . . The Place I propose, is in Blenheim Park with some plain, but magnificent & durable monument over him.[12]

Before the death of Vanbrugh in 1726, Lord Carlisle wrote in his will:

> I do design to build a burial place near my seat of Castle Howard, where I desire to be lay'd. . . . I think this Burial place should be built in ye form of a little chapple to hold about 40 or 50 people with a

Cupola, or Tower upon it & placed upon Lody Hill over against ye Hill where ye two high Beaches stand whereby it may be an ornament to ye Seat.[13]

With Vanbrugh's death the project of the mausoleum devolved to Nicholas Hawksmoor, who had assisted Vanbrugh at Blenheim and Castle Howard. The correspondence between Hawksmoor and Carlisle regarding the mausoleum is extensive from 1726 to 1729 and is principally concerned with famous historical precedents, such as the Mausoleum of Halicarnassus or the tomb of Porsenna. By mid-1728 the round Tomb of Cecilia Metella on the Via Appia at Rome was the favored model, but at Castle Howard Hawksmoor encircled the great drum first with an arcade and, by the spring of 1729, with a colonnade, which was particularly favored by Carlisle's son Lord Morpeth. By April 1729 enough agreement had been achieved with regard to the design that the foundations could be laid. The work was then pursued until about 1745, long after Hawksmoor's death in 1736 and Lord Carlisle's in 1738, who had to be temporarily buried in the parish church at Bulmer until his remains could be transferred to the new mausoleum in 1745.

The completed mausoleum stands isolated on a low hill about three-quarters of a mile southeast of the mansion (fig. 46). A colonnade of tightly spaced Doric columns encircles the cella, above which rises a drum with windows capped by a dome derived from Bramante's Tempietto at S. Pietro in Montorio in Rome. The narrowness of the intercolumniations of the colonnade was determined by Hawksmoor as a protection against possible cracking of the entablature, but it soon provoked criticism by Palladian critics such as Lord Burlington. After Hawksmoor's death in 1736 Palladian enthusiasts led by Lord Carlisle's son-in-law Sir Thomas Robinson altered the setting of the mausoleum by adding double-flight entrance stairs modelled on those at Lord Burlington's villa at Chiswick and outlying walls and bastions. The tautness of the lines of Hawksmoor's peristyle is now contrasted with the outward deployment of the podium.

The circular tomb silhouetted on the slight rise in the Yorkshire countryside must have recalled the Roman *campagna* to any Englishman who had experienced the Grand Tour, but the sullen skies of northern England often increased the gloomy aspect of the site. The mausoleum at Castle Howard is the first of many in eighteenth- and nineteenth-century England marking a gradual shift in the tradition of burial from urban and architectural sites to the natural landscape, to the garden, but it was at first only the nobility who could afford such mausolea.

46. Castle Howard (Yorks), Mausoleum

Some of the commonality continued to scorn and even scoff at the traditional burial customs. Richard Kay of Baldinstone near Bury in Lancashire records in his diary that his uncle John Kay of Gooseford died in 1734 and "according to his Desire was buried in his Garden ten Foot deep in a Square Plot of Ground which it seem'd he had designed for that Purpose."[14] The uncle was non-conformist in religion, adhering to the Unitarian faith. In another example there is no expressed reason for the action except that a contemporary denounced the perpetrator as "not a Christian." About 1746 the duchess of Portland wrote Mrs. Montagu:

> A hatter of Windsor left £ 100 to a man on condition he would bury him according to his desire under a mulberry tree in his own garden, 10 feet deep. The assistants to drink 12 bottles of wine over his grave, and French horns playing during the whole ceremony, and this was accordingly performed yesterday, to the great offence of Mr. Grosmith, who says he was not a Christian.[15]

The "Mr. Grosmith" of the duchess' account was the Reverend George Goldsmith, rector at Hedgerly. He was perhaps the kind of churchman whom Dr. William Martyn of Plymouth rebelled against when he ordered that he be buried in a field at Botusfleming in Cornwall marked by an obelisk with a long explanatory inscription.

> Here lieth the body of William Martyn of the Borough of Plymouth in the County of Devon, Doctor of Physick, who died the 22nd day of November in the year of our Lord Jesus Christ, 1762, aged 62 years. He was an honest, good-natured man, willing to do all the good in his power to all mankind; and not willing to hurt any person. He lived and died a Catholic Christian, in the true and not depraved Popish sense of the word, had no superstitious veneration for Church or Churchyard ground, and willing by his example if that might have any influence to lessen the unreasonable esteem which some poor men and women through prejudice of education often show for it in frequently parting with the earnings of many a hard day's labour, which might be better bestowed in sustenance for themselves and their families, to pay for Holy Beds for their kinsfolk's corpses, through a ridiculous fear lest their kinsfolks at the Day of Judgement should some way or other suffer because their corpses were wrongly situated or not, where the worldly advantage of their spiritual guides loudly called for them.[16]

Dr. Martyn's anti-clerical outburst echoes Sir John Vanbrugh's remark in his memorandum of 1722 about the "Priestcraft" getting "poor Carcasses into their keeping, to make a little money of," but this was a very ancient social cry against the clergy.

If most owners of gardens did not dare to flaunt religious tradition they had a satisfactory substitute in ceremoniously honoring their pet animals with garden burials. Any visitor to an English country house never fails to see in some obscure corner of the garden or park an animal burial ground often with individual markers extolling the virtues of the pets. Among a few notable examples in the eighteenth century is an old gravestone in a dog cemetery at Dunham Massey in Cheshire inscribed: "Here Lyes / Pugg / Als old vertue / who Dyed Feb: 17 / 1702." In the house is a portrait of a pug dog, undoubtedly the same pet, probably by Leonard Knyff of 1697.[17] Other examples are an obelisk in the woods of Nether Lypiatt in Gloucestershire commemorating a horse Wag, who died at the age of forty-two, or the tomb inscription at Marston in Somerset of Lord Orrery's horse King Nobby, who died in 1754 at age thirty-four. Perhaps the most famous example is the inscription carved on the rear of the Temple of the British Worthies at Stowe (fig. 61) and first recorded in 1735.

To the Memory of Signior Fido
an *Italian* of good Extraction
who came into *England*
not to bite us, like most of his Countrymen,
but to gain an honest Livelyhood.
He hunted not after Fame,
yet acquir'd it;
regardless of the Praise of his Friends,
but most sensible of their Love.
Tho' he liv'd amongst the Great,
he neither learnt nor flatter'd any Vice.
He was no Bigot,
Tho' he doubted of none of the 39 Articles
And, if to follow Nature,
and to respect the Laws of Society
be Philosophy,
he was a perfect Philosopher;
a faithful Friend,
an agreeable Companion,

a loving Husband
distinguish'd by a numerous Offspring,
all which he liv'd to see take good Courses.
In his old Age he retir'd
to the House of a Clergyman in the Country,
where he finish'd his earthly Race,
and died an Honour and an Example to the Whole Species
Reader
this Stone is guiltless of Flattery,
for he to whom it is inscrib'd
was not a Man,
but a
Grey-Hound[18]

The poet Joseph Spence claimed that Mrs. Racket, sister of Alexander Pope, who was a great frequenter of Stowe, told Spence that when Bounce, Pope's faithful dog, died the poet "had some thoughts of burying him in his garden, and putting a piece of marble over his grave with the epitaph: O RARE BOUNCE! and he would have done it, I believe, had not he apprehended that some people might take it to have been meant as a ridicule of Ben Jonson."

The strangest and rather morbid example of a garden burial is recounted by William Stukeley in a letter of October 14, 1728, to his friend Samuel Gale from Grantham just after the second miscarriage of Stukeley's wife. He relates that he and his mother-in-law and an aunt went into his garden laid out as a Druidic grove, as discussed previously, and there, "The embro, about as big as a filberd, I buryd under the high altar in the chappel of my hermitage vineyard; . . . with ceremony proper to the occasion."[19] Stukeley was apparently a promoter of garden burial, for among his drawings at Oxford is one dated September 7, 1742, for a mausoleum to stand on the great mount at Boughton in Northamptonshire (fig. 47). It was at this time that Stukeley was at Boughton offering advice to the duke of Montagu how to improve the grounds, including the creation of "serpentine ridings" in the woods and the design of an elaborate Gothic bridge which was never built.[20] In 1744 Stukeley noted in his diary: "I took some prospects in the garden, especially about the mausoleum, where the duke designs to be buryed in the plain earth above." Like the Gothic bridge, the mausoleum was never executed.

For William Shenstone the poet the nostalgic mood of burial in nature would be represented by the memory of a famous literary monument. He

The Mausoleum in the garden at Boughton.

7. sep. 1742.

47. Boughton (Northants), drawing of mausoleum by Stukeley, MS Top. gen. d. 14, f. 43v, The Bodleian Library, Oxford

himself wrote an account dated August 30, 1746, of the moment when his neighbor William Lyttelton brought James Thomson, the famous poet of *The Seasons*, to see Shenstone's *ferme ornée*. When they entered the little valley named Virgil's Grove by Shenstone, "I told him my then intention of building a model of Virgil's Tomb; which with the Obelisk and a number of mottoes selected from Virgil, together with the pensive idea belonging to the place, might vindicate, or at least countenance, the appellation I had given it."[21]

In the second half of the eighteenth century numerous family mausolea were erected at country estates. When Frederick, the prince of Wales, died suddenly in March 1751, William Chambers, then a young architect studying in Italy, prepared some eight designs for a mausoleum in a landscape setting, the last dated February 1752.[22] Chambers had met the prince and princess in 1749 and may have made some designs at that time for garden architecture at Kew. When word of the prince's death reached Chambers in Italy he probably prepared the drawings of a mausoleum to encourage future patronage by the dowager princess. Although the mausoleum was never executed, Chambers was later the architect of the dowager princess for her expansion of the gardens at Kew. The mausoleum designs feature a domed circular structure with references to famous ancient monuments, such as the Pantheon or the Tomb of Cecilia Metella, which Chambers was studying in Rome. As noted previously, one drawing of a section of the mausoleum was very unusual in being depicted as slightly ruined and overgrown (fig. 20). That Chambers would choose to design a landscaped mausoleum is probably not only a result of his Roman experience, but because he knew that the prince was an avid gardener. In fact, according to the account of George Vertue of the prince's death the unfortunate occurrence was a sad result of his gardening.

> [The prince] was first taken ill, being in his Gardens at Kew—where he was, directing the planting and setting of some exotic Trees—in which Gardens for their improvement he took great pains and pleasure, daily—for exercise and health—yet the unhappiness, to be there when a great prodigious storm of hail fell, that was so violent—that before he could get to his home indoors, he was wett thro & so bad from that cold he got and so continued daily that all the care & skill of the Physicians was in vain—

At the same time that Chambers was designing a mausoleum for the prince, in 1751, the Palladian architect Robert Morris published a small book of designs of "Ornamental Buildings . . . for Parks, Gardens, Woods, &c." with three of the fifty plates devoted to projects for two mausolea.

A combined chapel and mausoleum planned by the Palladian architect James Paine was erected from 1760 to 1766 as the last garden feature at Gibside in County Durham for George Bowes.[23] A terrace about a half mile in length, planted in 1746 to 1749, was at the center of the landscaping. An earlier architect, Daniel Garrett, had already built a Gothic Banqueting House and begun a Column of British Liberty to stand at the northeast end of the terrace, but in 1753 Paine was asked to advise on the column. His chapel with a mausoleum was then added at the other end of the terrace facing the column. The chapel of a rather ornate Palladian style is Greek cross in plan with a very shallow dome on a drum over the center (fig. 48). A freestanding portico of four Ionic columns with side stairs marks the entrance. The vaulted mausoleum under the podium of the chapel has access from the rear of the building. The centralized, domed structure at the end of a treed alley resembles a small Palladian villa in the tradition of Chiswick or Mereworth.

When the first earl of Shelburne died in May 1761, his widow immediately engaged the architect Robert Adam, recently returned from Italy, to design a mausoleum to stand in memory of her husband at their country estate of Bowood in Wiltshire.[24] Adam prepared four different projects for the tomb. All the designs had centralized buildings with Pantheon-type domes, all, except in the executed project, raised on drums. In two of the schemes the main chamber was a burial chamber with long niches for the storage of sarcophagi. In the other two the tombs were deposited in the podium of the structure. The executed mausoleum has a Greek cross plan with an entrance portico supported on four Doric columns, the entablature of which continues around the entire building tying the arms of the cross back to the cella (fig. 49). The architectural style is a very stark, neat mode with no mouldings outlining the exterior niches or inset panels. On the interior, Tuscan colonnades screen the arms of the cross. The white marble sarcophagus of the earl carved in the 1770s by Carlini is in the rear arm. The entrance to the catacombs, with the tombs below the main chamber, is at the rear or south side, as at Paine's mausoleum at Gibside.

A most unusual mausoleum was built at this same time at West Wycombe in Buckinghamshire for Sir Francis Dashwood, Lord le Despencer, but this might be expected given the remarkable career and reputation of Dashwood.[25] Many stories circulated about his youthful Grand Tour to Rome, including participation in a flagellation ceremony in the Vatican, but

48. Gibside (Co. Durham), Mausoleum

49. Bowood (Wilts), Mausoleum

he returned to England an impassioned amateur of antiquities and was one of the founders of the Society of the Dilettanti. As presumably a convivial offshoot of that society he formed the infamous Society of St. Francis of Wycombe which met biannually at the ruined Abbey of Medmenham. On the top of a hill at West Wycombe, overlooking the village and Dashwood's country estate, he rebuilt an old church and topped its spire with a huge copper globe visible as an eyecatcher for any visitor to the village. In 1762 George Bubb Dodington, Lord Melcome, one of Dashwood's companions in his social gatherings left him five hundred pounds, which Dashwood used to build a mausoleum set into the hillside just below the new church (fig. 50). The unroofed structure is a slightly elongated hexagon composed of six flint-stone walls built between April 1764 and September 1765 by the mason John Bastard, a year after Dashwood had become Lord le Despencer. The three front walls of the hexagonal enclosure are open, each with a large central arch flanked by two smaller arches, all separated by engaged Doric columns, obviously modelled on a Roman triumphal arch. On the interior walls in niches portrait busts and burial urns were originally set, many now lost or damaged. The statue commemorating Bubb Dodington is gone, but the yellow marble urn that once contained the heart of the poet Paul Whitehead, another friend of Dashwood, is preserved. Like the copper globe on the church, the mausoleum set into the hillside is visible from the main street of the village or from the extensive grounds of Dashwood's estate magnificently landscaped by a pupil of Capability Brown and later by Humphry Repton.

From the 1770s to the end of the eighteenth century there were numerous designs for mausolea that were never executed. Most of them are by very youthful architects exhibited at the Royal Academy.[26] This enthusiasm for the landscaped tomb marks the climax of interest in the elegiac Arcadian theme. Much earlier, as was noted previously, Sir William Chambers at the age of twenty-eight had prepared his mausoleum project for the late prince of Wales (fig. 20); so James Gandon, aged twenty-five, Thomas Hardwick and John Soane, both twenty-four, and the precocious Aaron Hurst, at seventeen, all exhibited projects at the Royal Academy. Many of the designs were for ideal mausolea with no specific commemoration, but some were to honor famous Englishmen. Chambers again led the way with his idea of a small aedicula, described by him as a "Mausoleum," to be erected in the garden at Kew of the dowager princess of Wales to the memory of the poet Alexander Pope. The illustration in Chamber's *A Treatise on Civil Architecture* of 1759 has the little garden building flanked by sphinxes, one dedi-

50. West Wycombe (Bucks), Mausoleum

cated to Swift, the other to Gay.[27] Several designs were proposed to honor the earl of Chatham, the national hero who died in May 1778.

Two of the loveliest of the eighteenth-century English mausolea were designed by the architect James Wyatt. In 1781, when the third earl of Darnley died, he left word in his will that he wished to have a mausoleum built for him and his wife at their country residence of Cobham Park in Kent.[28] From 1782 to 1783 Wyatt built the mausoleum on William's Hill some distance northeast of the house (fig. 51). The structure, however, was never used for burials and is now abandoned and somewhat ruinous. Built of Portland stone, the building is about thirty feet square with projecting, canted corners. The rusticated podium contains the catacomb with some sixteen recesses for sarcophagi. A Doric entablature encircles the building, supported on the sides by engaged columns and by pairs of freestanding columns on the projecting corners. Sarcophagi are carved above each corner and a stepped pyramid towers about the block of the building. The concept of a stepped pyramid rising from a colonnaded base is probably derived from the description by Pliny the Elder of the famous Mausoleum of Halicarnassus, from which the English word originates. The ancient building had haunted the minds of earlier architects, such as Wren and Hawksmoor, who had wrestled with reconstructions of it. The main floor of the Cobham Park building on the interior once comprised a rather rich chapel decorated with brocotello marble and stained glass. A shallow, coffered dome over the chapel masks the exterior pyramid.

The prime example of an English neoclassical tomb is that built at

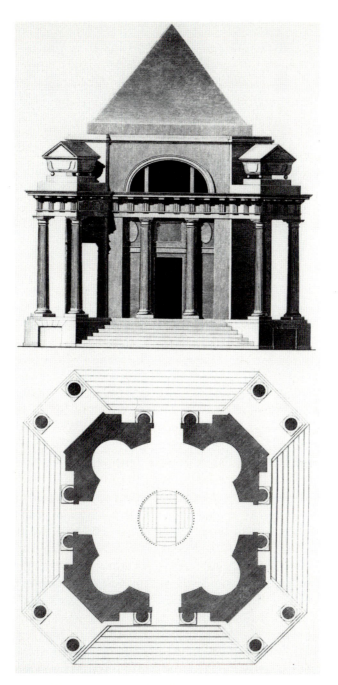

51. Cobham Park (Kent), Mausoleum, engraving

143

Brocklesby Park in Lincolnshire from 1786 to 1795 after the design of Wyatt.[29] With the sudden death of Sophia Pelham in January 1786, her husband Charles Anderson Pelham, later earl of Yarmouth, resolved to build a mausoleum in her memory on the site of an ancient Roman tumulus at Brocklesby. The building is a small, rather ornate and light-hearted version of Hawksmoor's Mausoleum at Castle Howard, but probably modelled on one of the ancient Roman round temples dedicated to Vesta in Rome and Tivoli and then influenced by Chambers' rather decorative version of neoclassicism (fig. 52). A rusticated ground floor or podium supports a peripteral colonnade of twelve Doric columns bearing an entablature of garland and bucrania rather than the traditional triglyphs and metopes. A balustrade above the colonnade softens the transition from the colonnade to the attic which is capped by a Pantheon-type dome. On the interior eight Corinthian columns bear the coffered dome which is lit by an oculus. In the rectangular niches between the paired columns are carved sarcophagi with figural groups. At the center stands a white marble statue by Nollekens of the lamented Sophia. The two mausolea designed by Wyatt are rather different from one another, but both offer an elegant, decorative version of neoclassicism rather unlike the neat, but stark mode of Adam's work at Bowood.

The most interesting English neoclassical mausoleum is the one erected at Blickling Hall in Norfolk.[30] After the death of the second earl of Buckinghamshire in September 1793 his daughter Caroline and her husband William Harbord charged the fashionable Roman architect Joseph Bonomi, who had worked with the Adam brothers, to plan a tomb for the earl. In 1794 a design was exhibited at the Royal Academy; work began that same year on the mausoleum set in the woods about a mile north-west of the house. In October 1797, the bishop of Norwich authorized the transference of the bodies of the earl and his first wife from the local parish church to the new mausoleum and consecrated the building. The tomb is a pyramid forty-five feet square and about forty feet tall (fig. 53). The entrance on the south-east side of the pyramid has a classical door frame surmounted by the earl's coat-of-arms. Deeply framed windows are set in the center of the remaining sides, except that the rear window is replaced by a commemorative inscription. The interior of the pyramid is a circular, domed chamber with eight large niches for the openings or for sarcophagi. The Blickling mausoleum represents the climax of the eighteenth-century reliance on the pyramidal form as a memorial or funerary symbol, seen much earlier at Stowe in Vanbrugh's pyramid of 1726 (fig. 60), as will be considered later.

52. Brocklesby Park (Lincs), Mausoleum

53. Blickling Hall (Norfolk), Mausoleum

IN AT LEAST one example the tomb set in a landscape was not intended for burial, but as a romantic device to emphasize the transience of life. Horace Walpole set the denouement of his Chinese fairy tale, *Mi Li*, published in 1785, in the landscape of General Conway's Park Place at Henley in Berkshire where Mi Li and the general's gardener stop at "a lonely [9] tomb, surrounded by cypress, yews, and willows that seemed the monument of some adventurous youth, who has been lost in tempting the current, and might have suited the gallant and daring Leander."[31] Walpole's footnote nine explains that it is a "fictitious tomb in a beautiful spot by the river, built for a point of view; it has a small pyramid on it." The idea of a "fictitious" pyramidal tomb in the landscape park was probably of French derivation, which ever since the Wood of the Tombs in the Parc Monceau at Paris, visited by Walpole in 1771, had become a favorite motif in French garden landscapes. Slightly later, General Conway's tomb was described in

Britton and Brayley's survey of the beauties of England as "an elegant tomb of white marble, composed in the Roman style, and perfectly in unison with the sequestered and lonely spot on which it stands."

Occasional garden burials of the third estate occurred into the early nineteenth century. According to an account of February 1786 Philip Thicknesse buried his youthful daughter Anna on the grounds of his hermitage at Bathampton near Bath, since "the idea of the procession of removing her remains down the hill [to burial in Bath] seemed to us but one remove less painful than that fatal remove between LIFE and DEATH."[32] Nearby were ancient Roman and Saxon graves and a monument with a small skull marked the grave of Jacko, a pet monkey. Betsy Sheridan, when she visited in June 1786, noted that Anna Thicknesse had died of consumption at age eighteen, but that the inscription was "taken from Pope's Lines on the Death of an Unfortunate Young Lady 'What tho' no Sacred Earth allow thee room, etc. etc.' but as Miss Thicknesse did not destroy herself I can not say I thought the selection judicious."

When John Wilkinson, the eminent ironmaster and brother-in-law of the scientist Joseph Priestley, died in July 1808 he left word that he should be buried in an iron coffin in the grounds of his country residence at Castle Head in Lancashire.[33] *The Gentleman's Magazine* for 1808 reported:

> On Thursday Aug. 25, the iron coffin, to hold the remains of the late Mr. Wilkinson, the great ironmaster, arrived at Ulverston, in a sloop, from his foundry at Bradley in Wales; together with an iron tomb and pyramid, with iron letters, gilt, for the inscription, which he had composed previous to his death. The whole of them was removed to his house at Castle Head. The rock in which the whole is to be placed fronts the house, and is completely exposed to view.

Wilkinson was an ardent follower of Tom Paine and, therefore, was reputed to be an atheist, which may explain his disregard for traditional churchyard burial. Much later his remains were removed from Castle Head and eventually came to rest in the churchyard at Lendal-in-Cartmel. Frequently the expressed wishes of a deceased were ignored. When the politician John Horne Tooke died in 1812 at Wimbledon in Surrey he left already prepared a burial vault in his garden, but his friends sent his remains to church burial at Ealing in Middlesex.[34] In contrast, when the eccentric and nonconformist John Norbury of Great Warford in Cheshire left instructions in 1822 to be buried in his own orchard at Heyhead, his wishes were respected by his daughter Ann Walkden, who later was also buried there.[35]

In 1785 the renowned Danish theorist C. C. L. Hirschfeld, who had been publishing a multivolume treatise, *Theorie der Gartenkunst*, promoting the English landscape mode, presented in the last volume his own design for a cemetery in the form of a landscaped garden, lending his authority to the concept. Parisians had long been concerned with the sanitary problems caused by their urban cemeteries.[36] The French Revolution, lessening the power of the Church, provoked a solution and in 1804 Napoleon as First Consul decreed that no more burials would be permitted within the city. Land was purchased outside the walls of Paris toward the east for a new cemetery laid out by the architect Brogniart. Popularly called the cemetery of Père-Lachaise, it soon became a model for cemetery reform in England and America, as well as on the Continent. In 1830 a non-denominational General Cemetery Company was formed at London, which in the following year purchased land at Kensal Green for a cemetery modelled on Père-Lachaise, and in 1837 the non-denominational, landscaped Norwood cemetery was consecrated, thus resolving the religious controversies that had previously dominated burials in England. After a long struggle with church tradition, mankind finally came to seek in death a harmony with nature, to return to the lost garden of Eden.

CHAPTER V

Monuments and Memorials

U NTIL the eighteenth century monuments honoring living notables, such as rulers, were exhibited in the public arena, most often in public squares, as memorials to the dead were displayed in churches or churchyards at the site of burial. In eighteenth-century England, however, gardens and garden parks, as they attracted public attention, often served as the habitat for such commemorative monuments.

Earlier, during the reign of Charles I, there had been one unusual example.[1] Letters commencing in December 1629 between the diplomat Balthazar Gerbier and the Lord Treasurer Sir Richard Weston discuss the project for an equestrian statue of the king, Charles I, by the sculptor Hubert Le Sueur to stand in the treasurer's garden of Mortlake Park at Roehampton in Surrey (fig. 54). By January 16, 1630, Le Sueur had contracted to fashion the bronze equestrian statue within a year and a half for six hundred pounds, as well as four large flower vases for the corners of the garden and thirty smaller ones like those of the queen at St. James's Palace. The statue, however, must have taken longer than contracted as its signature inscription is dated 1633. Unfortunately there is no evidence to determine the location or role of the equestrian statue in the garden. Its conception undoubtedly was meant to attract the king's support, which was realized in 1633 when Weston was created earl of Portland. With the commencement of the Civil War Parliament ordered that the image be sold in 1644 for the value of the bronze. Removed from Roehampton to Convent Garden in London, the work was purchased by the king's bronze founder, who pretended to destroy it, but hid it until the Restoration. In 1675 Charles II purchased the recovered portrait of his father, which was then set up at Charing Cross in London, where it still stands. Thus, the

54. London, Charing Cross, monument to King Charles I

usual tradition that such honorific monuments should have a public exhibition was reasserted.

During the seventeenth century monumental structures, such as pyramids, obelisks, or columns, could occasionally be employed as decorative features in a garden. In fact, John Worlidge, who, in his treatise of 1677, was uneasy about the proliferation of statuary in English gardens, suggested:

In the room of Statues in the midst of your Green Squares, Obelisks or single Columns may not be improper, so that the Workmanship be accordingly. Neither can there be a more proper use for an obelisk than to support a Globe with its Axis duely placed respecting both Poles, and its circumference on the Equinoctial Line, exactly divided into twenty four parts, and marked with twice twelve hours, that on it at a distance by the shadow only of the Globe on its self, you may discern the hour of the day, and obscure how the Day and Night, and Summer and Winter happen throughout the Universe.[2]

Probably the first commemorative monument of importance incorporated into the landscaping of an eighteenth-century country house was the obelisk that Lord Carlisle ordered Vanbrugh to design and erect in 1714 at Castle Howard to honor the duke of Marlborough and his deeds. A hundred feet in height, the obelisk stands at the junction of the two principal avenues leading to the house from the west (fig. 55) in a relatively public situation.[3] It was, however, at Stowe, the residence of Lord Cobham, with at least thirteen monuments or memorials and four commemorative temples as garden decoration, that the concept flourished and undoubtedly influenced its proliferation in other English gardens. In February 1723 the workshop of the sculptor John Van Nost was paid one hundred and fifty pounds for work, presumably the lead equestrian statue of King George I in Roman armor (fig. 56) which was originally set at the end of the canal at the entrance of the principal access avenue to the house at the north.[4] The setting, therefore, was at least semi-public, informing a visitor of the political fidelity of the owner. Later the statue was moved closer to the north facade of the house. Some of the commemorative features at Stowe had been anticipated at Cannons, a lavish estate in Middlesex. In about 1716 James Brydges, later duke of Chandos, had commissioned an assistant of Van Nost to create a portrait of King George I "on horseback in Armour and panells in the pedestall of Do. wth. Trophies of Warr," which was probably the model for the example at Stowe. This earlier version was erected in the north garden at Cannons at some distance from the house. The duke claimed that from his library window with the aid of a spyglass he could read "the letters on the garter round the King's arms of his Figure at the end of the walk, near half a mile long." In 1748 with the abandonment of the house and gardens, the equestrian statue was moved to Leicester Square where it remained in a gradually deteriorating condition until its destruction in 1872. The Inventory of Cannons dated June 19, 1725, now preserved at the Huntington Library in California, also records in the Plea-

55. Castle Howard (Yorks), obelisk to the duke of Marlborough

56. Stowe (Bucks), equestrian statue of King George I

sure Garden a marble statue of Queen Anne accompanied by a statue of her military hero the duke of Marlborough. The latter was particularly appropriate at Cannons as Brydges had served earlier as paymaster of Marlborough's troops.

At Stowe, in Home Park to the southwest of the house, a stone statue of the prince of Wales, the future King George II, stood in full regalia on a Composite, fluted column forty feet high and one of his wife, Princess Caroline, was posed on an entablature base supported by four Ionic columns (fig. 57). These statues attributed to Rysbrack were meant, of course, to display the owner's loyalty to the throne, as in the past painted portraits of royalty would be exhibited with family portraits in the long gallery of the house. Soon, however, Cobham's relationship with the reigning monarch

King George 2.　Queen Caroline.

57. Stowe (Bucks), Columns of prince and princess of Wales, engraving

became less auspicious. The prince of Wales's monument no longer survives. Somewhat later, in 1767, a succeeding owner, Earl Temple, erected at the entrance to the Elysian Fields at Stowe a Doric arch with a medallion of Princess Amelia, daughter of George II, commemorating her first visit to Stowe in 1766.

Already in 1701, during the reign of William III, the sculptor John Van Nost had been commissioned to design a fountain featuring a statue of the king to stand at Hampton Court, probably in Bushy Park.[5] The death of the king in 1702 presumably prevented realization of the work. Among drawings of the projected fountain by Van Nost in the British Museum one depicts, at the top of a tall pedestal, a standing figure of the king clad in Roman military costume holding a baton in his right hand against his thigh. An account of the auction of Van Nost's statuary in 1712 mentions a "King William, an excellent Statue, big as life . . . lead, with a very good pedestal," which may have derived from the Hampton Court commission. A similar statue exists at Wrest Park in Bedfordshire where the sculptor Andries Carpentière, once an assistant of Van Nost and known in England as Andrew Carpenter, furnished several statues in 1730 to decorate the formal gardens of the duke of Kent. The king's image is set on a pedestal in front of the domed banqueting pavilion built earlier by the architect Thomas Archer as a terminating feature at the end of the long canal running through the center of the garden (fig. 58).

A traditional example of a commemorative monument in the context of a garden is that of Sir Hans Sloane in the Chelsea Physic Garden in London (fig. 59). In the late seventeenth century the Apothecaries Company had leased about three and a half acres at Chelsea for their medicinal garden set on the bank of the Thames river. Sloane, having purchased the manor of Chelsea in 1712, ten years later gave the land of the garden to the Company. To honor the donor the Company voted in 1733 two hundred and eighty pounds for the sculptor Michael Rysbrack to carve a marble statue of Sloane in his doctor's regalia and wig. Completed in 1737 the statue was first located in the greenhouse, but in 1748 was moved to the center of the garden and placed on a tall pedestal overlooking the site. In 1985 the original statue was transferred to the British Museum and was replaced by a replica.

An intriguing monument at Stowe was a sixty-foot stepped pyramid designed by the architect Vanbrugh to stand on the north side of Home Park (fig. 60). When Vanbrugh died in 1726 Cobham dedicated the pyramid to Vanbrugh's memory with a Latin inscription carved on the exterior and on the interior a delightful quotation from Horace, which was translated in Bickham's *The Beauties of Stow* (1750).

> With Pleasure surfeited, advanc'd in Age
> Quit Life's fantastic, visionary Stage:
> Lest Youth, more fitly frolicksome, may join
> To push you, reeling under Loads of Wine.

The pyramid no longer exists, being destroyed in the late eighteenth century. There is no explanation why Vanbrugh originally chose a pyramid as a garden building.

58. Wrest (Bedfords), statue of King William III

59. London, Chelsea Physic Garden, statue of Sir Hans Sloane (replica)

In the previous year, 1725, the philosopher Francis Hutcheson remarked:

> In the *Monuments* erected in honour of deceased *Heroes*, altho a *Cylinder*, or *Prism*, or regular Solid, may have more *original Beauty* than a very acute *Pyramid* or *Obelisk*, yet the latter pleases more, by answering better the suppos'd Intentions of *Stability*, and being *conspicuous*. For the same reason *Cubes*, or square *Prisms*, are generally chosen for the *Pedestals* of *Statues*, and not any of the more *beautiful Solids*, which do not seem so secure from rolling.[6]

The principal types of commemorative monuments in eighteenth-century English gardens are pyramids, obelisks, and triumphal columns, the first two of which respond to Hutcheson's statement. By the third decade almost every avid gardener had some of these types in his garden. William Stukeley, for example, wrote his friend Samuel Gale in 1728 from Grantham: "Our neighbor, Sir Michael Newton, has lately set up a great column in his garden, & a circular temple of stone; he is going to make an

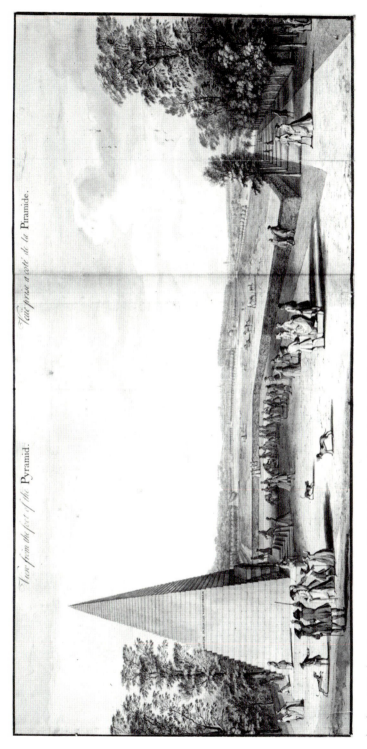

View from the foot of the Pyramid. Vuë prise à côté de la Piramide.

60. Stowe (Bucks), pyramid in memory of Sir John Vanbrugh, watercolor by Rigaud, 1746, The Metropolitan Museum of Art, New York

obelisk too."[7] All three types of monuments will be discussed later. At Stowe, however, were other unusual forms. The so-called Temple of British Worthies was erected in the Elysian Fields probably in 1734 after a design of William Kent intended for the exedra in the garden of the earl of Burlington at Chiswick (fig. 61). Set in niches in the exedra or curving wall are the busts of fifteen famous Englishmen and one of Queen Elizabeth I, representing eight figures associated with a life of active deeds, including Alfred, the Black Prince, Elizabeth I, Raleigh, Drake, John Hampden, William III, and Sir John Barnard, and eight men of thought or contemplative action, including Gresham, Shakespeare, Sir Francis Bacon, Inigo Jones, Locke, Milton, Newton, and Pope.[8] Eight of the busts had originally stood around the west side of a Temple of Fame built by Gibbs, which is now gone, to honor in general a group of famous Englishmen and Queen Elizabeth and King William III. With the creation by Kent of the area called the Elysian Fields, Cobham resolved to introduce a moral-political theme attacking the government and the Prime Minister Sir Robert Walpole. The eight new portrait busts were intended to sharpen this attack, the Black Prince being an obvious reference to the contemporary prince of Wales, whose opposition to his father and Walpole was supported by Cobham. The inscription glorifying King Alfred was a subtle jibe at George II, and Raleigh represented a contradiction of Walpole's policy toward Spain.

Queen Caroline had already employed Kent from 1730 to design her monument to eminent Englishmen in her hermitage at Richmond discussed previously (fig. 32).[9] The Englishmen she honored, Boyle, Locke, Newton, Samuel Clarke, and William Wollaston, were to represent her personal philosophy of the mutual interdependence of religion and science. With Lord Cobham's attack on Sir Robert Walpole, who was favored by Caroline and the king, she responded by commissioning Kent in the summer of 1735 to build at Richmond another garden folly called Merlin's Cave.[10] There waxwork figures, including Merlin, King Arthur's wizard and prophet, and Queen Elizabeth, were meant to emphasize the legitimacy of the present Hanover monarchy by reference to the throne of Arthur (fig. 40).

Probably in emulation of the queen, Henrietta St. John Knight, half-sister of the Tory politician Lord Bolingbroke, erected her own pantheon of notables in her gardens at Barrels in Warwickshire.[11] In June 1742 she wrote Lady Hertford: "I have also made a little summer-house that is stuccoed and adorned with the busts of my Brother Bolingbroke, Pope, Dryden, Milton, Shakespeare, Newton, and Locke." In 1771 the Rev-

61. Stowe (Bucks), Temple of British Worthies

erend William Mason, at the death of his close friend the poet Thomas Gray, placed on exhibition in the summerhouse of the garden of the rectory of Aston in Yorkshire a medallion portrait of Gray based on his memorial in Westminster Abbey.[12] Mason referred to the dedication at the beginning of Book III of his poem *The English Garden* and William Burgh in his commentary on the poem printed in a later edition of the poem claimed:

The three following lines [III, 12–14] allude to a rustic alcove the author was then building in his garden, in which he placed a medallion of his friend, and an urn; a lyre over the entrance with the motto from Pindar, which Mr. Gray had prefixt to his Odes, ΦΩΝΑΝΤΑ ΣΥΝΕΤΟΙΣΙ, and under it on a tablet this stanza, taken from the first edition of his Elegy written in a country church-yard.

Here scatter'd oft, the loveliest of the year,
By hands unseen, are showers of violets found;
The Redbreast loves to build and warble *here*,
And little footsteps lightly print the ground.

In 1736, at Lord Cobham's behest, Kent designed a most charming monument at Stowe in memory of the poet and dramatist William Congreve (fig. 62). The memorial, recently restored, now stands on a little peninsula of the Octagon Lake.[13] On the summit of a pyramid decorated on one side with relief sculpture of comic masks and other dramatic devices sits a monkey staring into a mirror with a Latin inscription to be translated: "Comedy is the Imitation of Life, and the Mirror of Fashion." Originally the poet's effigy reclined below on one side and on the other was his epitaph, dated 1736.

Many of the temples embellishing the grounds at Stowe were either built as celebrative memorials or were later dedicated as such. In 1739 the Temple of Friendship, designed by James Gibbs, was begun at the southern foot of Hawkwell Field.[14] Built of brick covered with stucco, the large central room had two side loggias and a tetrastyle, Tuscan entrance portico. Within the temple were portrait busts by Rysbrack of Lord Cobham and his friends and political allies, such as the prince of Wales, William Pitt, George Lyttelton, and the earls of Chesterfield, Westmorland, and Marchmont. The painting on the ceiling by Sleter made the political message obvious with a figure of Britannia proclaiming the glory of the reigns of Queen Elizabeth and Edward III, while frowning upon the contemporary reign whose name was discreetly hidden by Britannia's hand. The temple, therefore, reiterated the anti-government position previously demonstrated

62. Stowe (Bucks), monument to Congreve

63. Stowe (Bucks), Gothic Temple

in the Elysian Fields. Unfortunately the Temple of Friendship was later seriously damaged by fire leaving only ruins.

From 1741 to 1748 Gibbs built the so-called Gothic Temple or Temple of Liberty in the middle of Hawkwell Field (fig. 63). A triangular structure with towers, turrets, and pointed arches, the temple was an early example of the Gothic revival, an architectural style obviously chosen to recall the ancient "Gothic" liberties of England emphasized by the removal here of Rysbrack's statues of the seven Saxon gods, discussed previously. To match the masculine Temple of Friendship Gibbs constructed at the northern end of Hawkwell Field a structure known as the Lady's Temple as a center for Lady Cobham and her friends with decoration of ladies's diversions by Sleter. Gibbs's work, however, was completely refashioned later in the century, including the addition of a large Corinthian entrance portico approached by a wide flight of steps. In 1790 the garden structure was dedicated to Queen Charlotte and renamed the Queen's Temple.

North of Hawkwell Field and the Elysian Fields Lord Cobham planned and began in late 1746 a new landscaped area called the Grecian Valley, a dog-legged artificial valley of rolling nature lined by belts of trees. At the angle or hinge of the dog-leg the so-called Grecian Temple was erected from about 1749, modelled, however, on the Roman Maison Carrée at Nimes, and probably designed by Earl Temple himself. With the signing of the Peace of Paris in 1763 the temple was renamed the Temple of Concord and Victory to commemorate the moment of peace.

Constantly during the eighteenth century visitors criticized the quantity of garden buildings and monuments scattered through the Stowe landscape. Thomas Whately, a very perceptive critic, after complaining that "twenty or thirty capital structures, mixed with others of inferior note, do seem too many" then remarks:

> It is like one of those places celebrated in antiquity, which were devoted to the purposes of religion, and filled with several groves, hallowed fountains, and temples dedicated to several deities.[15]

Horace Walpole at the same time put it in contemporary terms. On July 7, 1770, Walpole wrote his friend George Montagu a charming, long description of the celebration he had just attended at Stowe in honor of a return visit of Princess Amelia to view her commemorative arch.*

> Every acre brings to one's mind some instances of the parts or of pedantry, of the taste or want of taste, of the ambition, or love of fame, or greatness, or miscarriages of those who have inhabited, decorated,

planned or visited the place. Pope, Congreve, Vanbrugh, Kent, Gibbs, Lord Cobham, Lord Chesterfield, the mob of nephews, the Lytteltons, Grenvilles, Wests, Leonidas Glover and Wilkes, the late prince of Wales, the king of Denmark, Princess Amelia, and the proud monuments of Lord Chatham's services, now enshrined there, then anathematized there, and now again commanding there, with the Temple of Friendship like the Temple of Janus, sometimes open to war, and sometimes shut up in factious cabals, all these images crown upon one's memory and add visionary personages to the charming scenes, that are so enriched with fanes and temples, that the real prospects are little less than visions themselves.[16]

In the 1740s inscribed urns and garden benches were two very popular forms of commemorative monuments, often used together. The poet William Shenstone particularly popularized these garden features at his country residence The Leasowes. Uninscribed urns and garden seats had furnished typical garden ornament, especially in the period of William and Mary. In 1701 John Van Nost was paid for two large vases for Hampton Court, obviously in emulation of the floral urns decorating the gardens at Versailles of the French King Louis XIV. Melbourne Hall in Derbyshire exhibits a magnificent lead urn with exuberant Baroque ornament, the Four Seasons Monument, cast by Van Nost in 1705. Costing one hundred pounds, the vase was presented by Queen Anne to her Vice Chamberlain Thomas Coke in gratitude for his services. The commemorative urn was set up at the junction of several alleys in the southeast extension of the formal, French-style garden. In November 1738 the poet Alexander Pope ordered six stone urns from his friend Ralph Allen of Prior Park at Bath. Later, in 1744, John Vardy in his book of designs by Jones and Kent reproduces vases designed by Kent for Pope's garden at Twickenham.[17] The Kent designs have blank plaques carved on their sides, suggesting that they were to be inscribed, but there is no evidence as to the execution of inscriptions. Vardy's book has plates illustrating urns designed by Kent for other patrons, such as Lord Mountford and Sir Robert Walpole, earl of Orford. By May 1739 William Biggs, a mason employed by Allen, had arrived at Twickenham to set up these urns and others given to Pope by the prince of Wales. Shenstone could afford only relatively small and simple urns carved by a local stonecutter "Old Pedley" and inscribed with the name of a friend or relative with a poetic epitaph composed by Shenstone himself. There are records or accounts of at least six such memorials at The Leasowes. Similarly there were at least four such commemorative benches located generally at a favorite viewing point of the recipient.[18] For Shenstone, whose income was modest, such urns or rustic benches were a relatively inexpensive mode of honoring his friends. In a letter of March 22, 1750, to Lady Luxborough Shenstone remarked on the problem:

> For I cannot agree to a Pyramid there, even if I c^d build one with rough stone as cheap as an urn—(Mr. Smith indeed proposed it, but it really were so diminutive so pitiful an Imitation of those in Egypt (covering 11 acres of ground to build one of 20 feet, y^t can't think of the latter with out contemning ye former; & sure one cannot view ye copy with out recollecting ye original—And yet a Pyramid has it's advantages—tis certainly a very solemn Ornament, & a very uncommon one. However, you will see by this y^t we vary in our Ideas of proportion, as he thinks a Pyramid not too large, where I esteem an Urn sufficient.

Cost did not determine the use of urns at the garden park of Hagley of Shenstone's neighbors the Lytteltons. There were, however, at least two inscribed urns in their landscaped park, one dedicated to Shenstone himself and the other to the poet Alexander Pope, who considered the landscape beauties of Hagley only excelled by Mount Edgecumbe. Pope's urn was dated 1744, early, therefore, in the series.[19] There was also a seat dedicated to the poet James Thomson, who had visited The Leasowes while staying at Hagley.

Although dedicatory urns were popular in many gardens, they were occasionally decried, probably because of their overabundance and often trite sentiment. Parson Allen, rector of Spernall, a neighbor of Lady Luxborough, wrote about 1750 *A Receipt for a Modern Urn* that commences:

> Forty five mottos full of odd Hints
> Nicely engrav'd on forty five Plinths
> An heart-melting epitaph scrawld on the urn
> With alas! & alack! he will never return.[20]

As might be expected it is Samuel Johnson who was most disparaging of urns as garden memorials. Johnson was accustomed to visit a draper, a Mr. Wickins, in his native Lichfield who gives an account of walking in his garden with Johnson when "we came to an urn which I had erected to the memory of a deceased friend. I asked him how he liked that urn—it was of the true Tuscan order. 'Sir,' said he, 'I hate urns; they are nothing, they *mean* nothing, convey no idea but ideas of horror—would they were beaten to pieces to pave our streets!' "[21] So in September 1777, when Mrs. Thrale wrote Johnson to inform him that Myddelton was erecting an urn in his memory at Gwynynnog, he could only reply:

> Mr. Myddeltons's erection of an urn looks like an intention to bury me alive. I would as willingly see my friend, however benevolent and hospitable quietly inurned. Let him think for the present of some more acceptable memorial.

An unusual group of monuments is concentrated at the Anson estate of Shugborough in Staffordshire.[22] From about 1748 to 1754 Thomas Anson employed the astronomer-architect Thomas Wright to make revisions to this house and presumably to design at least one garden monument, the Shepherd's Monument (fig. 64). A large marble relief carved by the sculptor Scheemakers after the famous painting in the Louvre by the French artist Nicolas Poussin entitled *Et in Arcadia Ego* is set into a rustic arch very like an illustration in Wright's book, *Six Original Designs of Arbours* (1755). Later, probably in 1763, a classical frame of Doric columns and entablature was added by the architect James Stuart around the rustic arch. The monument stands at the edge of the gardens just north of the house. Its purpose and commemoration are completely unknown. Below the relief is a very mysterious inscription of the letters OUOSVAVV subscribed with the presumably Latin initials D. M. for Diis Manibus, thus confirming the elegiac note suggested by the relief. Another singular monument is the Cat's Monument set on a little island beyond the Shepherd's Monument. On top of a large urn reclines a cat (fig. 65). A letter in 1749 from Anson's sister-in-law at Bath remarks that "you might have Kouli-Kan's monument made here" at Ralph Allen's quarry, suggesting that at least the idea of such a memorial was conceived then. Thomas Anson had a notable breed of Persian cats which is presumably commemorated here.

In the 1760s Anson, who was one of the founders of the Society of the Dilettanti, employed the neoclassical architect James "Athenian" Stuart, who had just returned from measuring antiquities in Athens, to design and erect several buildings or monuments in the park at Shugborough that were copies or derivatives of ancient Athenian works, including the front of the Temple of Hephaestus, often called the Theseum, the Tower of the Winds, and the Lanthorn of Demosthenes. Much of the new work was paid for by Anson's younger brother, Admiral George Anson, who had come into a fortune from his naval exploits. Stuart also designed in 1761 a Triumphal Arch based on the Arch of Hadrian in Athens to stand on an eminence about

64. Shugborough (Staffords), Shepherds' Monument

65. Shugborough (Staffords), Cat Monument

two-thirds of a mile south of the house. With the death of the admiral in the next year the arch was converted to a memorial. By at least 1764 the monument was decorated with symbols of war, such as the stern of a ship, and sarcophagi supporting busts of the admiral and his wife. The commemorative monuments at Shugborough are, therefore, very personal, only the Triumphal Arch having some public reference.

Thomas Wright was also involved with the landscaping of Stoke Park in Gloucester for Norborne Berkeley, Lord Botetourt, from about 1750, receiving payment in December 1750, until Berkeley left for Virginia in

North America in 1768.[23] Several unusual memorials were created at Stoke
Park during that time, as identified in Bishop Pococke's account of 1764. At
the entrance to a woods west of the house is a sepulchral monument decorated along its sides with a heavy Doric entablature. Its plinth has the
inscription "Fraterni Dignus Amoris" as a memorial to the fourth duke of
Beaufort, Berkeley's brother-in-law, who died in 1756. In the 1920s,
facing the house across the pond, were the remains of a ruined monument
then known as "Old Owl House," but which can be identified by Pococke's
report.

> We then went to a brow of a Hill, on which his Lordship has built a
> model of ye monument of ye Horatii at Albano, with four round
> Obeliscs upon an arch'd building adorn'd with a pediment every way.
> On ye Frieze round ye four sides is this inscription:
> Memoria Virtutis Heroicae S. P. Q. R.

The monument glorifying the heroic virtue of the Romans was inspired by
the remains of an ancient Roman tomb just outside of Albano on the road to
Ariccia south of Rome. The ruins of the ancient tomb, known traditionally
as the Tomb of the Horatii and Curiatii, consists of a massive square base
surmounted by a round drum with four elongated cones or obelisks on the
corners of the base. Bishop Pococke in an earlier trip in 1750 to Devon
claimed to have seen at Werrington, Sir William Morris' house at New-
port, "a model of what is called the Tomb of the Horatii, near Albano."
Similarly Arthur Young in the account of his visit to Studley Royal in
Yorkshire in 1768 records that on a "bank of wood stands the *Roman*
monument, the model of that erected to the *Horatii* and *Curiatii*; you look
down from it, into a winding valley, at a considerable depth, through which
the river takes its bending course; at one end it is lost most beautifully in the
hanging woods; and at the other under a wall of rocks."[24] The remains at
Albano were a tourist attraction for English visitors in the seventeenth and
eighteenth centuries. John Evelyn, for example, recorded in his diary that
he had visited the monument in 1645,[25] and the story of the two groups of
brothers was well known from Livy's history of ancient Rome. The significance of these copies of the ancient tomb for English sites is unknown,
beyond the fact that the Stoke Park example was to honor Roman republican
heroism.

In 1753 the renowned actor David Garrick resolved that he should have a
county villa near London and rented a house at Hampton on the London
road to Hampton Court, which he later purchased in 1754. The house
faced south with about an acre of land across the road running down to the

edge of the Thames river.[26] On the land along the river Horace Walpole noted in August 1755 that Garrick "is building a grateful temple to Shakespeare." A miniature Pantheon-type garden structure built of brick on an octagonal plan with a dome and Ionic portico (fig. 66), it has been attributed to the architect Robert Adam who was a friend of Garrick and would later revise Garrick's villa, but the attribution is unlikely as Adam was then in Italy. Capability Brown, the great landscapist, who was an even closer friend of Garrick and was at that moment "improving" the grounds at Hampton, was more likely the designer. It was Brown who suggested that rather than building a bridge over the road from the villa to the temple that an underground tunnel be excavated for access, probably inspired by the grotto-tunnel that the poet Pope had created for the same problem at his villa nearby at Twickenham. By October 1756 Horace Walpole was making his contribution to the temple.

> John [presumably Walpole's gardener, John Cowie] and I are just going to Garrick's, with a grove of cypresses in our hands, like the Kentish men at the Conquest. He has built a temple to his master Shakespeare, and I am going to adorn the outside, since his modesty would not let me decorate it within, as I proposed, with these mottoes:
>
> > Quod spiro et placeo, si placeo, tuum est,
> > That I spirit have and nature,
> > That sense breathes in ev'ry feature,
> > That I please, if please I do,
> > Shakespear, all I owe to you.

At about the same time Garrick commissioned the sculptor Roubiliac to carve a marble statue of Shakespeare for the interior of the temple. Signed and dated 1758, the statue, which is now in the British Museum, cost three hundred and fifteen pounds and depicts a standing figure, leaning on a desk in a pensive posture with his left hand to this chin. The memorial building also contained Shakespearean relics, including a glove and a signet ring. It was probably the painter Hogarth who designed an elaborate mahogany chair for the garden house which is portrayed in Hogarth's portrait of Garrick and his wife in 1756. The temple and museum served as a garden teahouse for the Garricks and their friends, as seen in a painting by Zoffany.

Later the Quaker doctor and botanist John Lettsom created a memorial to Shakespeare in his extended gardens of Grove Hill at Camberwell in Surrey.[27] In 1779 and 1780 Lettsom bought land at Camberwell and planted gardens with several greenhouses, comprising more than ten acres

66. Hampton, Garrick Mansion and Temple of Shakespeare, engraving

by 1794. The gardens were open to public access at certain times when a visitor could stroll along the walks decorated with statues of the Fates, Urania, and Eros, and view the unusual and exotic plants he nourished. A long path descending into a valley toward the north was known as Shakespeare's Walk with a statue of a standing Shakespeare holding a scroll in his right hand, identified on a map of the gardens published in 1794 as: "a statue of Shakespeare: it is covered by a thatched shed, supported by the trunks of eight oak trees, with the branches cropped, bearing festoons of foliage and flowers; and facing that statue is a pond well stored with fish."

Poets seem to have been honored more often in English gardens and parks than other artists. This may be occasioned in part because many of the owners were themselves poets, or at least amateur poets, whose friendship was governed by their interest. So the minor poet William Thompson, after earning his M.A. at Oxford, took up the living at the rectory of nearby Hampton Poyle, where he honored many English poets and the Romans, Vergil and Horace, usually with their busts accompanied by inscriptions which he published in 1757 in his collection of poetry.[28] Bowers were dedicated to Spenser, Chaucer, and Thomson, an alcove for Milton, arbors for Cowley and Bishop Taylor, and a walk named in honor of Shakespeare. Other inscribed memorials celebrated Horace, Philips, and Young. Busts of Vergil and Addison stood on a mount with Vergil's next to a cascade. A canal ran through the first half of the garden and at the end of the garden was a bust of Pope in a laurel grove on Laurel Hill.

The musician George Frederick Handel, however, was honored in at least two gardens. The first occasion was a logical one, for in May 1738 Jonathan Tyers, the owner of the public pleasure garden at Vauxhall Gardens in London, set up in the garden a marble statue of the musician by the young French sculptor Roubiliac (fig. 67).[29] Handel is depicted in informal, contemporary clothing, but still retains one Baroque allegorical device in that he is playing a lyre in the guise of Apollo. Handel was chosen, of course, as a contemporary musician whose music was often heard at Vauxhall. The success of the marble statue, which is now in the Victoria and Albert Museum in London, inspired Tyers to commission from Roubiliac a lead statue of Milton in the semblance of *Il Penseroso* seated on a little hill listening to music. This statue seems to have been lost.

After the death of Handel in 1759, Sir Samuel Hellier, a great music lover, commissioned the architect James Gandon to design a memorial to the musician to stand in the grounds of Hellier's country estate at Wodehouse Wombourne in Staffordshire.[30] In 1768 Gandon exhibited at the Society of Artists the elevation drawing of what he called a "Mausoleum to

67. F. Roubiliac,
statue of Handel
from Vauxhall Gardens,
Victoria and Albert
Museum, London

68. Stowe (Bucks), Cook's Monument and Grenville Column, watercolor by J. C. Nattes, Buckinghamshire County Museum, Aylesbury

the memory of Handel." A watercolor of 1773 illustrates a small, Pantheon-like temple with a tetrastyle portico, a semi-circular dome, and presumably a statue in a niche in the center of the portico. In the woods was also a small, cubelike music room provided with an organ where Handel's music, among others, could be played.

With the exception of royalty, as at Stowe and Wrest Park, portrait memorials to military heroes rarely decorated gardens. Their martial exploits were perhaps considered inappropriate to the peaceful ambiance of gardens, although abstract monuments, such as obelisks or columns, could have celebrated military achievements, such as those of the duke of Marlborough, as will be discussed later, or an occasional garden such as the Maastricht garden at Windsor or perhaps the mall at Blenheim could have been formed after battle designs. Two exceptional portrait statues of military heroes, however, stand now at Clifton Hampden where they were moved from the gardens of Glemham in Suffolk. Lead figures attributed to the sculptor Andrew Carpenter, they depict a proud duke of Marlborough, hand on hip, and his dashing colleague Prince Eugene of Savoy brandishing a sword.[31] Carpenter had included a statue of Marlborough, six feet tall at twenty-eight pounds, on his price list sent in about 1723 to Lord Carlisle.

Political sentiments also inspired commemorative monuments, as apparent in some of Cobham's memorials at Stowe. The politician Henry Fox, first Lord Holland, who surrounded his rented house at Kingsgate with numerous ruins which earned William Gilpin's scorn, also erected there several memorials.[32] One was a tower honoring Thomas Harley, Lord Mayor of London in 1768 and Tory opponent of the popular John Wilkes. The circular tower set on a square base decorated with eagles was destroyed during World War II. Fox remarked in August 1768: "My tower in honor of Mr. Harley is built, I believe, more for my private amusement than from public spirit. But he is really almost the only man that has not been a coward." Another monument, a slender tower bearing an urn, was not political but honored Robert Whitfield, a builder praised in the inscription on the tower as "The Adorner of Kingsgate."

The adventures and unfortunate death of the explorer Captain James Cook inspired several memorials. Originally on an island in the Elysian Fields at Stowe was a small monument consisting of a cubical pedestal supporting a terrestrial globe and on its base was a marble medallion portrait of the captain dated 1778, just before his death (fig. 68).[33] Later the memorial was moved to the Shell Bridge and the globe was replaced by an ancient sarcophagus. After Cook's tragic death in February 1779 Sir Hugh Palliser had a commemorative monument, consisting of a small, quadrifrons-arched, flint tower under which is exhibited a marble pedestal and globe, probably inspired by the Stowe monument, erected at his estate of The Vache near Chalfont St. Giles in Buckinghamshire.

The two marquises of Rockingham and their heir the fourth Earl Fitz-william raised at their country residence at Wentworth Woodhouse in Yorkshire a rather extraordinary group of monuments, often labelled follies, including a triumphal column and several versions of an obelisk, some of which will be discussed later.[34] When the second marquis of Rock-ingham died in 1782 the estate passed to his nephew Earl Fitzwilliam, who soon commissioned the architect John Carr of York to design a monument to the memory of Rockingham, often identified as a mausoleum, but with no burial (fig. 69). Several drawings dated 1783 portray a project with a square base decorated with Doric entablature on engaged, paired columns and supporting a tall, hollow obelisk rising over one hundred feet. The base was to contain a circular, domed chamber. The executed memorial, com-pleted about 1790, abandoned the obelisk and is instead a three-storied cenotaph adapted from the ancient Roman Tomb of the Julii at St. Remy in southern France. Above the simplified square base, which still has an unobtrusive Doric entablature, is a quadrifrons arch where a sarcophagus is exhibited, and a third story that consists of a domed rotunda with Corin-thian columns. Two years after its completion four small obelisks were set around the building at its corners. The circular chamber is decorated with a life-size marble statue of the marquis in his regalia of the Order of the Garter carved by Nollekens. The eight busts were to have been portraits of Rockingham's political friends, such as Edmund Burke, James Fox, and Admiral Keppel. The memorial was not only a personal commemoration by his heir, but a political testimonial, a Temple of Friendship, rather like that at Stowe. On the four sides of the pedestal of the portrait of the marquis would have been extensive inscriptions detailing and praising his public service.

Thomas Jefferson in the diary of his visits to English gardens in 1786 remarks at Stowe on the project to erect there a memorial to an eminent English politician who had been a great friend of Earl Temple: "The Egyptian pyramid [honoring Vanbrugh] is almost entirely taken down by the late Lord Temple, to erect a building there, in commemoration of Mr. Pitt, but he died before beginning it, and nothing is done to it yet."[35]

In contrast to the monuments to prominent political figures was the memorial that Philip Thicknesse created after 1774 at St. Catherine's Hermitage in the village of Bathampton near Bath to the young poet Thomas Chatterton of Bristol who took his own life in 1770 at the age of

69. Wentworth Woodhouse (Yorks),
Mausoleum, engraving

eighteen.[36] In Thicknesse's own description of his hermitage published in 1787, he gives an account of the memorial.

> Now do not wonder! for I must inform you, that for some years since I had scooped out a cave on the side of the dingle, under the spreading roots of an ash tree, and turned a rude arch in front of it; and there placed, cut in relief, the head of that wonderful genius Thomas Chatterton, with the following lines beneath it:

Sacred to the Memory of
THOMAS CHATTERTON
Unfortunate Boy!
Short & Evil were thy Days,
But the vigour of thy genius shall immortalize thee
Unfortunate Boy!
Poorly wast thou accommodated
During thy short sojourning among us,
Thou livedst unnoticed
But thy Fame shall never die.

The *Ladies Magazine* published a print of the memorial in 1784 (fig. 70). A rough cast, arched frontispiece was let into the hillside "raised between the bosom of two hills." Cut into the upper part of the grotto face was a pedestal supporting a medallion with Chatterton's profile and above that a freestanding urn. A small stream flowed immediately in front of the entrance which was gained from a bridge.

THE PYRAMID

IN 1540 the Italian architect Sebastiano Serlio published in the third book of his treatise on architecture a depiction of the Great Pyramid of Egypt after the drawing and measurements of the Venetian Marco Grimani. Serlio's book, published in numerous later editions, including an English version in 1611 of the first five books, was extremely popular in England. In 1603 the Italian writer Cesare Ripa, in his publication *Iconologia*, the standard handbook on the meaning of art for European artists for the next two centuries, published under the entry "Glory of Princes" the image of a woman holding a pyramid which he asserts "signifies the clear and great glory of Princes, who with magnificence make sumptuous and large buildings, with which they show their glory."[37] In England Henry

Peacham, inspired by Ripa, included in his emblem book, *Minerva Britanna* of 1612, an image dedicated to the earl of Pembroke of a crowned woman embracing what seems to be an obelisk but which Peacham identifies as "a huge and stately Pyramis," which "is of their [Princes's] fame, some lasting Moniment."

Soon English explorers were studying the Egyptian pyramids. In 1610 George Sandys began a journey to the Near East during which he examined the Great Pyramid, publishing an account in 1615, to be succeeded by at least seven more editions.[38] John Greaves, a mathematician and professor of astronomy at Oxford, left in 1637 to visit Rome where he measured the ancient, pyramidal Tomb of Cestius, as well as the Pantheon, and then continued on to Constantinople and Egypt where in 1638 and 1639 he measured the pyramids. As a result of his studies he published in 1646 a treatise, *Pyramidographia, or a Discourse of the Pyramids of Egypt*, offering a detailed report of their history and his account of their construction with views and a section of the Great Pyramid.

The pyramidal form was used as a decorative motif in the garden of Sir John Danvers at Chelsea in London from about 1622–23.[39] John Aubrey

70. Bathampton (Avon), St. Catherine's Hermitage, memorial to Thomas Chatterton, engraving

in his description of the garden notes that the entrance gateway was flanked by "two, spacious elegant Pyramides of brick covered with finishing mortar, but pointed with freestone: about twenty foure foot high, which stood on the spires of the Gate." He adds "The Pyramides are the most beautifull, and taking of any that ever I saw: for there is a criticall proportion in them, that is neither too high or too low." The idea of pyramidal finials on entrance piers was very traditional, but Aubrey's emphasis on their size, "about twenty-foure foot high," and their careful proportions would seem to cast them into the company of the robust pyramids that Vanbrugh and Hawksmoor used much later as decoration at Castle Howard.

The architects Sir John Vanbrugh and Nicholas Hawksmoor would seem to have been the major exponents in the early eighteenth century of the use of the pyramidal form as a feature in architecture and gardening. At Castle Howard in Yorkshire Vanbrugh built massive, bastioned walls south of the house flanking the approach road and constructed an entrance gateway consisting of a cubical block cut by an arched passageway and surmounted by a heavy pyramid. The gate bears the coat-of-arms of the earl and the date 1719. The pyramid in this case presumably was used as Ripa suggested, to honor a building "Prince." Perhaps the last building designed by Vanbrugh for Stowe was the stepped pyramid some sixty feet high, discussed previously (fig. 60). It was already in place in 1724 when Viscount Perceval visited Stowe: "The Pyramid at the End of one of the walks is a copy in miniature of the most famous one in Egypt, and the only thing of its kind I think in England."[40] Two years later with the death of Vanbrugh the pyramid was dedicated to his memory, thus creating a funerary monument. It is difficult to guess its original purpose unless it too was to commemorate the building activities of Lord Cobham.

At the same time Vanbrugh's colleague Hawksmoor was designing pyramids to decorate the landscape of Castle Howard.[41] In Pretty Wood to the southeast of the mausoleum is a small, decorative, rusticated pyramid on a square plinth which, probably contributed by Hawksmoor, was in place in the woods by 1727. Then on June 3, 1728, Hawksmoor sent to the builder Mr. Etty of York a drawing of a larger pyramid to be erected on a small hill a little more than half a mile south of the house, but slightly east of the central axis (fig. 71). In this position it must have been meant to function as an eye-catcher making a visitor more aware of the expanse of landscape surrounding the house. Hawksmoor himself in a letter regarding the ornaments decorating the pyramid's enclosure indicated his concern for the visual effect, noting that the enclosure should be so low "that it may not

71. Castle Howard (Yorks), Howard Pyramid

hinder the view of ye Elevation of ye bodey of ye pyramide." The idea may have been inspired by William III's garden at Het Loo in Holland where a large, wooden pyramid was erected about a half mile away on the heath on axis with the garden front of the house. The pyramid at Castle Howard, however, was also a commemorative monument as it contained in its conical interior chamber a large, stone bust of Lord William Howard (1563–1640), the founder of the fortunes of Lord Carlisle's branch of the family. An inscription on the exterior of the pyramid records the dedication with the date 1728.

The poet Alexander Pope in that same year, 1728, wrote his friend Lord Bathurst at Cirencester in September to advise him to consider building a pyramid there.[42] On his arrival at Cirencester Pope had been dismayed to find that Bathurst had cut down a large timbered area in his woods. Somewhat caustically Pope wrote:

> Nevertheless my Lord (to prove I am not angry, but with s mixture of charity inclind to rectify, what I disapprove) I would not advise you to an obelisque which can bear no Diameter to fill so vast a Gap unless it literally touch'd the Skies; but rather to a solid Pyramid of 100 ft square, to the end there may be Something solid and Lasting of your works.

Pope's letter indicated that the more common provision for a large garden feature was normally an obelisk like the one Lord Carlisle erected at Castle Howard in 1714 to honor the duke of Marlborough (fig. 55). Bathurst, however, built neither an obelisk nor a pyramid in the great opening in Oakley Wood called the Seven Rides, but did erect later a triumphal column in the center of Home Park.

A tall pyramid, surmounted by a copy of Gianbologna's statue of a flying Mercury, once stood on a small island in one of the series of ponds at the north end of the water garden behind Ebberston Hall in Yorkshire.[43] Colen Campbell, who designed the charming, little casino, records in his *Vitruvius Britannicus* that it was built in 1718, standing "in a fine Park well planted, with a River which forms a Cascade and Canal 1200 feet long and runs under the Loggio into the back-pond." All that remains of the water garden is a rather unkempt canal and cascade behind the house. A series of later paintings, now attributed to John Setterington, depict the water garden as it existed toward the middle of the century with the pyramid on an island in a pond beyond the canal. The date of the pyramid, as well as the name of the author of the water garden, is unknown, with attributions to William Benson, Stephen Switzer, and Charles Bridgeman.

James Gibbs, who succeeded Vanbrugh as architect at Stowe in 1726, designed large pyramids as features in two gardens undoubtedly inspired by Vanbrugh's pyramid at Stowe. The landscapist Charles Bridgeman was called in by William Gore, earlier Lord Mayor of London, to lay out formal gardens at Tring Park in Hertfordshire in the 1720s, including a large canal which a visitor in 1724 said was planned but not yet created.[44] Gibbs then added a large stepped pyramid at the end of the canal in front of the house illustrated in the birdseye view published in 1739 in the fourth volume of the *Vitruvius Britannicus*, but now destroyed (fig. 72). A little

72. Tring (Herts), pyramid, engraving

later Gibbs may have erected another stepped pyramid in the wilderness at Hartwell in Buckinghamshire. It too has been demolished, but its image is preserved in one of the several charming paintings of 1738 by the artist Balthzar Nebot of garden views at Hartwell.[45] There is no evidence of the purpose of these pyramids other than the probable proclamation of the eminence of the owners.

William Kent, however, very aware of the meanings associated with the pyramidal form, in about 1735 placed a stepped pyramid over the central block of his Temple of British Worthies at Stowe (fig. 61). Within an oval niche in the pyramid was exhibited originally a bust of the Roman deity Mercury, the guide to the ancient Elysian Fields as the Latin inscription noted below: *Campos Ducat Ad Elysios*. Thus, the pyramid functioned both as a funerary monument and as a commemoration of outstanding leaders.

The architect Henry Flitcroft, who later was to design and build the triangular tower dedicated to King Alfred at Stourhead in Wiltshire, was employed by the marquis of Rockingham to create a singular commemorative monument at Wentworth Woodhouse in Yorkshire, the first of several unusual follies there.[46] In October 1746 Rockingham, having just been created marquis, wrote his son:

> I have had Mr. Flitcroft here and fixed the Plan of a Pyramid for Hoober Hill, which is to be begun next Summer, it is to rise 70 foot, no Room only a Staircase to carry you to the top. The Base 40 Foot diminishing as it rises.

Work on the "fine Pyramid" was begun in November 1747. The monument as built on an eminence northeast of the house is a triangular, tapering stone structure about ninety feet high capped by a hexagonal domed lantern. A spiral stair within the pyramid mounts to the top where a railing around the lantern protects a viewer who can enjoy the magnificent vistas offered from there. Several windows in a line above the entrance light the stairs. An inscription dated 1748 states:

> This Pyramidal Building was Erected by his Majesty's most Dutiful Subject, Thomas, Marquess of Rockingham in Grateful Respect to the Preserver of our Religion, Laws and Liberties, King George the Second. Who by the Blessing of God having subdued a most Unnatural Rebellion in Britain, Anno 1746 Maintains the Balance of Power and Settles A Just and Honourable Peace in Europe.

The monument is, of course, an unspoken thank offering to George II for raising Rockingham to the marquisate as well as a commemoration of the Peace of Aix-la-Chapelle in 1748 and the suppression of the Jacobite rebellion in 1745.

After the death of his father in 1742, William Aislabie, inheriting the splendid gardens that his father had planted at Studley Royal in Yorkshire, rededicated the Temple of Hercules which peers prominently over the Moon Ponds as a Temple of Piety in memory of his father and erected a pyramid at the end of the avenue pointing to Ripon Minster to honor him.[47] In 1807 the pyramid was replaced by an obelisk now hidden by the late nineteenth-century church of St. Mary. In 1750 Robert Tracy set up a pyramid in memory of his father on Lidcome Hill at Stanway in Gloucestershire. The pyramid, sixty feet tall, rises on an open-arched base about twenty feet square.[48] Originally the memorial stood in a water garden with a cascade and canal, but its garden setting has now been destroyed. About the same time, as noted previously, Francis Wise, the Radcliffe librarian, had decorated his garden at Ellesfield with miniature copies of antique structures, including "an Egyptian pyramid."[49]

Later Sir Watkin Williams-Wynn, the patron of many artists, commissioned the architect Robert Adam at the death of the actor David Garrick on January 20, 1779, to design a memorial to Sir Watkin's friend to stand in the park at Wynnstay in Denbighshhire in Wales. Never carried out, there are, however, several drawings for it including an interesting one in the British Museum (fig. 73), dated June 5, 1779.[50] The drawing depicts a ruined pyramid, whose point has been destroyed, accompanied by a shattered column and a large, strigillated sarcophagus bearing a relief bust, presumably of Garrick. A small temple portico seems to project from the entrance face of the pyramid.

Most of the eighteenth-century pyramids, commencing with Vanbrugh's pyramid at Stowe, are rather attenuated in their proportions, presumably derived from the Roman pyramid of Caius Cestius, an exception being the pyramid by Vanbrugh over the gate at Castle Howard. In fact, the Hoober monument of the marquis of Rockingham at Wentworth Woodhouse would seem rather unlikely as a pyramid except that the marquis himself so described it. In the seventeenth and eighteenth centuries the terms pyramid and obelisk were often not clearly differentiated. A truly Egyptian pyramid in form and function was, however, the mausoleum that the architect Joseph Bonomi built in the woods at Blickling Hall (fig. 53).[51] Unlike most commemorative pyramids this one at Blickling was a burial monument with the heavy proportions of the Great Pyramid in Egypt.

72   Robert Adam, drawing for memorial to Garrick at Wynnstay (Denbighs), 1779, British Museum, London

THE OBELISK

THE POET William Shenstone remarked to Lady Luxborough in 1750 that the pyramid as a garden feature was "a very uncommon one," a comment that could not be said of the obelisk.[52] Indeed, the form of the obelisk was well known to the English in several capacities. Funerary architecture, especially in the Elizabethan and Stuart periods, often favored obelisks.[53] Wall tombs might have obelisks decorating the architectural frame at the upper sides, or a freestanding tomb, such as that of the second earl of Southampton at Titchfield in Hampshire, dating from 1592, would have freestanding obelisks at each corner of the monument. A more special occasion would be obelisks used as decoration on temporary triumphal arches featured at royal entries. The obelisks in these situations were used to proclaim the glory identified with the recipient of the tomb or the person honored by the arch. The emblematist Achille Bocchi devised an emblem published in 1574 to "True Glory" (*Vera Gloria*) employing an obelisk.[54]

Obelisks were also used occasionally in Elizabethan gardens as part of their heraldic decoration. Laneham in his account of the wonderful pageants prepared by the earl of Leicester for Queen Elizabeth's visit to Kenilworth in 1575 notes that the terrace of the new gardens was decorated at "sundry equal distances, with obelisks, and spheres, and white bears, all of stone upon their curious bases," the white bears being Leicester's personal device.[55] Sometime after 1579, when Lord Lumley inherited the former royal palace of Nonsuch in Surrey, and before 1592, he erected several unusual monuments in the Privy Garden around the palace. Immediately behind the palace on the south side was a fountain with a column surmounted by Diana. Flanking the fountain were two columns capped by popinjays, Lumley's device. In the Parliamentary survey of 1650 the columns are described as "marble pinacles or pyramids called the Fawlcon perches," but an engraving of 1610 depicts them as columns.[56] Towards the west side of the palace at the left edge of the engraving is an obelisk identified in the 1650 survey as "one piramide or spired pinacle of marble set vppon a basis of marble grounded vppon a rise of free stone." The obelisks at Kenilworth and at Nonsuch, in company with the personal devices of the owners, are part of the heraldic decoration of the garden visible so often in other Tudor gardens such as those of Hampton Court or Whitehall Palace. The decoration was to honor the owner and his family; the obelisk with its meaning of glory was appropriate to this tradition.

The obelisk form was prominent also in seventeenth- and eighteenth-century gardens as part of the topiary decoration. It was very common to trim into an obelisk shape the single evergreens standing at the corners of grassed plots or along their edge or isolated in the center of the plot. By this time the overt meaning of the form was generally lost and it had become merely a decorative shape. However, the emblem in Francis Quarles's book of 1635, which featured a sundial in a garden as a symbol of transience (fig. 2), also depicted at the rear of the garden an obelisk, presumably to emphasize that the mortality of man would overwhelm even glory and fame.

In the eighteenth century it seems to have been the circle of Vanbrugh and Hawksmoor who revived the obelisk as a monumental form. Already in 1702 Hawksmoor designed for John Aislabie, who was then the mayor of Ripon and was soon to create the extensive garden at Studley Royal, an obelisk to stand in the center of the Market Place at Ripon in Yorkshire.[57] The Ripon obelisk, which still stands, was the progenitor of urban obelisks planned by Hawksmoor for Cambridge, which were never executed, and for several public obelisks erected by John Wood the Elder in the city of Bath.

Perhaps about 1714 the duke of Marlborough considered memorializing the history of Woodstock Manor, the royal manor presented to him as a site for his new Blenheim Palace.[58] Marlborough apparently envisioned mounting an obelisk at the location of the ancient manor house which "would please Sr John [Vanbrugh] best, because it would give an opportunity of mentioning that King whose Scenes of Love He was so much pleas'd with." The fate of the project was foreshadowed by the sarcastic comment the duchess appended, "but if there were obelisks to bee made of what all our Kings have don of that sort the country would bee stuffed with very odd things."

As noted previously Lord Carlisle engaged Vanbrugh to design early in 1714 an obelisk one hundred feet high on the approach road to Carlisle's country residence at Castle Howard in Yorkshire (fig. 55) to commemorate the deeds of the duke of Marlborough.[59] Although the monumental obelisk was part of the landscaping of the estate, its location at the junction of two principal access avenues offered a more public function than an obelisk in a garden or even in an open park. In 1731, as much of the landscaping at Castle Howard was being completed, Carlisle added an inscription at the bottom of the west side of the obelisk celebrating his own efforts in building Castle Howard, its "out-works," and plantation. A series of letters to Lord Carlisle from Vanbrugh commencing in February 1721 and continuing until April 1724 were concerned with the decoration of the garden parterre immediately behind the house to the south.[60] The earliest proposal was to have a fluted Doric column in the center of the parterre with four large obelisks at the corners near the column and four small ones at the outer corners. Vanbrugh then suggested not to flute the obelisks, but to put balls upon them which "Will make them Gay, without being Tawdry." By mid-1722 it was decided that the four obelisks built were too small to accompany the Doric column which was not yet erected. Eventually the upper part of each of the obelisks was enlarged to a height of about forty feet. The work must have been completed by May 1725 when the earl of Oxford reported during his visit seeing "a small plantation of young obelisks on our right, which are in number four, and have a fluted pillar in the centre."[61] The decoration associated with Vanbrugh was soon decried, as in the comment by Philip Yorke in 1744: "In general the gardens are overcrowded with Vanbruggian statues and obelisks, particularly a lawn before the house." Later in the century the parterre and the wooded wilderness behind it would be destroyed.

Early in the eighteenth century several interesting examples of obelisks were set in the center of a pool as garden decoration, as in Lord Burlington's garden at Chiswick. Burlington himself with the aid of the architects Gibbs and Campbell began laying out the gardens perhaps as early as 1715. One of the garden buildings was a version of the ancient Pantheon in Rome in the form of a small, domed temple with a tetrastyle Ionic portico (fig. 74), which was receiving its finishing touches in 1719 while Burlington was visiting Italy.[62] According to a written account in 1728 the area near the temple was complete as is visible in a painting of Rysbrack. A round, formal pool in front of the temple was surrounded by an amphitheater of terraces where Burlington's collection of potted orange trees could be exhibited in summer. A small obelisk in the center of the pool served as a focus for the encircling artificial orange grove. Later William Kent began to revise the garden, leaving the obelisk rather forlornly abandoned in the pool in front of the garden temple. In November 1732 Kent also introduced a monumental obelisk at the Burlington Lane entrance to the gardens at the southwest. This obelisk, like those erected earlier in the piazzas of Rome, served to mark the junction of garden alleys as they approached the gate.

About the same time that Burlington created his round pond with an obelisk, several similar projects associated with the architect Vanbrugh appeared in notable gardens, but unfortunately none of them survive. The most prominent example was the "Guglio" at Stowe, named for the Italian word *guglia* for an obelisk or pinnacle. From about 1719 the garden designer Charles Bridgeman, probably on the recommendation of Vanbrugh, began an expansive, formal garden at Stowe with Vanbrugh providing designs for the garden architecture. South of the house Bridgeman organized a wide axis ending in a large, octagonal pool. It was presumably Vanbrugh who conceived the idea of an obelisk seventy feet tall set in the center of the pond with water gushing forth from its summit and cascading down its sides (fig. 75). The concept may have been inspired by the ancient fountain of the *Meta Sudans* (the sweating goalpost) once near the Colosseum in Rome, but destroyed in 1936. An intermediary model may have been the Dupérac engraving of 1573 of the gardens at the Villa d'Este at Tivoli which illustrated and identified two *Mete Sudanti*, standing in two of the fishpools in the gardens of the Renaissance villa, although never executed in the pools.[63] Building accounts at Stowe indicate that work on the fountain was underway in June 1722. The "Guglio" at Stowe was in dramatic contrast with Burlington's obelisk and pool at Chiswick. The latter had all the restrained elegance, especially with the orange trees in bloom, appropriate to the Palladian style worshipped by Burlington. The "Guglio," on the other hand, must have had all the dramatic energy, boldness, and monumentality that Vanbrugh sought. At Stowe, after General Wolfe was killed at the seizure of Quebec in 1759, the formal octagon pond was transformed into a seemingly natural lake appropriate to changes in the landscape of Stowe and the "Guglio" was dismantled. The stones of the old obelisk were recut to lose their rustication and were reassembled on a pedestal. Set on a hill in the park north of the house, the new obelisk, over one hundred feet tall, was dedicated and inscribed to the memory of General Wolfe.

At the time they were working at Stowe Bridgeman and Vanbrugh were involved with new gardens for the duke of Newcastle at Claremont in Surrey. There Bridgeman excavated a large, round, formal pool in the center of the new garden and, probably, Vanbrugh, along with designs for benches, reared in the center of the pond an obelisk originally topped by the lead figure of a peacock.[64] Bridgeman's pool, like the one at Stowe, was naturalized by William Kent about 1734 and an artificial island with a garden pavilion was substituted for the obelisk, which was removed to the stable area.

Two other instances of obelisk fountains in Yorkshire gardens are probably derived from Vanbrugh's examples.[65] In Bramham Park on the Broad Walk running across the west front of the house toward the south is a large, rectangular pool known as Obelisk Pond because of the obelisk that once stood in it serving as a visual accent for the vista along the Broad Walk south toward the Black Fen, but also marking a cross vista from the Gothick Temple at the west down the slope over the Obelisk Pond into the surrounding countryside. The waterworks were probably the work of the architect

74. Chiswick, Ionic Temple and Orangery, painting by P. A. Rysbrack, c. 1729, Devonshire Collection, Chatsworth

View of the Great Baſon, *from the Entrance of the* Great Walk *to the* Houſe. *Vüe du Grand Baſin, prise et l'entree de la Grand Allee qui mente au Chateau.*

75. Stowe (Bucks), *guglio*, watercolor by Rigaud, 1746, The Metropolitan Museum of Art, New York

John Wood the Elder who was called in to improve the water supply, excavating in 1728 a large reservoir known as the T-canal. About forty years later a succeeding owner, the second Lord Bingley, erected a second, more monumental obelisk surmounted by an urn in the densely wooded Black Fen in memory of his only son, who died in 1768. The first obelisk in the pond was strictly an ornamental feature, serving as an eye-catcher to enhance the several vistas, in contrast to the later commemorative obelisk. At about the same time that the first Lord Bingley was creating his Obelisk Pond, John Aislabie, his neighbor at Studley Royal, raised an obelisk fountain in the center of the large formal lake he had created near his house by damming the Skell river. In August 1728 a payment was recorded for the construction of a "large Ingin" to pump water to the house "and to serve the obelisk in the large Bason." A slightly later painting by Balthazar Nebot of the lake and obelisk depicts the latter hidden under the envelop of water gushing from its summit. John Aislabie was a friend of Vanbrugh so that it is very likely that these Yorkshire fountains resulted from this friendship. Kent's introduction in the 1730s of a more naturalistic gardening, however, was prejudicial to the formal motif of an obelisk rising from a geometrically designed pool.

The idea of an obelisk in the park at Blenheim Palace was revived after the death of the duke of Marlborough in June 1722, but this time with the enthusiastic support of the duchess.[66] The architect Hawksmoor prepared several designs for an obelisk to commemorate the duke and submitted a memorandum entitled *Explanation of the Obelisk*. In the latter he gave detailed measurements of the parts of the projected obelisk which would be more than one hundred feet tall. The obelisk would be surmounted by a star, as is also seen in one of his drawings. After mentioning several historical obelisks, such as the one honoring King Louis XIV of France at Arles and several of the Roman obelisks, Hawksmoor discussed several locations where the obelisk might be sited. By 1725 the duchess had presumably changed her mind and resolved to erect a triumphal column rather than an obelisk. The latter idea was probably also Hawksmoor's as there is among his obelisk drawings one of a fluted Doric column surmounted by a figure of the duke and in Hawksmoor's memorandum on the obelisk he advocated that it be decorated with Roman eagles and laurels as "upon the Pedestal of the column of ye Emperour Trajan. One of the best of the Roman Emperours."

In the third decade of the eighteenth century the proliferation of obelisks in gardens, both as decorative features and as commemorative monuments, flourished. When the poet Alexander Pope visited Sherborne Park in Dorset, probably in 1724, he was enchanted by the site overshadowed by the ruins of Sherborne Castle.[67] In his descriptive letter to Martha Blount he noted how the ruins "do no small honor" to the family of Lord Digby: "I would sett up at the entrance of 'em an Obelisk, with an inscription of the Fact: which would be a Monument erected to the very ruins; as the adorning & beautifying them in the manner I have been imagining, would not be unlike the Egyptian Finery of bestowing Ornament and curiosity on dead bodies."

James Gibbs, who was closely aware of the ideas and work of Vanbrugh and Hawksmoor, helped to popularize both obelisks and triumphal columns as garden ornaments with his book on architecture published in 1728. Just previously, sometime after 1723, Gibbs had built an obelisk for Sir Thomas Lee at Hartwell in Buckinghamshire.[68] This obelisk was included as the third obelisk on plate LXXXV of his book, illustrating the three different proportions he proposed for obelisks. The following plate depicted three more obelisks each surmounted by an urn, resulting in obelisks "more ornamental than the former." Gibbs also planned for Kedleston in Derbyshire "a Vista proposed to be cut through a Wood, and to be terminated with an Obelisque upon a Hill fronting the House," but the plan was abandoned with the death in 1727 of the patron Sir John Curzon.

William Kent designed an obelisk for Thomas Coke for his country estate of Holkham Hall in Norfolk (fig. 76).[69] By 1729, before work was begun on a new house, a large obelisk of stone facing attached to a brick core some eighty feet tall and relatively massive was raised on a mound south of the site for the house as the first step of Coke's new works. In addition to commemorating the beginning of his building activities at Holkham, it served as a visual focus for several vistas, including the long approach avenue to the house. A tall obelisk, perhaps the result of improvements of about 1728 by Viscount Tyrconnel, once stood in the center of the wide alley leading up to the north or garden facade of Belton House in Lincolnshire, as depicted in volume four of *Vitruvius Britannicus* of 1739 (fig. 77).

Another Palladian architect, Colen Campbell, was probably the designer of the obelisk raised by Harry Waller in the gardens of his grandfather, the poet Edmund Waller, at Hall Barn in Buckinghamshire.[70] Edmund Waller sometime after his return in 1651 from exile in France began to lay out formal gardens which Christopher Hussey has suggested may be the first of formal landscapes in England inspired by Versailles. At the end of the principal lake is Waller's Grove, a wilderness of beechwood with alleys lined by laurel hedges radiating from a Temple of Venus in the center. A long approach avenue leads to the entrance of the grove where Harry

76. Holkhan Hall (Norfolk), obelisk

Waller set up a tall obelisk about 1725 (fig. 78). Relief panels on the pedestal of the obelisk depict garden tools and the Waller family coat-of-arms, probably to honor Edmund Waller and his beloved garden just as the obelisk supported by four skulls stands above his tomb in the churchyard at Beaconsfield.

One of the most magnificent obelisks erected as a visual accent, without any specific dedication, is at Farnborough Hall in Warwickshire.[71] By July 1742 William Holbech the owner had begun an extensive grassed terrace east of the house which would soon be remodelled probably by his neighbor the architect Sanderson Miller. The s-shaped terrace about a half mile long mounts gently upwards from the house along a natural ridge. The inner side of the terrace was masked by a screen of beech and elm trees, while a

77. Belton House (Lincs), obelisk, engraving

laurel hedge lined the edge of the terrace with originally elm trees, now replaced by limes, set regularly on small protruding bastions. Several delightful summer pavilions, presumably designed by Miller, were set along the terrace, but the climax was a slender obelisk raised on a tall pedestal at the end of the terrace (fig. 79). First mentioned in 1746, the obelisk bears the date 1751, which probably marks the completion of the terrace, whose labors were celebrated in Richard Jago's poem, *Edge-Hill* (1767).

> Hear they the master's call? In sturdy troops,
> The jocund labourers hie, and, at his nod,
> A thousand hands or smooth the slanting hill
> Or scoop new channels for the gath'ring flood.

An inscription on the obelisk relates that it collapsed in 1823 but was completely rebuilt in its original form. There are magnificent vistas from the terrace across the Warwickshire plain at least three miles to Edgehill where the architect Miller, who undoubtedly planned the obelisk, lived. Although the obelisk bears no dedication, its position dominating the entire countryside proclaims it a monument in the old Renaissance tradition to "true glory."

Another obelisk serving as the visual termination of a broad terrace is the so-called Obelisk of the Sun which a Latin poem by one "J. S. Academicus," perhaps Joseph Spence, in the December 1748 issue of *The Gentleman's Magazine* records was "not yet finished" at Henry Hoare's extensive gardens at Stourhead in Wiltshire.[72] A terrace, described by Sir John Parnell in 1768, continued northward for some five hundred yards along a ridge between the house at Stourhead and the artificial lake Henry Hoare created in the valleys at the center of his vast garden. About forty feet wide, the terrace, called the Fir Walk, was densely framed by spruce firs through which were occasional glimpses of the lake below, but not the broad open vista offered at the Farnborough terrace. In 1755 James Hanway described the obelisk on the highest point at the end of the terrace as one hundred and twenty feet tall surmounted by a gilded copper sun or "*mythra*" six feet in diameter and noted that it "is divided from the garden by an *haha*." This may be explained by a note in Joseph Spence's description of 1765, where he remarks on "the obelisk and Turkish tent in the old (Bridgeman) part of the gardens," although this is the only known reference to possible work by Charles Bridgeman at Stourhead. The sun symbolism of the obelisk was continued in the garden when Henry Hoare built a temple to Apollo on the heights across the lake, but the major purpose of the

78. Hall Barn (Bucks), obelisk

79. Farnborough (Warwicks), obelisk

obelisk was again as an eye-catcher terminating the terrace, as well as being visible occasionally from viewing points on the other side of the lake. Parnell in his account observes that the Fir Walk is an "old fashioned" feature introduced into "a new improvement."

> But a single one, fine as this is, introduc'd on the top of a hill, after a winding walk apparently the work of nature, has given you in its turns all the beauties of prospect, and retirement of shade, has a noble effect; whether produced by contrast or the power of perspective strongly striking you on the first entrance is no way material, but so it is. I never mett a better instance of the good effect of introducing a fine walk of this kind than here.

Parnell then compared it with the grassed terrace terminating in Vanbrugh's belvedere or mount that Bridgeman contrived at Claremont in Surrey for the duke of Newcastle.

The function of obelisks as visual accents in gardens and parks is emphasized by the poet William Shenstone in letters to Lady Luxborough in 1749 regarding the obelisk in Lord Archer's park at Umberslade in Warwickshire.[73] Noting that the obelisk was intended to be viewed from the "Salon" of the house, Shenstone considered the obelisk too small for that vista—"yᵉ Obelisk continues to appear small to me, & I shou'd think must do so, at yᵉ Place from which it shou'd be seen. It has a good effect from some Lanes adjoining to yᵉ Park, and it is no doubt capable of being made good use of, from yᵉ Woods on each side his House."

The obelisk at Hagley Park in Worcestershire holds a very dramatic position as an eye-catcher in the Clent hills that rise above the house (fig. 80).[74] The principal efforts at beautifying the park were begun by George Lyttelton after a visit to Mount Edgecumbe in 1747. Over the years he added garden buildings and ornaments throughout the park, such as seats and urns, ensuring that the summit of each of the hills enclosed within the park should be marked by a building or monument serving as an eye-catcher. One of the last buildings erected was the Doric Temple designed by James "Athenian" Stuart in 1758 to stand on a hill toward the northwest. Sometime after that but before Thomas Martyn's description of Hagley in 1767 a tall obelisk was raised on the summit of the hill north of the temple, where it is dramatically outlined on the horizon, or as Joseph Heely described it in 1777:

> and on the left of the building [Doric Temple], on a yet higher swell, in the midst of an irregular area of lawn, proudly stands an obelisk,

80. Hagley (Worcester), obelisk

rearing its ample head beyond which, at the farthermost extremity of
the ground, a venerable grove of ancient oaks stretching down, and
almost losing itself behind the shrubbery and limes that grace the
foreground, compleats one of the most ravishing views that ever was
held up to the eye.

The poet Aaron Hill created a strictly decorative obelisk of shell work in his
garden at Petty France in London as he observed in a letter to Alexander
Pope on November 7, 1773.

The last time I had the pleasure of seeing you, at Westminster, you
were observing among some rude beginnings of rock-work, which I
am designing in my garden, a little obelisk of Jersey Shells, over a
grotesque portico for Pallas, against the park-wall. You then express'd
some thoughts of improving such a use of those shells, into a nobler
obelisk, among your beauties, at Twittenham. Allow me to bespeak
for myself against next spring, the permission of presenting you the
shells, materials, and workmanship.[75]

It may be significant that Pope is reported considering raising an obelisk in
his garden at Twickenham just five months after the death of his mother, for
later he would fashion an obelisk in her memory in the garden, but certainly not a shell-encrusted one as Hill's letter suggests.

Pope with great filial devotion took care of his mother who lived with
him for many years.[76] By 1724, in her mid-eighties, she was reported to be

in frail condition, inspiring a melancholic mood in Pope who wrote his friend Lord Digby on September 8, 1729: "I have of late been conversant with nothing but melancholy Subjects, my own Mother's Decay giving me a daily Dejection of Mind, which has very much affected my own state of Body." Despite her health Edith Pope lived to the age of ninety-three, dying on June 7, 1733, but it was not until March 22, 1735, that Pope wrote William Fortescue: "I am building a stone obelisk." The death of Pope's mother, and later that of his close friend Lord Peterborough in October 1735, as well as the collapse in 1735 of the Shell Temple in Pope's garden, caused a protracted period of melancholy for the poet associated with his garden and that of Peterborough at Bevis Mount near Southampton. In October 1735 Fortescue was informed by Pope that he was off to Bevis Mount "where I am to put the last hand too to the Garden he begun, & lived not to finish. It is a place that always made me Contemplative, & now Melancholy; but is a Melancholy of that sort of which becomes a Rational Creature, & an Immortal Soul."[77] By November 1738 the painter Jonathan Richardson had painted a portrait of Pope which William Kent, who was taken by Pope to the studio to view it, described as "Pope in a mourning gown with a strange view of the garden to shew the obelisk as in memory to his mothers Death . . . the alligory seem'd odde to me" (fig. 81). Kent's bewilderment at viewing the portrait is understandable as Pope is represented in the deshabille of the Tudor tradition of the melancholic sitting with a glimpse of his garden behind him focusing on the obelisk.

The obelisk at Twickenham stood on a slight rise at the far west end of the garden terminating the central vista (fig. 82). Embowered by dark cypress trees, the classic tree of mourning, the pedestal of the obelisk carried a simple, poignant epitaph, one line on each side of the plinth:

Ah! Editha
Matrum Optima
Mulierum Amantissima,
Vale
[Ah, Edith, Best of Mothers,
Most Beloved Wife, Farewell]

As Pope had suggested earlier to Digby at Sherborne, the obelisk was to be a family memorial. Set at the far end of the garden cut off from the more frivolous Shell Temple at the east end of the garden by a screen of trees, the obelisk marked a somber, elegiac climax to one's experience of the garden. In the nineteenth century the obelisk and several garden urns were removed to Penn House at Amersham in Buckinghamshire.

81. J. Richardson, *Portrait of Alexander Pope*, 1738, Paul Mellon Coll., Yale Center for British Art, New Haven

The events commemorated by obelisks in gardens in the mid- and late eighteenth century were extraordinary in their variety. In 1739 Lord Guilford, who was lord of the bedchamber to Frederick, prince of Wales, erected an obelisk south-east of his house at Wroxton Abbey in Oxfordshire to celebrate a visit by the prince coming to view the nearby Banbury races.[78] An inscription on the obelisk, as Horace Walpole remarked, claims that the obelisk was "erected to the honour and at the expense of 'optimus' and

82. Twickenham, Pope's Garden, obelisk, watercolor by S. Lewis, c. 1785, Twickenham Reference Library, Twickenham

'munificentissimus' the late Prince of Wales, 'in loci amoenitatem et memo-riam adventus eius.'" Perhaps the more significant commemoration was marked by an obelisk raised at Wentworth Castle in Yorkshire by the second earl of Strafford about 1743 to celebrate the earlier introduction into England by Lady Mary Wortley Montague of innoculation against small-pox.[79] Occasionally a proposed recipient might urge moderation in the proffered praise. So when Sir William Draper wrote in 1768 to William Pitt, earl of Chatham, enclosing a long, grandiloquent Latin epitaph prais-ing Pitt that Draper proposed to inscribe on an obelisk in the garden of Manilla Hall near Bristol, Pitt begged Draper to reduce the epitaph to its last four lines which rather prosaically recorded that the obelisk was erected by him to honor his friend Pitt.[80]

The rage for obelisks as garden decoration was incredible. In John Lockman's description in 1752 of Jonathan Tyers' famous Vauxhall Gar-dens in London for public entertainment, a "Gothick *Obelisk*" stood at the end of the so-called Lovers' or Dark Walk on the south side of the gardens, but by 1762 it was moved to a more prominent position at the termination of the wide Grand Walk running from the entrance across the garden.[81] The monument, like so much at Vauxhall, was fashioned of several upright boards covered with canvas giving the semblance of an obelisk. At the same time, Thomas Percy wrote the poet William Shenstone offering as an example of bad taste the pursuits of a Mr. Weaver at Morville Hall near Bridgnorth in Shropshire.

> He [Mr. Weaver] came into possession of an Old Mansion that commanded a fine view down a most pleasing Vale, he contrived to intercept it by two straight rows of Elms that ran in an oblique direction across it, and which led the Eye to a pyramidal Obelisk composed of one single board set up endways and painted by the Joiner of the Village: this obelisk however was soon removed by the first puff of wind.
>
> In view of one of his windows grew a noble large, Spreading Ash, which tho' the spontaneous gift of Nature, was really a fine object; and by its stately figure and chearful Verdure afforded a most pleasing relief to the eye; you will stare when I tell you that Mr W. had this Tree painted *white*—leaves and all: it is true the leaves soon fell off, and the tree died, but the Skeleton still remains, as a Monument of the owner's Wisdom and Ingenuity.[82]

The poet Aaron Hill noted in 1733 that the obelisk that he erected in his garden in London was decorated with "Jersey Shells," whereas Dr. Charles

Grevile was more practical using for decoration of the obelisk in his garden at Barton Street in Gloucester bits of "old broken China," as the artist Thomas Robins inscribed on his drawing of the obelisk.[83] Robins depicts a tall obelisk supported on a pedestal decorated with ogival arches set up on a conical mound planted with small trees.

Obelisks of wood were erected even in the parks of wealthy nobility. A wooden obelisk visible in Moses Griffith's panoramic view of the park at Shugborough in Staffordshire was raised about 1760 by Thomas Anson on Brocton Hill, but unfortunately collapsed in a strong wind very early in the nineteenth century.[84] Presumably the Shugborough obelisk perched on the summit of the hill far distant from the house was to serve as an eye-catcher emphasizing the broad expanse of the estate. The drawings for a fifty-foot, wooden obelisk prepared about 1765, probably by the Norwich architect-builder William Ivory, for the second earl of Buckinghamshire to stand at Blickling Hall in Norfolk identify the obelisk as a viewing tower with an interior staircase by which a single person could climb up to enjoy the vista.[85] No longer extant, there is uncertainty as to whether the Blickling tower was ever built.

THE TRIUMPHAL COLUMN

THE TRIUMPHAL COLUMN as a commemorative monument in the garden seems strictly to be an eighteenth-century phenomenon in England. The gardens at Nonsuch that Lord Lumley developed in the time of Elizabeth did have several columnar shafts surmounted by the Lumley popinjay. They, however, were not triumphal columns, nor strictly speaking commemorative monuments, but merely part of the traditional, family-oriented, heraldic decoration of a Tudor garden. The two great triumphal columns in Rome were well known to English on the Grand Tour as public monuments of celebration and were available to others in the engravings and books of Roman antiquities. Equally important was the great Monument of London built from 1671 to 1677 in commemoration of the restoration of the city of London after the Great Fire of 1666.[86] Sir Christopher Wren, the designer, wished the column, a fluted Doric column of Portland stone, to be surmounted by "a *Coloss* Statue of Brass Gilt of *King Charles the Second*, as Founder of the new City; in the manner of the *Roman* Pillars, which terminated with the Statues of their Caesars." Despite Wren's disapproval, an urn was substituted for the statue. The ambiguity of the use of the several terms—pyramid, obelisk, and column—is again revealed in official accounts, as the minutes of a City Committee of July 14, 1675, refer to the column as "the new erected Obelisq in Memoriall of the Fire."

An early eighteenth-century example of a column decorating a garden was in the first garden layout of the earl of Burlington at Chiswick near London from the period 1715–20.[87] As the terminating feature of the vistas along one of the long alleys in the garden, Burlington, probably with the assistance of the architect James Gibbs, raised a rather plain Doric column supporting a copy of a famous piece of antique sculpture, the so-called Venus de'Medici. Later, in 1728, Gibbs in addition to publishing designs of several obelisks devoted one plate in his book on architecture to "Three Designs for columns, proper for publick Places or private Gardens." The column at Chiswick is obviously not a commemorative monument, but is of decorative origin providing a focus within the visual variety of the garden as well as lending a classical note.

Among the earliest examples of triumphal columns decorating a garden were those at Stowe dating from before 1724. One was a figure of the prince of Wales, the future George II, on a fluted column forty feet tall, and the other the Princess Caroline, his wife, on a cluster of four Ionic columns, both statues probably carved by the sculptor Rysbrack (fig. 57).[88] Later two more unusual columnar monuments were erected at Stowe. In 1747 a column was raised first in the Grecian Valley, but soon moved to the Elysian Fields, to the memory of Cobham's nephew Captain Thomas Grenville, who had died in a naval engagement with the French (fig. 68). Appropriate to a naval captain, the Doric column was a version of the ancient Roman rostral columns that once stood in the Roman Forum with shafts featuring the prows of Roman galleys. Surmounting the column, however, was originally a statue of Hercules, soon to be replaced by a figure of Heroic Poetry holding a scroll with the inscription *Non nisis Grandia Canto* (Heroic Deeds alone my Theme). The other commemorative monument was in honor of Lord Cobham himself, erected in 1747 after his death by his widow, being probably the first architectural project of the landscapist Capability Brown (fig. 83). The rather awkward octagonal, Tuscan pillar has an interior spiral stair leading to an open lantern, from which there were superb vistas over the garden. The lantern was originally surmounted by a statue of Cobham in Roman armor. The January 1748 issue of *The Gentleman's Magazine* noted that "an Octagon Pillar" was being erected that "will be 115 feet high, with a brass or copper figure of his lordship on the top" and quoted the inscriptions on the column. Lions of artificial Coade stone were added later by the painter Valdre to strengthen the base, but in 1957 the

83. Stowe (Bucks), Cobham's Pillar

pillar was struck by lightning severely damaging the lions and destroying Cobham's statue, which has been replaced by an urn.

The most famous commemorative column set up in a garden or park was undoubtedly the one in memory of the duke of Marlborough at Blenheim. As previously noted the duchess had first considered a gigantic obelisk for which the architect Hawksmoor made several designs, but by 1725 she had finally decided on a triumphal column, probably on Hawksmoor's suggestion.[89] From at least 1727 contracts and correspondence were conducted between the duchess and an Oxford mason and builder William Townesend regarding the column, which was completed by October 1731 when Hawksmoor visited Blenheim, who also remarked that the work was "conducted by my Ld Herbert." The Palladian architect Lord Herbert, later earl of Pembroke, is also mentioned in a letter of 1727 of the duchess to Townesend. That a Palladian-inclined architect and critic of the architectural style of Vanbrugh and Hawksmoor would oversee the work must have been galling to Hawksmoor. As the work began on the monument the duchess had an anxious period seeking a proper epitaph to grace the commemorative monument. So many proffered drafts remained unsatisfactory that she finally sought help by intermediaries from her bitter enemy Lord Bolingbroke. By July 1728 he sent a draft that moved the duchess very much with its terse military cadence. The duchess did not acknowledge the author to her friends, but Bolingbroke ensured his authorship by publishing the complete inscription in the periodical *The Craftsman*, issued by his partisans.

The monument, standing across the bridge in front of the palace about three-quarters of a mile from the entrance, is a gigantic Doric column set on a tall, marble revetted pedestal (fig. 84). Engraved on three sides of the dado are the several acts of Parliament authorizing the gift of the manor and new palace to the duke and his progeny. The fourth or south side facing the house bears Bolingbroke's panegyric, commencing:

The Battle was bloody: The Event decisive. The Woods were pierced:
the Fortifications trampled down. The Enemy fled

Surmounting the column, which is one hundred and thirty-four feet tall, is a round, Roman altar surrounded by Roman eagles at the four corners of the capital and supporting a lead statue by Robert Pit portraying Marlborough in Roman armor holding a winged figure of Victory. In 1735 a visitor to the nearby mansion of Ditchley, about four miles away, remarked that from there he had "a fine Prospect of Blenheim, the Park & Obelisk. A most agreable View certainly to an English Peer, which puts him in Mind of the Glorious Day, to which we owe our Lives, Liberties, & present happy Establishment."[90] Again we encounter the equivocality of terminology, identifying the column as an obelisk.

Most of the early eighteenth-century triumphal columns in gardens were associated with monarchs or members of the royal family. In 1735 a Doric column supporting a statue of King William III, carved of Portland stone by Henry Cheere, was raised on the central alley of the formal garden at Hartwell House in Buckinghamshire.[91] In 1702, during the reign of William III, Sir Thomas Lee had inherited Hartwell House. In 1757, however, the column was moved to the east side of the house and a statue of the current monarch, George II, was substituted. Allen Lord Bathurst, a close friend of Alexander Pope, was an ardent Tory, his family having faithfully supported the crown during the Civil War. In 1712 he had been enobled by Queen Anne, but the accession of George I in 1714 defeated any political ambitions of Bathurst, who was viewed suspiciously as a Jacobite. Meanwhile he devoted his attention to his huge estate at Cirencester.[92] It was only as late as 1741 that Bathurst felt safe enough to proclaim his political beliefs by building a triumphal column in memory of his bene-factress Queen Anne (fig. 85). A large Doric column set on a rather low, simple plinth stands in the center of Home Park on the long axis from the house that runs for miles through Home Park and the adjacent Oakley Park. On the summit of the column is a regal portrait of the queen stand-ing, wearing her crown. In contrast, about 1750 Sir George Lyttelton, who had been secretary to Frederick, prince of Wales, raised at Hagley in honor of the prince a tall Corinthian column with a statue of the prince in the guise of a Roman emperor (fig. 86).[93] Bishop Pococke, when he visited Hagley in June 1751, just after the death of the prince, mentioned "the Corinthian pillar with its entablature of Bath stone called the Prince's pillar, because it was presented to Mr. Lyttelton by the late Prince of Wales." As usual, Lyttelton's neighbor, the poet William Shenstone, decried the column even to its designer the architect Sanderson Miller, who had earlier planned the Gothic Ruin at Hagley. Having dined at Hagley, Shenstone rather smugly wrote his confidante Lady Luxborough in the fall of 1751:

> Mr. Miller unluckily asked me at Table, how I liked the new Situa-tion of their Column; which threw me under the necessity of offend-ing either against the Rules of Politeness, or (what is more sacred with me) the Laws of Sincerity. The Truth is, I do not like it upon many Accounts; and I am persuaded before many Years are past, they will be of the same Mind.

Perhaps a more judicious object of commemoration than a politically tainted member of the royal family was the concept of British liberty which George Bowes honored at his Gibside estate in County Durham.[94] The architect Daniel Garrett presumably designed the Doric column, some one hundred and fifty feet tall, which was begun in 1750 at the northeast end of

84. Blenheim (Oxon), Column of Victory

the long terrace at Gibside, although the landscapist Capability Brown offered some advice, including details on the column at Stowe where he had been employed. Work on the column at Gibside continued until 1757, but already in October 1753 the architect James Paine was paid for "Advice relating to the Column," which was apparently his first duty there. In 1757 he also appraised the design for the figure of British Liberty which was to surmount the column. The sculptor Christopher Richardson of Doncaster completed the statue in 1757 at a cost of forty pounds, the total cost of the monument being about two thousand pounds. By June 1760 the architect

85. Cirencester (Glos), Column of Queen Anne

Gibbs had submitted the designs for the Palladian mausoleum at the south-west end of the terrace, previously discussed (fig. 48).

Other columnar monuments served as personal family memorials, such as the column created by the second earl of Strafford at Wentworth Castle in Yorkshire to honor his father-in-law, who died in 1743. The column was described by Bishop Pococke in 1750 as "a Corinthian pillar, in imitation of that of St Maria Majore at Rome, with this inscription on the pedestal: 'To the memory of his Grace John, Duke of Argyle and Greenwich [should be Greenoch], this column was dedicated in 1744.'" The bishop, however, mistakenly identified the figure of Minerva surmounting the column as "the statue of Fame."[95] Such familial memorials may have had an uneasy existence. In 1760 George Bubb Dodington, Lord Melcombe, erected in memory of his wife an Ionic column one hundred feet tall on the grounds of La Trappe House in Hammersmith, but twenty years later his heir removed the monument and sold it to the earl of Ailesbury for Tottenham Park in Wiltshire.[96] Raised at the end of a mile-long avenue, the column had a new inscription.

> This column was erected by Thomas Bruce, Earl of Ailesbury, as a testimony of gratitude to his ever honoured uncle Charles, Earl of Ailesbury and Elgin, who left to him the estates, and procured for him the Barony of Tottenham, and of loyalty to his most gracious sovereign George the Third, who unsolicited conferred upon him the honour of an earldom, but above all of piety to God, first, highest, best, whose blessing consecrateth every gift, and fixeth its true value, MDCCLXXXI.

The column served several memorials, for in 1789 the earl had another inscription added on the north side of the plinth celebrating the recovery, although only temporary, of George III from his attack of insanity.

Even landscapists could be awarded commemorative monuments. In 1758 the famous Capability Brown was commissioned by the marquise de Grey and her husband, the second Earl Hardwicke, to "improve" the magnificent formal gardens that the marquise had inherited at Wrest Park in Bedfordshire.[97] In contrast to other examples of Brown's "improvements" he left untouched the formal center of the old garden with its long canal, the Long Water, terminating in a pavilion by the architect Thomas Archer, limiting his work to the periphery and particularly to a serpentine stream surrounding the formal garden. East of the Long Water hidden in the trees the owners erected a small, Tuscan column outlining the history of the gardens (fig. 87).

86. Hagley (Worcester), Column of prince of Wales

87. Wrest (Bedfords), Column to Capability Brown

These Gardens were begun in the year 1706 by the Duke of Kent, who continued to beautify them until the year 1740; the work was again carried on by Philip Earl of Hardwicke and Jemima, Marchioness de Grey, with the professional assistance of Lancelot Brown Esq. 1758–60.

Another monument honoring Brown's landscaping once stood in the park at Croome Court in Worcestershire where he had begun work as early as

1748.[98] An account from the early nineteenth century records a memorial inscribed:

> To the memory of Lancelot Brown
> who by the power of
> his inimitable and creative genius
> formed this garden scene out of a morass.

Brown himself designed a memorial column on the commission of William Pitt, the earl of Chatham.[99] Sir William Pynsent, dying in January 1765 without heirs, left his estate of Burton Pynsent in Somerset to Pitt. By September Pitt had plans to improve the house, raise a memorial to his benefactor, and eventually to landscape the grounds. Capability Brown was engaged to design the commemorative monument, while Pitt himself would handle the landscaping, primarily after his retirement from government in 1767. Work on the column began in the spring of 1766 and was completed by September 1767. A Tuscan column of Portland stone one hundred and forty feet high, the monument stands at the end of an avenue about a quarter of a mile from the house on a knoll overlooking a steep drop to the adjacent moor. At this location it was to be the principal focus of the landscape, as well as a memorial. In his original plans Brown informed Pitt that the "figure I have put on the pedestal is that of Gratitude conveying to Posterity the name of Pinsant," but as executed by the mason John Ford of Bath for about two thousand pounds an urn was substituted for the figure. When Pitt himself died in 1778 his widow dedicated in the gardens in 1781 a white marble urn with a delightful inscription, making up for the Latin epitaph Pitt had requested Sir William Draper to modify in 1768.

> Sacred to pure affection, this simple urn stands a witness of unceasing grief for him, who, excelling in whatever is most admirable, and adding to the exercise of the sublimest virtues the sweet charm of refined sentiment and polished wit, by gay and social commerce, rendered beyond comparison happy the course of domestick life and bestowed a felicity inexpressible on her, whose faithful love was blessed in a pure return, that raised her above every other joy but the parental one—and that still shared with him. His generous country, with publick monuments, has eternalized his fame. This humble tribute is but to sooth the sorrowing breast of private woe.

On the back of the urn was written:

> To the memory of William Pitt, earl of Chatham, this marble is inscribed by Hester his beloved wife, 1781.

Another honorary column to celebrate an inheritance of property stands at Audley End in Essex.[100] In 1762 Sir John Griffin inherited the estate from his aunt, the countess of Portsmouth. Immediately in April 1763 Griffin contracted with the eminent landscapist Capability Brown to replace the old formal gardens with new landscapes and by August the architect Robert Adam was submitting designs for garden structures, including a bridge, a circular Grecian temple to honor the end of the Seven Years War with France, and a column to commemorate the countess. By 1767 Brown withdrew from the landscape supervision because of a quarrel with Sir John over the work and fees, but the landscaping continued under the supervision of Joseph Hicks. The architectural work of Adam was therefore delayed. His Ionic Grecian temple begun in 1771 to the west of the house was completed about 1775 and in March 1774 the foundations were excavated for the triumphal column. Later in 1774 payment was made for a marble inscription tablet and for a Portland stone urn to surmount the tall Doric column raised on a hill some distance north of the house. Later, from 1790 to 1792, another commemorative structure was built after the design of R. F. Brettingham. This was the Temple of Concord, set on a hill east of the house to celebrate the recovery of George III from his first attack of insanity. By 1792, therefore, there were commemorative monuments set as distant eye-catchers on natural eminences around the house, temples on the east and west, and the column on the north.

Many gardens and parks had commemorative columns of only local or personal interest. When the second Sir Watkin Williams-Wynn died in 1789 his mother engaged the architect James Wyatt to design and erect a column in his memory at their country estate at Wynnstay in Wales.[101] The fluted Doric column, one hundred and sixteen feet tall, stands on a slight promontory at the end of the upper lake almost half a mile northwest of the house. Surmounted by a railed walkway and a bronze urn, the inscription at its base, composed by Sir Watkin's brother-in-law, Lord Grenville, reads: "Filio Optimo Mater—Eheu—Superstes." At Hawkstone Park in Shropshire Sir Richard Hill erected in 1795 an unfluted, red sandstone Doric column, one hundred and twelve feet high, to honor his ancestor Sir Rowland Hill, the first Protestant Lord Mayor of London. The column originally bore a statue of Sir Rowland by the sculptor John Nelson of Shrewsbury, but the statue was destroyed in the 1930s, leaving only its feet. English Heritage, however, has just had the twelve-foot statue replaced.

A more significant memorial was undertaken by the second marquis of Rockingham at Wentworth Woodhouse.[102] In 1773 the architect John Carr of York began a huge, Tuscan column, some one hundred and fifteen feet tall, in the center of Scholes Wood south of the house where it is identified on a map of 1778 as "Scholes Column," without any further indication of its purpose. In the fall of 1778 a close political friend of the marquis, Admiral Augustus Keppel, was charged by a politically motivated government with improper military duties and desertion in a French naval engagement. With a great public outcry against the government the admiral was acquitted of the charge early in 1779, whereupon the marquis dedicated the column to commemorate the acquittal of his friend.

THE THREE PRINCIPAL TYPES of commemorative monuments are all of antique derivation, very appropriate for the neoclassic age of the second half of the eighteenth century when most were erected. Although the pyramid was much more rarely employed than the others, all three were used together at the same locations without much apparent significance to the type utilized. The triumphal column, however, seems more often associated with royalty and military heroes. Even Lord Cobham's memorial dedicated by his wife depicts him as a military leader in Roman armor, undoubtedly suggested by the figure of the duke of Marlborough. Yet the pacific pursuit of gardening and its protagonist Capability Brown was honored by a column. Although in a few examples, as in the parterre at Castle Howard or at Chiswick, a column might be limited to a decorative function with no apparent commemorative character, it was the obelisk and even the pyramid that often served as decorative features in the landscape to identify or focus vistas.

The mixture of the three types of monuments is reminiscent of engravings of Rome and her antiquities, which the English gentry collected, except that the ancient examples were viewed in urban settings. The eighteenth-century contribution was to transport the monuments to a pastoral ambience, evoking themes such as *Et In Arcadia Ego* or the Elysian Fields. The gardens of Cobham's Stowe would seem to be the inspiration for other eighteenth-century gardens. At Stowe there was a confluence of factors that promoted such commemorative monuments. The owner and first creator of the gardens, Richard Temple, Lord Cobham, was a renowned military leader and an ardent politician. In both roles he was supported by large groups of friends and colleagues. The Temple of Friendship at Stowe, begun in 1739, with its numerous busts of Cobham's political allies most abundantly commemorates the role of his friends in his political concerns. Like other leading Whig politicians, Cobham was also a member of the political-literary Kit-Cat Club, whose literary members such as Congreve and Vanbrugh, to whom Cobham erected memorials, looked to their political colleagues for patronage as the political aims of the nobility were furthered by the propaganda offered by the writers. The earliest monuments at Stowe were appropriately dedicated to the reigning house of Hanover with portraits of King George I and the prince and princess of Wales. Yet at the same time menial garden foremen at Stowe, such as Nelson, John Gurnet, and Rogers, were honored with walks, and in one case a seat, bearing their names.[103]

The imperial inclinations of the Whig faction led by Cobham, which eventually caused disaffection with the policies of the Whig Prime Minister Robert Walpole, were already apparent in the equestrian form of King George's monument, recalling those of the Roman emperor Marcus Aurelius or the French king Louis XIV, and the triumphal columns of the prince and princess of Wales. Such imperial connotations continued at Stowe with the rostral column memorializing Cobham's nephew, Captain Thomas Grenville, deceased in a naval engagement furthering English interests against the French, as the later obelisk dedicated to General Wolfe commemorated his tragic victory over the French at Quebec or the monument to Captain James Cook honored his explorations expanding the political power and scientific knowledge of England. In addition, Cobham had at least six nephews, including by marriage William Pitt the Elder and two great-nephews, several of whom wrote poetry celebrating the gardens at Stowe and three of whom perpetuated the political power of the Temple brood by serving as Prime Ministers.[104] Two of the nephews, Lord Lyttelton and Pitt the Elder, emulated their uncle's predilection for commemorative monuments at their estates at Hagley and Burton Pynsent, thus furthering the concept.

Conclusion

ENGLISH GARDENING of the eighteenth century was very much involved in the creation of several of the important aspects of the Romantic movement of the late eighteenth and early nineteenth century. The essence of Romanticism was escape through the imagination from the reality of the moment. English gardens and landscapes were sites where this imagination was particularly nourished. The variety of architectural styles that would evoke the spectator's imagination was introduced first in garden architecture whose practical functionalism, unlike most other architecture, was minor, often serving only as visual eye-catchers terminating vistas in the garden-parks or as evocative settings for teas such as those Gilbert White set in his hermitage at Selborne. The exotic style of China, as seen at Stowe or Shugborough, or that of Islam at Kew, would recall lands far distant from the islands of Great Britain. This geographical escapism was accompanied by a specific, appropriate concern for the historical moment particularly identified by the ardent pursuit of archaeology both in the ancient classical world and in the native past of England. The antiquities of Athens, through "Athenian" Stuart's publication, were reconstructed in the follies at Shugborough. The Temple of Venus from Robert Wood's *Rules of Balbec* was the source of garden temples at Kew and Stourhead. On the other hand, the Gothic style, seen first at Shotover, revived a nationalistic past foreign to the traditional classical style of the Renaissance architect Palladio. This concern for England's past was also aroused by evocative images of hermits and Druids, and their rude dwellings and temples. Even the vision of nature itself changed from the gentle, rolling nature of Capability Brown to the awesome picturesqueness of William Gilpin and Uvedale Price. At the end of the century Humphry Repton in a letter to Price published in Repton's first treatise, *Sketches and Hints on Landscape Gardening* (1795), equated the English mode of landscaping with English civil liberty that the Gothic mode of architecture had also recalled.

The neatness, simplicity, and elegance of English gardening, have
acquired the approbation of the present century, as the happy medium
betwixt the wildness of nature and the stiffness of art; in the same
manner as the English constitution is the happy medium between the
liberty of savages, and the restraint of despotic government.[1]

The appearance in 1757 of Edmund Burke's *A Philosophical Enquiry
into the Origin of our Ideas of the Sublime and Beautiful,* followed in 1759 by
its second edition with its added "Essay on Taste," marked the end of the
classical Renaissance, especially as it denied the Renaissance principle that
proportion was the source of beauty. Burke's treatise signified the final
victory of Locke's sensationist philosophy that knowledge was founded on
sensate experience.[2] Ten years previously the poet Joseph Spence, in his
dissertation *Polymetis,* rejected the Renaissance bible of allegory, Cesare
Ripa's *Iconologia.* Both Burke's and Spence's writings would have consequences for later English gardening. Visual imagery even earlier revealed a
shift away from classical allusion and heroic portraiture to contemporary
reality. Early in the century noble military heroes, such as Marlborough
and Cobham, were garbed in Roman armor, but by 1738 an artist such as
Handel was portrayed in contemporary clothing in an informal pose, the
only suggestion of the past being the lyre of Apollo he held.

In 1770 the very perceptive critic Thomas Whately in the section of his
book, *Observations on Modern Gardening,* entitled "Of Character" criticized the prevalent mode of gardening.

The heathen deities and heroes have therefore had their several places
assigned to them in the woods and the lawns of a garden; natural
cascades have been disfigured with river gods; and columns erected
only to receive quotations; the compartments of a summer-house have
been filled with pictures of gambols and revels, as significant of gaiety;
the cypress, because it was once used in funerals, has been thought
peculiarly adapted to melancholy; and the decorations, the furniture,
and the environs of a building have been crouded with puerilities
under pretence of propriety. All these devices are rather *emblematical*
than expressive; they may be ingenious contrivances, and recal absent
ideas to the recollection; but they make no immediate impression; for
they must be examined, compared, perhaps explained, before the
whole design of them is well understood.[3]

Whately's derogation of triumphal columns as billboards of commemorative inscriptions could apply to all the earlier famous eighteenth-century

gardens. His castigation of summerhouses decorated with gambols could refer to Stowe and his disparagement of the use of cypresses to convey melancholy could be Pope's Twickenham garden. Whately also decries the loss of functionalism in garden buildings and their reduction to mere "objects."[4]

A few years later, in 1779, Lord Thomas Lyttelton would be more personal in his depreciatory remarks on his own father's gardening at Hagley.

> Our climate is not suited to the deities of Italy and Greece, and in an hard winter I feel for the shuddering divinities. At Hagley there is a temple of Theseus, commonly called by the gardener the temple of Perseus, which stares you in the face wherever you go, while the temple of God, commonly called by the gardener the parish church, is so industriously hid by trees from without that the pious matron can hardly read her prayer-book within. This was an evident preference of strange gods, and, in my opinion, a very blasphemous improvement. Where nature is grand, improve her grandeur, not by adding extraneous decorations, but by removing obstructions. Where a scene is in itself lovely, very little is necessary to give it all due advantage, especially if it be laid into park, which undergoes no variety of cultivation.[5]

Lyttelton continues by including in his diatribe the gardens of his relatives at Stowe.

> Stowe is, in my opinion, a most detestable place, . . . A classical park or a classical garden is as ridiculous an expression as a classical plumb-pudding or a classical sirloin of beef. It is an unworthy action to strip the classics of their heroes, gods, and goddesses, to grow green amid the fogs of our unclassical climate.

By 1806 the horticultural writer and designer John Claudius Loudon, who was soon to be most eminent British authority on gardening, in his treatise on the improvement of country residences endorsed the comments of Whately and Lyttelton. In Loudon's chapter "Of the Principles of the Picturesque Movement," he decreed:

> A scene not composed of many parts, and tending to simplicity, will be improved in character with much more ease and effect by removing some of these, and increasing simplicity, than by adding others to produce richness. In picturesque improvement, the character appro-

priated should always be a natural one, or one justified by propriety, in opposition to such as have been called emblematical and imitative. Emblematical characters may succeed in poetry or painting, but can never succeed in rural scenery, and seldom in architecture.[6]

Loudon then derides the Elysian Fields and Grecian Valley at Stowe, claiming that "When the whole is once seen, all the charms of illusion vanish, and the obvious want of utility, renders such scenery nauseous and tiresome, and only worth preservation for its singularity and antiquity."

NOTES

Introduction

1. H. Walpole, *Correspondence*, vol. 10, ed. W. S. Lewis and R. S. Brown, Jr. (New Haven, 1941), 313–16, letter to George Montagu, July 7, 1770; also H. Walpole, *Correspondence*, vol. 4, ed. W. S. Lewis and W. H. Smith (New Haven, 1939), 432–35, to Mme du Deffand, July 8, 1770; and vol. 39, ed. W. S. Lewis (New Haven, 1974), 127, to Conway, July 12, 1770. For Cliveden, see *The Gentleman's Magazine* 10 (August 1, 1740): 411 and R. Fiske, "A Cliveden Setting," *Music and Letters* 47 (1966): 126–29.

2. P. H. Goodchild, "'No phantasticall utopia, but a reall place,' John Evelyn, John Beale and Backbury Hill, Herefordshire," *Garden History* 19 (1991): 119.

3. J. Cordey, *Vaux-le-Vicomte* (Paris, 1924), 114–21 and E. Magne, *Les fêtes en Europe au XVIIe siècle* (Paris, 1930), 107–22.

4. Magne, *Les fêtes en Europe*, 144–58. For the relationship between French gardens and the theater, see the survey in W. H. Adams, *The French Garden 1500–1800* (New York, 1979), 63–73.

5. [C. Fontana], *Risposta del Signor Carlo Fontana alla lettera dell'Illustriss. Sig. Ottavio Castiglioni* (Rome, 1668) and D. R. Coffin, *Gardens and Gardening in Papal Rome* (Princeton, 1991), 230–31.

6. [Carmontelle], *Jardin de Monceau* (Paris, 1779), 3–4 (Jardin de Flore reprint, n.p., c. 1979).

7. The bibliography on melancholy, particularly in regard to literature, seems inexhaustible, but some useful items are A. L. Reed, *The Background of Gray's Elegy: A Study in the Taste for Melancholic Poetry 1700–1751* (New York, 1924); O. Doughty, "The English Malady of the Eighteenth Century," *The Review of English Studies* 5 (1926): 257–69; L. Babb, *The Elizabethan Malady* (East Lansing, Mich., 1951); J. F. Sena, "The English Malady: The Idea of Melancholy from 1700 to 1760" (Ph.D. diss., Princeton University, 1967); and B. G. Lyons, *Voices of Melancholy* (New York, 1971).

8. See especially R. Klibansky, E. Panofsky, and F. Saxl, *Saturn and Melancholy* (London, 1964), 254–74.

9. A. du Laurens, *A Discourse of the Preservation of the Sight* (London, 1599), 82 and T. Walkinton, *The Optick Classe of Humors* (London, 1607), 68. For Bushell and Harvey, see below, chapter II.

10. R. Burton, *The Anatomy of Melancholy*, ed. H. Jackson (New York, 1977), 237–41. See [J. B.] Le Blanc, *Lettres de Monsieur l'Abbé Le Blanc*, rev. ed. (Amsterdam, 1751), I: 7 and O. Goldsmith, *Collected Works of Oliver Goldsmith, II. The Citizen of the World*, ed. A. Friedman (Oxford, 1966), 365 and 368–69.

11. M. Ficino, *Three Books on Life*, trans. C. V. Kaske and J. R. Clark (Binghamton, N.Y., 1989), 135 and Burton, *The Anatomy of Melancholy*, 74–75.

12. For English portraiture and melancholy, see R. Strong, "The Elizabethan Malady: Melancholy in Elizabethan and Jacobean Portraiture," *Apollo* 79 (1964): 264–69 and R. Strong, "Nicholas Hilliard's Miniature of the 'Wizard,'" *Bulletin van het Rijksmuseum* 31 (1983): 54–62.

13. G. Keynes, *John Evelyn: A Study in Bibliophily with a Bibliography of His Writings*, 2nd ed. (Oxford, 1968), 5 and J. Evelyn, *The Diary of John Evelyn*, ed. E. S. de Beer (Oxford, 1955), I: 55.

14. M. M. Verney, ed., *Verney Letters of the Eighteenth Century from the MSS. at Claydon House* (London, 1930), I: 82.

15. I. Walton, *Walton's Lives*, rev. ed., ed. A. H. Bullen (London, 1903), 74–75.

16. D. M. Bergeron, *English Civic Pageantry 1598–1642* (Columbia, S.C., 1971), 148–56.

17. See especially K. Thomas, *Man and the Natural World* (New York, 1983), 236–37. See also J. Lawrence, *Gardening Improv'd* (London, 1718 [Garland facsimile, 1982]), unpaginated prefaces.

Chapter I

1. J. Melton, *Astrologaster, or the Figure-Caster* (London, 1620 [Augustan Reprint Society, special no. 174X, Los Angeles, 1975]), 2–3; partially quoted in S. Stewart, *The Enclosed Garden* (Madison, Milwaukee and London, 1966), 115.

2. J. Parkinson, *Paradisi in Sole: Paradisus Terrestris* (London, 1629), sig. **3v.

3. G. Herbert, *The English Works of George Herbert*, ed. G. H. Palmer (Boston and New York, 1905), III: 321.

4. F. Quarles, *Emblemes* (London, 1635), 173–74; quoted in Stewart, *The Enclosed Garden*, pp. 103–104.

5. [M. S.] Gatty, *The Book of Sun-Dials*, 4th ed., ed. H. K. F. Eden and E. Lloyd (London, 1900), 294–95, no. 506 (Stanwardine) and 456–58, no. 1530 (Dereham) and E. S. Rohde, *The Story of the Garden* (London, 1933 [1989 reprint]), 76 (Manington).

6. T. Fowler, *The History of Corpus Christi College*, Oxford Historical Society Publications, 25 (Oxford, 1893), 85 and 381; J. D. North, "Nicolaus Kratzer—The King's Astronomer," in *Science and History: Studies in Honor of Edward Rosen*, Studia Copernica, XVI (Wroclaw, 1978), 205–34; P. Pat-

tenden, *Sundials at Oxford College* (Oxford, 1979), 12–24; and W. Hackman, "Nicolaus Kratzer: The King's Astronomer and Renaissance Instrument-Maker," in *Henry VIII: A European Court in England*, ed. D. Starkey (Greenwich, 1991), 70–73.

7. Regarding clocks, see L. Mumford, *Technics and Civilization* (New York, 1934), esp. 12–18 and C. M. Cipolla, *Clocks and Culture 1300–1700* (London, 1967).

8. London County Council, *Survey of London*, vol. 13, pt. 2 (London, 1930), 89–90; H. M. Colvin, ed., *The History of the King's Works*, vol. 3, pt. 1 (London, 1975), 94 and vol. 4, pt. 2 (1982), 314–17; and R. Strong, *The Renaissance Garden in England* (London, 1979), 34–38. For early descriptions, see G. von Bülow, "Journey through England and Scotland made by Lupold von Wedel in the Years 1584 and 1585," *Transactions of the Royal Historical Society* 9, new ser. (1895): 234–36 and P. Hentzner, *Paul Hentzner's Travels in England*, trans. H. Walpole (London, 1797), 23–24.

9. Mrs. E. Cecil, *A History of Gardening in England*, 3rd ed. (London, 1910), 79–90; Strong, *The Renaissance Garden in England*, 25–28; and H. M. Colvin, ed., *The History of the King's Works*, vol. 4, pt. 2 (London, 1982), 138–39.

10. W. L. Spiers, *The Notebook and Account Book of Nicholas Stone*, Walpole Society, VII (Oxford, 1919), 49, 50, 87, and 88.

11. [E. Gunter], *The Description and Use of His Maiesties Dials in Whitehall Garden* (London, 1624). Charles I's interest in sundials is reported in Gatty, *The Book of Sun-Dials*, 95.

12. R. Plot, *The Natural History of Oxford-shire* (Oxford, 1677), 261. See also H. Baskerville, ed., "Thomas Baskerville's Account of Oxford, c. 1670–1700," *Collectanea* 4 (1905): 191–92; [S. Sewall], *Diary of Samuel Sewall 1674–1729*, Collections of the Massachusetts Historical Society, ser. 5, vol. V (Boston, 1878), I: 260–61; and C. Fiennes, *Through England On a Side Saddle in the Time of William and Mary* (London, 1888) 29.

13. Rohde, *The Story of the Garden*, 147. Presumably the 1692 date instead of 1672 is an error in Rohde; the 1672 edition of Hughes has the addition to its title, "Whereunto is now added the gardiners or planters dialling, how to draw a horizontall diall, as a knot in a garden, on a grass-plot, or elsewhere, the life before not extant."

14. J. E. B. Mayor, ed., *Cambridge under Queen Anne* (Cambridge, 1911), 367. In the nineteenth century and later, floral and boxwood sundials were revived as at Broughton Castle, near Banbury, see *Country Life* 4 (Dec. 17, 1898): 756–62.

15. London County Council, *Survey of London*, vol. 13, pt. 2 (London, 1930), 92–93 and [Great Britain, P. R. O.], *Calendar of Treasury Books, 1685–1689*, vol. 8, pt. 3, ed. W. A. Shaw (London, 1923), 2121, Nov. 10, 1688, and 2139, Dec. 4, 1688.

16. C. Reilly, *Francis Line S. J.: An Exiled English Scientist 1595—1675*, Bibliotheca Instituti Historici S. I., XXIX (Rome, 1969); see also Gatty, *The Book of Sun-Dials*, 100—101; and A. M. Earle, *Sun Dials and Roses of Yesterday* (New York, 1922), 115—19. Two contemporary descriptions are F. Line, *An explication of the diall sett up in the King's Garden at London, a. 1669. in which very many sorts of dyalls are contained* (Liege, 1673) and W. Leybourn, *Dialing* (London, 1682), 323—30.

17. [Great Britain], Hist. Mss. Comm., *Report on the Laing Manuscripts* (London, 1914), 405 and J. Aubrey, *Brief Lives*, ed. A. Clark (Oxford, 1898), II: 34.

18. A. Marvell, *The Poems and Letters of Andrew Marvell*, 3rd ed., ed. H. M. Margoliouth (Oxford, 1971), 200.

19. Gatty, *The Book of Sun-Dials*, 233, other mottoes on 270—71, 354, 428, and 456; also P. Yorke, *The Royal Tribes of Wales* (Wrexham, 1799), quoted in J. Marsden, "The Garden at Erddig," *Journal of Garden History* II (1991): 142.

20. Earl of Romney, *Diary of the Times of Charles the Second*, ed. R. W. Blencowe (London, 1843), I: xcv.

21. J. Boswell, *Boswell's Life of Johnson*, ed. G. B. Hill and L. F. Powell (Oxford, 1934), IV: 59—60. The full quotation from Horace, *Odes*, II, xiv, 1—2 reads: *Eheu! fugaces, Postume, Postume, Labuntur anni* [Alas, O Postumus, Postumus, the fleeting years glide by].

22. J. W[orlidge], *Systema Horti-culturae* (London, 1677), 67.

23. J. Moxon, *A Tutor to Astronomy and Geography*, 4th ed. (London, 1686), 180 and Gatty, *The Book of Sun-Dials*, 106.

24. For Van Nost and Cheere, see R. Gunnis, *Dictionary of British Sculptors 1660—1851*, rev. ed. (London, 1968), 279—82 (Van Nost) and 99—100 (Cheere) and T. Friedman, *The Man at Hyde Park Corner* (Leeds, 1974), 23—24. For the Hampton Court sundial, see H. M. Colvin, ed., *The History of the King's Works*, vol. 5 (London, 1976), 173; recently the sundial has been rediscovered and is now on the art market, see *The Garden History Society Newsletter* 37 (spring 1993): 20. The 1725 Inventory of Cannons is in the Huntington Library in California. For the Fetcham Park statue, see C. Fiennes, *The Journeys of Celia Fiennes*, 2nd ed., ed. C. Morris (London, 1949), 353. Other examples of the Moor or Indian sundials are in J. P. Davis, *Antique Garden Ornament* (Woodbridge, Suffolk, 1991), 49 (Arley Hall, Dunham Massey, and Okeover Hall); G. J[ackson-]S[tops], *The Anglo-Dutch Garden in the Age of William and Mary*, *Journal of Garden History* 8 (1988): 319 (Dunham Massey, Norton Conyers, and West Green); A. Oswald, "Okeover Hall, Staffordshire, I," *Country Life* 135 (Jan. 2, 1964): 175; M. Whinney, *Sculpture in Britain 1530 to 1830* (Baltimore, 1964), 262 (Okeover Hall); Earle, *Sun Dials and Roses of Yesterday*, 215 (Enfield Old Park); H. A. Triggs, *Formal Gardens in England and Scotland* (London and New York, 1902), 57 and pl. 115 (Enfield Old Park, Arley, Guys Cliff, and Hampton Court,

Herefordshire); and Gatty, *The Book of Sun-Dials*, 109–10 (London, Clement's Inn).

25. J. Marsden, *Belton House, Lincolnshire* ([London], 1985), 45; see also Triggs, *Formal Gardens in England and Scotland*, 116.

26. C. Hussey, *English Gardens and Landscapes 1700–1750* (London, 1967), 141.

27. Davis, *Antique Garden Ornament*, 50 (Blair Atholl and St. Paul's Walden Bury) and *Country Life* 184 (June 14, 1990): 219 (ex-Fonthill House).

28. G. B. Clarke, ed., *Descriptions of Lord Cobham's Gardens at Stowe (1700–1750)*, Buckinghamshire Record Society, no. 26 (n.p., 1990), 72. For Father Time, see *County of Cambridge II. North-East Cambridgeshire* (London, 1972), 80.

29. T. Hull, ed., *Select Letters Between the Late Duchess of Somerset, Lady Luxborough* . . . (London, 1778), I: 228–29; translation from *Virgil*, Loeb Classical Library, trans. H. R. Fairclough (London and New York, 1920), I: 175.

30. Earl of Ailesbury. *Memoirs of Thomas, Earl of Ailesbury* (Westminster, 1890), I: 75.

31. For ruins in general, see R. Macaulay, *Pleasures of Ruins* (London, [1935]); M. Baridon, "Ruins as a Mental Construct," *Journal of Garden History* 5 (1985): 84–96; and R. Zimmermann, *Künstliche Ruinen* (Wiesbaden, 1989).

32. [T. Whately], *Observations on Modern Gardening* (London, 1770), 132.

33. Ibid., 155.

34. F. L. Huntley, *Bishop Joseph Hall and Protestant Meditation in Seventeenth-Century England* (Binghamton, N.Y., 1981), 163–64, the meditation on a sundial on 124.

35. A. à Wood, *The Life & Times of Anthony à Wood*, ed. L. Powys (London, 1932), 56.

36. J. Dryden, *The Poems and Fables of John Dryden*, ed. J. Kinsley (London, 1962), 239.

37. W. Harison, *Woodstock Park, A Poem* (London, 1706), 4–5.

38. Sir J. Vanbrugh, *The Complete Works of Sir John Vanbrugh*, ed. B. Dobree and G. Webb (London, 1928), IV: 29.

39. Hussey, *English Gardens and Landscapes*, 132–39; The National Trust, *Fountains Abbey and Studley Royal, Yorkshire* ([London], 1985); G. Headley and W. Meulenkamp, *Follies* (London, 1986), 426–28; and R. Haslam, "Studley Royal, North Yorkshire," *Country Life* 179 (March 27, 1986): 802–5.

40. [T. Gent], *The Antient and Modern History of the Royal Town of Rippon* (York, 1733), 23–37. For Peter Aram, see P. Aram, *A Practical Treatise of Flowers*, ed. F. Felsenstein (Leeds, 1985).

41. W. Gilpin, *Observations, Relative Chiefly to Picturesque Beauty, Made in the Year 1772* . . . *of Cumberland, and Westmoreland* (London, 1786), II: 178–89.

42. J. Dyer, *Poems* (London, 1761), 12–13.

43. B. Langley, *New Principles of Gardening* (London, 1728), xv. For the comparison with the Villa Doria Pamphili, see J. D. Hunt, *William Kent: Landscape Garden Designer* (London, 1987), 28.

44. J. Lees-Milne, *Earls of Creation* (London, 1962), 37–56; Hussey, *English Gardens and Landscapes*, 78–83; and P. Martin, *Pursuing Innocent Pleasures: The Gardening World of Alexander Pope* (Hamden, Conn., 1984), 74–94.

45. J. Swift, *The Correspondence of Jonathan Swift*, vol. 4, ed. R. Williams (Oxford, 1965), 199–200.

46. R. A. Aubin, *Topographical Poetry in XVIII-Century England* (New York, 1936), 134–35.

47. J. Colton, "Kent's Hermitage for Queen Caroline at Richmond," *Architectura* (1974): 181–91 and C. M. Sicca, "'Like a Shallow Cave by Nature Made': William Kent's 'Natural' Architecture at Richmond," *Architectura* (1986): 68–82.

48. In the extensive bibliography, see especially G. Clarke, "Grecian Taste and Gothic Virtue: Lord Cobham's Gardening Programme and its Iconography," *Apollo* 97 (1973): 566–71; Hunt, *William Kent*, 62–64; Clarke, ed., *Descriptions of Lord Cobham's Gardens at Stowe*, 39 (G. West, 1732), 61 (J. Milles, 1735), 67–68 (Anonymous, 1738) and 180 (Bishop Herring, 1738); and G. Bickham, *The Beauties of Stow* (London, 1750), 4–6.

49. Hunt, *William Kent*, 147 and 149–50.

50. [W. Gilpin], *A Dialogue Upon the Garden at Stowe in Buckinghamshire* (London, 1748), 5–6.

51. *The British Poets* (Chiswick, 1822), LXVIII: 57.

52. F. M. Kearney, *James Hervey and Eighteenth Century Taste* (Muncie, Ind., 1969).

53. E. J. Climenson, ed., *Elizabeth Montagu: The Queen of the Blue-Stockings* (London, 1906), II: 52.

54. *The British Poets*, LXIV: 27–28.

55. For Miller, see M. McCarthy, *The Origins of the Gothic Revival* (New Haven and London, 1987), 51–55. For Radway, see B. Jones, *Follies & Grottoes*, 2nd ed. (London, 1974), 54–55, and for the ruin at Hagley, see D. Watkin, *The English Vision* (New York, 1982), 51 and Headley and Meulenkamp, *Follies*, 129. Shenstone's letters are from *The Letters of William Shenstone*, ed. M. William (Oxford, 1939), 112 and 149.

56. H. S. Hughes, "Shenstone and the Countess of Hertford," *Publications of the Modern Language Association of America* 46 (1931): 116.

57. T. Mowl, "The Case of the Enville Museum," *Journal of Garden History* 3 (1983): 136.

58. H. Walpole, *Correspondence*, vol. 35, ed. W. S. Lewis (New Haven, Conn., 1973), 148. Heely's comments in J. Heely, *Letters on the Beauties of Hagley, Envil, and the Leasowes* (London, 1777), I: 173.

59. Jones, *Follies & Grottoes*, 56–58; D. Stroud, *Capability Brown*, rev. ed. (London, 1975), 140–41; G. Jackson-Stops, *Wimpole Hall, Cambridgeshire* ([London], 1982); Headley and Meulenkamp, *Follies*, 338–39; and McCarthy, *The Origins of the Gothic Revival*, 53. For the letters to Miller, see L. Dickins and M. Stanton, eds., *An Eighteenth Century Correspondence* (London, 1910), 271–72.

60. J. Riely, "Shenstone's Walks: The Genesis of the Leasowes," *Apollo* 110 (1979): 202–209 and H. F. Clarke, *The English Landscape Garden*, 2nd ed. (Gloucester, 1980), 57–65. For Shenstone's letter, see *The Letters of William Shenstone*, 407–8.

61. W. Shenstone, "Unconnected Thoughts on Gardening," in *Essays on Men and Manners* (London, 1868), 131.

62. Riely, "Shenstone's Walks," 207–8.

63. For Wright, see E. Harris, "The Architecture of Thomas Wright," *Country Life* 150 (Aug. 19, 1971): 492–95, (Sept. 2, 1971): 546–50, and (Sept. 9, 1971): 612–15; T. Wright, *Arbours & Grottoes*, ed. E. Harris (London, 1979); and McCarthy, *The Origins of the Gothic Revival*, 42–48. For Shugborough, see The National Trust, *Shugborough, Staffordshire* ([London], 1983); S. E. Pybus, *Shugborough: A Guide to the Monuments* (Shugborough, 1984); Headley and Meulenkamp, *Follies*, 310; and G. Worsley, "The Baseless Roman Doric Column in Mid-Eighteenth-Century English Architecture: A Study in Neo-Classicism," *The Burlington Magazine* 128 (1986): 336.

64. J. Nichols, *Illustrations of the Literary History of the Eighteenth Century* (London, 1817), I: 639, Davies poem on 640–41.

65. W. Gilpin, *Observations, Relative Chiefly to Picturesque Beauty, Made in the Year 1772 . . . of Cumberland and Westmoreland* (London, 1786), I: 65–66.

66. R. Warner, *The Topographical Works of the Rev. Richard Warner* (Bath, 1802 [–1809]), III: 73–80; M. Girouard, "Mount Edgecumbe, Cornwall—II," *Country Life* 128 (1960): 1598–1601; and Headley and Meulenkamp, *Follies*, 10.

67. Earl of Ilchester, *Henry Fox, First Lord Holland* (London, 1930), II: 279–82, and H. Honour, "An Epic of Ruin Building," *Country Life* 114 (Dec. 10, 1953): 1968–69. For the letter of Lady Holland, see Duchess of Leinster, *Correspondence of Emily, Duchess of Leinster*, vol. 1, ed. B. Fitzgerald (Dublin, 1949), 408.

68. A. Hodges, "Painshill Park, Cobham, Surrey (1700–1800): Notes for a History of the Landscape Garden of Charles Hamilton," *Garden History* 2, no. 1 (autumn 1973): 39–68 (Gilpin's comments), and N. B. Kitz, *Pains Hill Park* (Cobham, 1984), Walpole's comments.

69. W. Chambers, *Plans, Elevations, Sections, and Perspective Views of the Gardens*

and Buildings at Kew (London, 1763) and J. Harris, *Sir William Chambers, Knight of the Polar Star* (University Park, Penn. and London), 32–39.

70. Henry Home, Lord Kames, *Elements of Criticism* (Edinburgh, 1762), III: 313.

71. W. Mason, *The English Garden*, rev. ed. (York, 1789), 104–5. In the same edition, 185–86, a commentary on this passage by William Burgh ends: "the idea of a Greek ruin in England being a contradiction both in history and experience."

72. [A. Young], *A Six Months Tour through the North of England*, 2nd ed. (London, 1771), II: 301–2.

73. P. Martin, *Pursuing Innocent Pleasures: The Gardenng World of Alexander Pope* (Hamden, Conn., 1984), 95–115. For Pope's letter, see A. Pope, *The Correspondence of Alexander Pope*, vol. 2, ed. G. Sherburn (Oxford, 1956), 236–39.

74. J. McDonnell, ed., *A History of Helmsley, Rievaulx and District* (York, n.d.), 190; Hussey, *English Gardens and Landscapes*, 145–46; and The National Trust, *The Rievaulx Terrace* ([London], 1989).

75. [Young], *A Six Months Tour*, II: 82.

76. F. Cowell, "Richard Woods (?1716–93): A Preliminary Account, II," *Garden History* 15 (1987): 19–23; D. A. Crowley, ed., *A History of Wiltshire*, Victoria County History, XIII (Oxford, 1987), 221–23: M. Cowan, "The Wardour Castles and Their Landscape," *The Hatcher Review* 3 (1988): 211–16; and M. Girouard, "Wardour Old Castle," *Country Life* 185 (Feb. 14, 1991): 44–49, and (Feb. 21, 1991): 66–79.

77. R. W. King, "Joseph Spence of Byfleet, IV," *Garden History* 8, no. 3 (winter 1980): 87.

78. H. Trump, "A Dutchman's Visits to Some English Gardens in 1791," *Journal of Garden History* 2 (1982): 41–58.

79. Mrs. E. Cecil, *A History of Gardening in England*, 3rd ed. (London, 1910), 254–56 (Brown's contract); M. Girouard, "Sandbeck Park, Yorkshire—III," *Country Life* 138 (Oct. 21, 1965): 1024–27; D. Stroud, *Capability Brown*, rev. ed. (London, 1975), 138–40; R. Turner, *Capability Brown and the Eighteenth-Century English Landscape* (New York, 1985), 132–34; and T. Hinde, *Capability Brown* (New York and London, 1987), 126–27.

80. W. Gilpin, *Observations . . . on Several Parts of Great Britain; Particularly the High-lands of Scotland* (London, 1789), I: 21–27.

81. J. Britton and E. W. Brayley, *The Beauties of England and Wales*, vol. 1 (London, 1801), 267–68; A. Dale, *James Wyatt* (Oxford, 1956), 180–81; and O. Hedley, *Queen Charlotte* (London, 1975) 179–87. For contemporary accounts, see R. F. Greville, *The Diaries of Colonel the Hon. Robert Fulke Greville*, ed. F. M. Bladon (London, 1930), 281 and J. Farington, *The Diary of Joseph Farington*, vol. 3, ed. K. Garlick and A. MacIntyre (New Haven and London, 1979), 918–19.

Chapter II

1. H. Latimore, *Sermons by Hugh Latimer*, The Parker Society XXVII, vol. 1, ed. G. E. Corrie (Cambridge, 1844), 225 and 236. It was on March 17, 1548, that a pulpit was first "set up in the *King's privie Garden* at Westminster, and therein Doctor Latimer preached before the King, where he might be heard of more then foure times so many people as could have stood in the King's Chappell." See London County Council, *Survey of London*, vol. 13, pt. 2 (London, 1930), 89.

2. R. Rogers, *Seven Treatises* (London, 1603), unpaginated preface; the chapter on meditation is on 235–59.

3. B. K. Lewalski, *Protestant Poetics and the Seventeenth-Century Religious Lyric* (Princeton, 1979), 150–52, and R. A. McCabe, *Joseph Hall: A Study in Satire and Meditation* (Oxford, 1982). For some examples of Hall's horticultural meditations, see J. Hall, *The Works of the Right Reverend Joseph Hall, D. D.*, rev. ed., ed. P. Wynter (Oxford, 1863), I: 14–15; II: 683; X: 145–46 and 161–62.

4. W. Roper, *The Lyfe of Sir Thomas More, Knighte*, Early English Text Society Original Series, no. 197, ed. E. V. Hitchcock (London, 1935), 20–21.

5. M. Hoby, *Diary of Lady Margaret Hoby 1599–1605*, ed. D. M. Meads (Boston and New York, 1930), 66 and 117. See, in general, L. Forster, "Meditation in a Garden," *German Life and Letters* 31 (1977–78): 23–35.

6. Lady Anne Clifford, *The Diaries of Lady Anne Clifford*, ed. D. J. H. Clifford (Stroud, Glos., 1990), 32, 50–52, 57, and 62.

7. T. Bright, *A Treatise of Melancholy*, Facsimile Text Society no. 50 (New York, 1940), 263–64. See also L. Babb, *The Elizabethan Malady* (East Lansing, Mich., 1951). For Burton, see R. Burton, *The Anatomy of Melancholy*, ed. H. Jackson (New York, 1977), II: 74–75, and for Evelyn, see J. Evelyn, *The Diary of John Evelyn*, ed. E. S. de Beer (Oxford, 1955), I: 55.

8. Sir Henry Slingsby, *The Diary of Sir Henry Slingsby, of Scriven, Bart.*, ed. D. Parson (London, 1836), 288.

9. Anne Viscountess Conway, *Conway Letters*, ed. M. H. Nicolson (New Haven, 1930), 76 (to More) and 229 (to Conway).

10. R. T. Gunther, *Early British Botanists and Their Gardens* (Oxford, 1922), 265.

11. J. Aubrey, *Brief Lives*, ed. A. Clark (Oxford, 1898), I: 70 and 83 (Bacon), 298 (Harvey), and II: 110 (Arundel).

12. [H. Hawkins], *Partheneia Sacra* (Aldington, Kent, 1950), 11.

13. Ibid., 2.

14. R. Josselin, *The Diary of Ralph Josselin 1616–1683*, ed. A. MacFarlane (London, 1976), 449.

15. J. Batchiler, *The Virgins Pattern in the Exemplary Life and Lamented Death of Mrs. Susanna Perwich, Daughter of Mr. Robert Perwich, Who Departed This*

Life, Every Way a Rarely Accomplished Virgin in the Flower of Her Age, at Her Father's House in Hackney, Near London, in the County of Middlesex, July 3, 1661 (London, 1661), 13–14.

16. Sir Thomas Browne, *The Works of Sir Thomas Browne*, ed. G. Keynes (Chicago, 1964), IV: 275.

17. C. F. Smith, *Mary Rich, Countess of Warwick (1625–1678): Her Family & Friends* (London, 1901) and M. E. Palgrave, *Mary Rich, Countess of Warwick (1625–1678)* (London and New York, 1901). For the diary, see Mary Rich, Lady Warwick, *Memoir of Lady Warwick Also Her Diary* (London, n.d.).

18. Hall, *The Works of the Right Reverend Joseph Hall*, X: 121.

19. F. Peck, *Desiderata curiosa* (London, 1779), II: 475; see also S. H. Mendelson, *The Mental World of Stuart Women* (Brighton, Sussex, 1987), 93–94.

20. [J. Aubrey], *The Natural History and Antiquities of the County of Surrey* (London, 1718), II: 160; see also P. Henderson, "Adorning the Arbour," *Country Life* 184 (March 8, 1990): 105–6.

21. R. Thoresby, *The Diary of Ralph Thoresby*, ed. J. Hunter (London, 1820); John Thoresby's letter is in the preface, I: xv.

22. W. Turner, *A Compleat History of the Most Remarkable Providences* (London, 1697), 53.

23. T. Nourse, *Campania Foelix* (London, 1700), 341–42.

24. Duke of Buckingham, *The Works of John Sheffield* (London, 1723), II: 277–78.

25. For eighteenth-century accounts, see "Some Account of the Parish of Dorking and its Environs," *Gentleman's Magazine* 33 (1763): 222; *The Scots Magazine* 29 (1767): 456; and *Gentleman's Magazine* 51 (1781): 123–24; see also N. Penny, "The Macabre Garden at Denbies and Its Monument," *Garden History* 3, no. 3 (summer 1975): 58–61, and B. Allen, "Jonathan Tyer's Other Garden," *Journal of Garden History* 1 (1981): 215–38.

26. E. Young, *The Works of Edward Young, D. D.* (London, 1813), III: 258.

27. J. Boswell, *Boswell's Life of Johnson*, ed. G. B. Hall and L. F. Powell (Oxford, 1934), IV: 120.

28. G. Whitefield, *Whitefield's Journals*, ed. W. Wale (London, 1905), 45.

29. J. Wesley, *The Journal of the Rev. John Wesley, A. M.*, vol. 1, ed. N. Curnock (London, 1938), 181. All other references to Wesley's journals are to this edition.

30. Oct. 5, 1771; Oct. 8, 1779 (with a further comment on Oct. 13); and Oct. 2, 1790.

31. Wesley, *The Journal of the Rev. John Wesley*, VI: 257.

32. J. Dent, *The Quest for Nonsuch* (London, 1962), 59–60.

33. M. E. Blackman, ed., *Ashley House (Walton-on-Thames), Building Accounts 1602–1607*, Surrey Record Society XXIX (Guilford, 1977), 77.

34. J. Caley, "A Survey of the Manor of Wymbledon, alias Wimbleton . . . in the Moneth of November 1649 . . . ," *Archaeologia* 10 (1792): 424–25. For

Meager, see L. Meager, *The English Gardener* (London, 1670), pls. 18, 23, and 24.

35. Palgrave, *Mary Rich*, 204. For Knole, see V. Sackville-West, *Knole and the Sackvilles*, 4th ed. (Tonbridge, Kent, 1958), 116.

36. W. G. Hiscock, *John Evelyn and his Family Circle* (London, 1955), 28–32. For the Berkeley letters, see J. Evelyn, *Diary and Correspondence of John Evelyn, F. R. S.*, rev. ed., ed. W. Bray (London, 1859), III: 273 and 284.

37. J. G. Dunbar, "The Building-activities of the Duke and Duchess of Lauderdale, 1670–82," *The Archaeological Journal* 132 (1975): 202–30; M. Tomlin, *Ham House*, 5th ed. (London, 1982); and J. Y[orke] in *The Anglo-Dutch Garden in the Age of William and Mary*, *Journal of Garden History* 8 (1988), 255–58. Batty Langley's comment in *New Principles of Gardening* (London, 1728), vi. See also J. Badeslade and J. Rocque, *Vitruvius Britannicus*, vol. 4 (London, 1739), pls. 65–66.

38. R. Strong, *The Renaissance Garden in England* (London, 1979), 117. For French bosquets, see J. Boyceau, *Traité du jardinage selon des raisons de la nature and de l'art* ([Paris], 1638) and A. Mollet, *Le Jardin du plaisir* (Stockholm, 1651).

39. P. J. Drury, "No other palace in the kingdom will compare with it: The Evolution of Audley End, 1605–1745," *Architectural History* 23 (1980): 1–39.

40. J. D. H[unt], "Hampton Court, Middlesex," in *The Anglo-Dutch Garden in the Age of William and Mary*, *Journal of Garden History* 8 (1988), 211–20.

41. J. M. Steane, "The Development of Tudor and Stuart Garden Design in Northamptonshire," *Northamptonshire Past & Present* 5, no. 5 (1977): 383–405 and T. Sladen, "The Garden at Kirby Hall 1500–1700," *Journal of Garden History* 4 (1984): esp. 149–54.

42. J. Johnson, *Excellent Cassandra: The Life and Times of the Duchess of Chandos* (Gloucester, 1981), 66, with the comments of Cassandra Willoughby; D. Jacques and A. J. van der Horst, *The Gardens of William and Mary* (London, 1988), 158–61 and 175–76; and J. D. H[unt], "Badminton House," in *The Anglo-Dutch Garden*, 242–244, see esp. cat. no. 98b for the plan of a wilderness.

43. Earl of Ilchester, *The Home of the Hollands, 1605–1820* (London, 1937), illus. opp. 32 and D. Hudson, *Holland House in Kensington* (London, 1967), endpapers.

44. J. Morton, *The Natural History of Northamptonshire* (London, 1712), 491–92 and J. M. Steane in *Northamptonshire Past & Present* 5, no. 5 (1977): 383–405.

45. A. Mitchell, *The Park and Garden at Dyrham* ([London], 1977) and A. M[itchell], "Dyrham, Gloucestershire," in *The Anglo-Dutch Garden*, 258–60.

46. S. Switzer, *Ichnographia Rustica* (London, 1718), III: 126.

47. A. Pope, *The Correspondence of Alexander Pope*, vol. 2, ed. G. Sherburn (Oxford, 1956), 237.

48. T. Nourse, *Campania Foelix* (London, 1700), 321–22.

49. M. Jermin, *A Commentary upon Ecclesiastes* (London, 1639), 36.

50. E. Flügel, "Kleinere Mitteilungen aus Handschriften," *Anglia* 14 (1892): 473–74; see also M. E. James, *A Tudor Magnate and the Tudor State*, Bothwick Papers, no. 30 (York, 1966), esp. 37–38.

51. N. Breton, *The Works in Verse and Prose of Nicholas Breton*, ed. A. B. Grosart (Edinburgh, 1879), I: 6.

52. [St. Bonaventure], *The Mirrovre of the Blessed Life of Ovr Lorde and Saviovre Iesus Christe* [Douai, c. 1609], 176–78.

53. [F. Hutcheson], *An Inquiry into the Original of our Ideas of Beauty and Virtue*, 2nd ed. (London, 1726), 83.

54. B. Langley, *New Principles of Gardening* (London, 1728), xi [in error for iv].

55. P. Miller, *The Gardeners Dictionary*, 6th ed. (London, 1752), s.v. Wilderness. The same article was repeated in the eighth edition of 1768, the last edition during Miller's life, see T. Hinde, *Capability Brown* (New York and London, 1987), 167–68.

56. D. Defoe, *A Tour Thro' the Whole Island of Great Britain*, 3rd ed. (London, 1742), III: 292.

57. J. M. Steane in *Northamptonshire Past & Present* 5, no. 5 (1977): 393.

58. G. H. Williams, *Wilderness and Paradise in Christian Thought* (New York, 1962), 73.

Chapter III

1. G. Kipling, *The Triumph of Honour* (The Hague, 1977), 123–26.

2. R. Greene, *The Dramatic and Poetical Works of Robert Greene & George Peele*, ed. A. Dyce (London, 1861), 577–78.

3. J. Aubrey, *Brief Lives*, ed. A. Clark (Oxford, 1898), I: 131–34; see also R. Plot, *The Natural History of Oxford-shire* (Oxford, 1677), 236–39; A. à Wood, *Athenae Oxoniensis*, rev. ed., ed. P. Bliss (London, 1817), II: cols. 1007–1008; J. W. Gough, *The Superlative Prodigall: A Life of Thomas Bushell* (Bristol, 1932), 23–34; and C. Thacker, "'An Extraordinary Solitude,'" in *Of Oxfordshire Gardens* (Oxford, 1982), 25–48. For Lt. Hammond's account of 1635, see L. G. W. Legg, ed., "A Relation of a Short Survey of the Western Counties," *Camden Miscellany* 16, Camden Third Series, LII (London, 1936).

4. J. D. Hunt, *The Figure in the Landscape: Poetry, Painting, and Gardening during the Eighteenth Century* (Baltimore and London, 1976), 1–9, and E. Harris, "Hunting for Hermits," *Country Life* 182 (May 26, 1988): 186–89.

5. T. Parnell, *Poems on Several Occasions* (London, 1722), 164, and T. M. Woodman, *Thomas Parnell* (Boston, 1985).

6. A. Pope, *The Correspondence of Alexander Pope*, vol. 2, ed. G. Sherburn (Oxford, 1956), 238.
7. See chapter I and note 47.
8. G. B. Clarke, *Descriptions of Lord Cobham's Gardens at Stowe (1700–1750)*, Buckinghamshire Record Society, no. 26 (n.p., 1990), 39 (West), 61 (Milles), and 67 (Anonymous), and D. Defoe, *A Tour Thro' the Whole Island of Great Britain*, 3rd ed. (London, 1742), III: 273 and 275.
9. W. Stukeley, *The Family Memoirs of the Rev. William Stukeley, M.D.*, Surtees Society, 73 (Durham, London, and Edinburgh, 1882); A. K. Owen, *The Famous Druids* (Oxford, 1962); B. Allen, "Gardens of an Enquiring Mind: William Stukeley: From Hermitage to Mausoleum," *Country Life* 174 (Nov. 3, 1983): 1243–50; and S. Piggott, *William Stukeley*, rev. ed. (New York, 1985).
10. F. Tolson, *Hermathenae, or Moral Emblems and Ethnick Tales*, vol. 1 (n.p. [c. 1740]), 137.
11. B. H. Davis, *Thomas Percy* (Philadelphia, 1989).
12. W. Shenstone, *Letters of William Shenstone*, ed. D. Mallam (Minneapolis and London, 1939), 66. See also R. Pococke, *The Travels through England of Dr. Richard Pococke*, Camden Society, n.s., 42, vol. 1, ed. J. J. Cartwright (London, 1888), 224–25, and J. Heely, *Letters on the Beauties of Hagley, Envil, and The Leasowes* (London, 1777), I: 191–93. Walpole's comment in H. Walpole, *Correspondence*, vol. 35, ed. W. S. Lewis (New Haven, 1973), 148.
13. M. S. Røstvig, *The Happy Man*, 2nd ed. (Oslo and New York, n.d.), II: 117.
14. Shenstone, *Letters of William Shenstone*, 318.
15. *The Gentleman's Magazine* 16 (Dec. 1746): 665.
16. Shenstone, *Letters of William Shenstone*, 149; see also [R. Dodsley, ed.], *A Collection of Poems in Six Volumes* (London, 1758), IV: 345–46, and [R. Dodsley, ed.], *The Works in Verse and Prose of William Shenstone Esq.* (London, 1764), II: 333–71 for Dodsley's description of The Leasowes.
17. Shenstone, *Letters of William Shenstone*, esp. 137, 139, and 144. For Spence, see T. Hull, ed., *Select Letters Between the Late Duchess of Somerset, Lady Luxborough . . .* (London, 1778), I: 242.
18. W. Cole, *The Blecheley Diary of the Rev. William Cole, M.A., F.S.A., 1765–67*, ed. F. G. Stokes (London, 1931), 315. The hermitage is illustrated opp. xix and the Chinese-Gothic seat opp. xxii.
19. J. G. Southworth, *Vauxhall Gardens* (New York, 1941), 36, and J. D. Hunt, "Theatres, Gardens, and Garden-theatres," *Essays and Studies*, n.s., 33 (1980): 101. For the location of the "hermitage," see "X" on map of the gardens in O. Manning and W. Bray, *The History and Antiquities of the county of Surrey*, vol. 3 (London, 1814), opp. 492.
20. E. Harris, "Hunting for Hermits," *Country Life* 182 (May 26, 1988), 186–89. See also E. Harris, "Architect of Rococo Landscape: Thomas Wright—III," *Country Life* 150 (Sept. 9, 1971): 612–15; B. Jones, *Follies & Grottoes*,

2nd ed. (London, 1974), 179–80; T. Wright, *Arbours & Grottoes*, ed. E. Harris (London, 1979); and M. McCarthy, "Thomas Wright's 'Designs for Temples' and Related Drawings for Garden Buildings," *Journal of Garden History* 1 (1981): 55–66.

21. D. Lambert and S. Harding, "Thomas Wright at Stoke Park," *Garden History* 17 (1989): 68–82.

22. Jones, *Follies & Grottoes*, 180–82, 342, and 358, and Headley and Meulenkamp, *Follies*, 181 and 349–50.

23. See J. Rykwert, *On Adam's House in Paradise* (New York, 1972). For Adam's hermitage at Kedleston, see L. Harris and G. Jackson-Stops, "When Adam Delved: Robert Adam and the Kedleston Landscape," *Country Life* 181 (Mar. 5, 1987): 100, and L. Harris, *Robert Adam and Kedleston* ([London], 1987), 86, no. 73.

24. R. Pococke, *The Travels through England of Dr. Richard Pococke*, Camden Society, n.s., 44, vol. 2, ed. J. J. Cartwright (London, 1889), 40–41.

25. W. Mason, *The English Garden* (York, 1783), 115; for the commentary, see 186–87.

26. J. Sambrook, "Painshill Park in the 1760's," *Garden History* 8, no. 1 (spring 1980): 93 (1763 visit) and 101–102 (1769 visit). For the advertisement, see Notes and Queries, *Milledulcia* (New York, 1857), 119.

27. K. Woodbridge, *Landscape and Antiquity* (Oxford, 1970), 61–62. See also O. Siren, *China and Gardens of Europe* (New York, 1950), 50–51, and E. Harris in *Country Life* (May 26, 1988): 189. For the letter to Fanny Burney, see F. Burney, *The Early Diary of Frances Burney, 1768–1778*, ed. A. R. Ellis (London, 1907), II: 322.

28. For Marcham, see Notes and Queries, *Milledulcia*, 119, and for Derwent Water, see Sir W. Gell, *A Tour in the Lakes made in 1797 by William Gell*, ed. W. Rollinson (Newcastle upon Tyne, 1968), 16. See also A. Taylor, "Compulsive Lakeland Builder: Joseph Pocklington," *Country Life* 178 (Sept. 5, 1985): 614–17.

29. P. Gosse, *Dr. Viper: The Querulous Life of Philip Thicknesse* (London, 1952), 123–26 (Harwich) and 216–236 (Bathampton); for Bathampton, see also B. S. Allen, *Tides in English Taste* (Cambridge, Mass., 1937), I: 174, and E. Sheridan, *Betsy Sheridan's Journal*, ed. W. Le Fanu (Oxford, and New York, 1986), 89. Richard Graves' account of the Rivers garden is in R. Graves, *The Spiritual Quixote*, ed. C. Tracy (London, 1967), 186.

30. E. Harris in *Country Life* 182 (May 26, 1988): 188. One of Robins' drawings of the hermitage, dated May 27, 1760, is reproduced in J. Harris, *Gardens of Delight: The Rococo English Landscape of Thomas Robins the Elder* (London, 1978), 64, fig. 124.

31. J. Houseman, *A Descriptive Tour, and Guide to the Lakes, Caves, Mountains, and other Natural Curiosities in Cumberland, Westmoreland, Lancashire, . . .* (Carlisle, 1800), 67–68.

32. J. Bull, *John Newton of Olney and S. Mary Woolnoth* (London, [1868]), 276.

33. [Victoria County History], *A History of the County of Stafford*, vol. 20 (Oxford, 1984), 206 and illus. opp. 193, and S. Markham, *John Loveday of Caversham, 1711–1789* (Wilton, 1984), 448.

34. Jones, *Follies & Grottoes*, 68–84; R. Haslam, "Rescue of a Masterpiece: Future of Hawkstone Park, Shropshire," *Country Life* 177 (May 9, 1985): 1244–47; Headley and Meulenkamp, *Follies*, 185–87; and A. C. Dixon, "Hermits for Hire," *Country Life* 182 (June 2, 1988): 161.

35. J. Byng, *The Torrington Diaries*, vol. 2, ed. C. B. Andrews (London, 1935), 382.

36. G. White, *The Natural History & Antiquities of Selborne & A Garden Kalendar*, ed. R. B. Sharpe (London and Philadelphia, 1900), I; R. Holt-White, *The Life and Letters of Gilbert White of Selborne*, 2 vols. (London, 1901); C. S. Emden, *Gilbert White in His Village* (London, 1956); H. Le Rougetel, "Gilbert White's Beechen Grove: The Landscaping of Selborne," *Country Life* 148 (July 23, 1970): 247–51; and R. Mabey, *Gilbert White* (London, 1986).

37. G. White, *The Journals of Gilbert White*, ed. F. Greenoak (London, 1986), I: 68–69.

38. Holt-White, *The Life and Letters of Gilbert White*, I: 129–35.

39. White, *The Journals of Gilbert White*, I: 131.

40. W. Cowper, *The Letters and Prose Writings of William Cowper*, vol. 1, ed. J. King and C. Ryskamp (Oxford, 1979), 502–3.

41. Ibid., IV: 372 and 380.

42. H. L. Piozzi, *Anecdotes of the Late Samuel Johnson, L. L. D.* (Dublin, 1786), 203–204. For *Rasselas*, see S. Johnson, *The History of Rasselas, Prince of Abissinia* (Harmondsworth, N.Y., 1976), 86.

43. S. Johnson, *Poems*, ed. E. L. McAdam and G. Milne (New Haven and London, 1964), 294–95.

44. [R. Graves], *Euphrosyne* (London, 1776), 261–62.

45. H. Walpole, *The History of the Modern Taste in Gardening* (New York and London, 1982), 275–76; the history was printed in 1771, but not issued to the public until 1780. See I. W. U. Chase, *Horace Walpole, Gardenist* (Princeton, 1943), xix.

46. In general, see S. Kliger, *The Goths in England* (Cambridge, Mass., 1952); A. L. Owen, *The Famous Druids* (Oxford, 1962); and S. Piggott, *The Druids* (London, 1968). For Stowe, see S. Moore, "Hail! Gods of Our Forefathers," *Country Life* 176 (Jan. 31, 1985): 250–51; and J. Kenworthy-Browne, "Rysbrack's Saxon Deities," *Apollo* 122 (1985): 220–27.

47. [G. West], *Stowe, The Gardens of the Right Honourable Richard Lord Viscount Cobham* (London, 1732), 24. For Boringdon House, see G. Jackson-Stops, *An English Arcadia 1600–1990* (Washington, D.C., 1991), 61–62.

48. Quoted in Kliger, *The Goths in England*, 7–8, and M. Baridon, "Ruins as a Mental Construct," *Journal of Garden History* 5 (1985): 95 n. 21.

49. M. Batey, *Oxford Gardens* (Amersham, 1982), 106–108, and M. McCarthy, *The Origins of the Gothic Revival* (New Haven and London, 1987), 27.

50. J. Colton, "Merlin's Cave and Queen Caroline: Garden Art as Political Propaganda," *Eighteenth-Century Studies* 10 (1976): 1–20.

51. *The Craftsman* 14, no. 478 (Sept. 6, 1735), 104.

52. K. Woodbridge, *Landscape and Antiquity: Aspects of English Culture at Stourhead, 1718 to 1838* (Oxford, 1970), 51–70; K. Woodbridge, *The Stourhead Landscape* (n.p., 1974), 13 and 22; and M. Kelsall, "The Iconography of Stourhead," *Journal of the Warburg and Courtauld Institutes* 46 (1983): 141–43.

53. J. Thomson, *The Poetical Works of James Thomson*, ed. D. P. Tovey (London, 1897), II: 88–89.

54. W. Warburton, *The Works of the Right Reverend William Warburton, Lord Bishop of Gloucester* (London, 1788), V: 243. His theory on the origins of Gothic architecture is in A. Pope, *The Works of Alexander Pope, Esq.*, with notes of Drs. Warburton and Warton, ed. W. L. Bowles (London, 1806), III: 328–29. For Stukeley, see Piggott, *The Druids*, 143.

55. W. Collins, *The Poems of William Collins*, ed. E. Blunden (London, 1929), 117.

56. M. Drayton, *The Works of Michael Drayton*, vol. 4, *Poly-Olbion*, ed. J. W. Hebel (Oxford, 1961), 122 and 193.

57. Owen, *The Famous Druids*, 41–42.

58. G. W. Johnson, ed., *The Fairfax Correspondence* (London, 1848), I: cxxiii–cxxv.

59. *The British Poets*, vol. 27 (Chiswick, 1822), 89–102, see also R. I. Cook, *Sir Samuel Garth* (Boston, 1980), 100–104.

60. W. Stukeley, *The Family Memoirs of the Rev. William Stukeley, M.D.*, Publications of the Surtees Society, LXXIII (Durham, 1882), 209, the letters on religion on 216 and 228. For Stukeley in general, see S. Piggott, *William Stukeley*, rev. ed. (New York, 1985).

61. M. J. Bevington, "Henry Hoare and the Creation of his 'Demy-Paradise,'" *Studies in Iconography* 12 (1988): 145 n. 51, and P. L. Powys, *Passages from the Diaries of Mrs. Philip Lybbe Powys*, ed. E. J. Climenson (London, 1899), 53.

62. Rev. W. Huddesford, "Memoirs of the Rev. Francis Wise, . . . 1771," in J. Nichols, *Illustrations of the Literary History of the Eighteenth Century* (London, 1822), IV: 479.

63. T. Gray, *The Complete Poems of Thomas Gray*, ed. H. W. Starr and J. R. Hendrickson (Oxford, 1966), 18–24, and for the correspondence with Mason, T. Gray, *Correspondence of Thomas Gray*, ed. P. Toynbee and L. Whibley (Oxford, 1935), II: 465–603, *passim*. For Gray and Macpherson, see Gray, *Correspondence*, II: 672, 680, and 702.

64. Pococke, *The Travels through England*, II: 161–62.

65. G. Jackson-Stops, "Arcadia under the Plough: The Garden at Halswell, Somerset," *Country Life* 183 (Feb. 8, 1989): 85.

66. Pococke, *The Travels through England*, II: 215; Hull, ed., *Select Letters*, I: 269 (Dodsley letter); and R. W. King, "Joseph Spence of Byfleet, IV," *Garden History* 8 no. 3 (winter 1980): 110.

67. *The Gentleman's Magazine* (June 1774): 263–65, and J. J. Bagley, *The Earls of Derby 1485–1985* (London, 1985), 144.

68. G. Cumberland, *An Attempt to Describe Hafod* (London, 1796), 31. The description of the site for the Druid Temple is on pages 10–11. For Hafod, see also B. H. Malkin, *The Scenery, Antiquities, and Biography, of South Wales* (London, 1804), 338–64; E. Inglis-Jones, *Peacocks in Paradise* (Shoreham-in-Sea, Sussex, 1971); and C. Kerkham, "Hafod: Paradise Lost," *Journal of Garden History* 11 (1991): 207–16.

69. [Victoria County History], *A History of the County of Stafford*, XX: 206 and illus. opp. 193.

70. Gell, *A Tour in the Lakes*, 15, and A. Taylor in *Country Life* (Sept. 5, 1985): 615.

71. R. H. Clutterbuck, *Notes on the Parishes of Fyfield, Kimpton, Penton Mewsey, Wyhill and Wherwell*, ed. E. D. Webb (Salisbury, 1898), 12.

72. J. Britton and E. W. Brayley, *The Beauties of England and Wales*, vol. 1 (London, 1801), 189–90; Chase, *Horace Walpole*, 221–25; and B. Jones, *Follies & Grottoes*, 2nd ed. (London, 1974), 237–38.

73. H. Walpole, *Correspondence*, ed. W. S. Lewis (New Haven, 1965–74), XXXIV: 14–15 (Sept. 6, 1788), XXXV: 395–96 (Aug. 2 and Sept. 12, 1788), and XXXIX: 460–61 (Nov. 11, 1787).

74. G. Jackson-Stops, "Plas Newydd," *Transactions of the Ancient Monuments Society*, n.s., 29 (1985): 11-35.

75. A. Kelly, *Mrs. Coade's Stone* (Upton-upon-Severn, Worcs, 1990). For the Druid at The Vyne, see H. Walpole, *Correspondence*, XXXV: 642, and The National Trust, *The Vyne, Hampshire* ([London], 1983), illus. on page 35. For the Chichester figure, see Rev. T. D. S. Bayley, "Lady Mary May's Monument in Mid Lavant Church," *Sussex Archaeological Collections* 107 (1969): 10–11 and figs. 7A and 7B, there misidentified as Moses.

76. J. Cornforth, "Swinton, Yorkshire—III," *Country Life* 139 (April 21, 1966): 944–48.

Chapter IV

1. *Diogenes Laertius*, Loeb Classical Library, trans. R. D. Hicks (London and New York, 1925), I: 505–507 (V, 53).

2. J. Evelyn, *The Diary of John Evelyn*, ed. E. S. De Beer (Oxford, 1955), II:

337. See also, D. Chambers, "The Tomb in the Landscape: John Evelyn's Garden at Albury," *Journal of Garden History* 1 (1981): 37–54; J. B. Trapp, "The Grave of Vergil," *Journal of the Warburg and Courtauld Institutes* 47 (1984): 1–31; and [J. D. Hunt], "Editorial: A Garden and a Grave," *Journal of Garden History* 4 (1984): 209–10.

3. J. Evelyn, *Silva*, 4th ed. (London, 1706), 342–44.

4. F. Quarles, *Hosanna or Divine Poems on the Passion of Christ and Thenodes*, English Reprints Series no. 15, ed. J. Harden (Liverpool, 1960), 6, and M. Jermin, *Commentary, Upon the Whole Booke of Ecclesiastes or the Preacher* (London, 1639), 35.

5. Earl of Romney, *Diary of the Times of Charles the Second*, ed. R. W. Blencowe (London, 1843), I: xcv. See also W. Gilpin, *Observations on the Western Parts of England, Relative Chiefly to Picturesque Beauty* (London, 1798), 41, and G. Burnet, *History of His Own Time*, rev. ed. (London, 1818), I: 423.

6. Evelyn, *Silva*, 344. See also W. Burton, *A Commentary on Antoninus His Itinerary or Journies . . .* (London, 1658), 136–38; J. Nightingale, *The Beauties of England and Wales*, vol. 13, pt. 1 (London, 1813), 97–98; and D. Stroud, *Humphry Repton* (London, 1962), 133–34.

7. F. de Bassompierre, *Memoirs of the Embassy of the Marshal de Bassompierre*, trans. J. W. Crocker (London, 1819), 18 n. 15.

8. R. Clark, *Sir William Trumbull in Paris, 1685–1686* (Cambridge, 1938), 32 and 62–68, and [Great Britain], Hist. Mss. Comm., *Report of the Manuscripts of the Marquess of Downshire*, vol. 1, pt. 1 (London, 1924), 223.

9. S. C. Morland, ed., *The Somersetshire Quarterly Meeting of the Society of Friends 1668–1699*, Somerset Record Society, vol. 75 (n.p., 1975), 20. See especially K. Thomas, *Man and the Natural World* (New York, 1983), 237–38.

10. T. F. Thiselton-Dyer, *Old English Social Life As Told by the Parish Registers* (London, 1899), 164, and G. Omerod, *The History of the County Palatine and City of Chester* (London, 1819), III: 92.

11. [C. Wren], *Parentalia* (London, 1750), 318–21, and K. Downes, *Vanbrugh* (London, 1977), 257–58.

12. Sir J. Vanbrugh, *The Complete Works of Sir John Vanbrugh*, ed. B. Dobrée and G. Webb (London, 1928), IV: 147, no. 140.

13. C. S. Smith, *The Making of Castle Howard* (London and Boston, 1990), 168–69. Other references to the mausoleum are to ibid., 159–92. For English mausolea in general, see D. Stillman, "Death Defied and Honor Upheld: The Mausoleum in Neo-Classical England," *Art Quarterly*, n.s., 1 (1978): 175–213, and *Mausoleen des 18. Jahrhunderts in England*, Berichte und Forschungen zur Kunstgeschichte 7 (Freiburg i. Br., 1984).

14. R. Kay, *The Diary of Richard Kay, 1716–51 of Baldingstone, near Bury*, Chetham Society, ser. 3, XVI, ed. W. Brockbank and F. Kenworthy (Manchester, 1968), 60.

15. E. J. Climenson, *Elizabeth Montagu* (London, 1906), I: 85, and E. Young, *The Correspondence of Edward Young 1683–1765*, ed. R. Pettit (Oxford, 1971), 128 n. 2.

16. B. Jones, *Follies & Grottoes*, 2nd ed. (London, 1974), 297–98.

17. J. Swarbrick, "Dunham Massey Hall," *Transactions of the Lancashire & Cheshire Antiquarian Society* 42 (1925): 69, and G. Jackson-Stops, "Dunham Massey, Cheshire—II," *Country Life* 169 (June 11, 1981), 1666. For Nether Lypiatt, see G. Headley and W. Meulenkamp, *Follies* (London, 1986), 171, and for Marston, see Countess of Cork and Orrery, *The Orrery Papers* (London, 1903), II: 320.

18. G. Clarke, "Signior Fido and the Stowe Patriots," *Apollo* 122 (1985): 248–51. The inscription was first recorded in T. Hearne, *Remarks and Collections of Thomas Hearne*, Oxford Historical Society, 72, ed. H. E. Salter (Oxford, 1921), XI: 438–39. The comment on Pope is in J. Spence, *Anecdotes, Observations and Characters of Books and Men* (London, 1964), 163.

19. W. Stukeley, *The Family Memoirs of the Rev. William Stukeley, M.D.*, Publications of the Surtees Society, LXXIII (Durham, 1882), 209, and S. Piggott, *William Stukeley*, rev. ed. (New York, 1985), 77.

20. Stukeley, *Memoirs*, I: 367 and III: 66–67, and Piggott, *William Stukeley*, 119 and 122–23; see also T. Murdoch, "Boughton House, Northamptonshire," *Antiques* (June 1986): 1253–54.

21. J. Thomson, *James Thomson (1700–1748): Letters and Documents*, ed. A. D. McKillop (Lawrence, Kansas, 1958), 186.

22. J. Harris, *Sir William Chambers, Knight of the Polar Star* (University Park, Penn. and London, 1970), 24–25. Regarding the death of the prince, see *Walpole Society*, vol. 30 (Oxford, 1955), 156. For Robert Morris, see R. Morris, *The Architectural Remembrancer* (London, 1751), pls. XXIV, XXVIII, and XXIX.

23. *Mausoleen des 18. Jahrhunderts in England*, 57–66; Headley and Meulenkamp, *Follies*, 424; and P. Leach, *James Paine* (London, 1988), 185.

24. A. T. Bolton, *The Architecture of Robert & James Adam* (London, 1922), I: 204–14; D. Stillman in *Art Quarterly* (1978): 192–93; and *Mausoleen des 18. Jahrhunderts in England*, 72–82.

25. Jones, *Follies & Grottoes*, 106–107; Stillman in *Art Quarterly*, 193; Headley and Meulenkamp, *Follies*, 225; and *Mausoleen des 18. Jahrhunderts in England*, 67–71.

26. Stillman in *Art Quarterly*, 181–82 and Appendix II: 205–207, with list of exhibited designs.

27. W. Chambers, *A Treatise on Civil Architecture* (London, 1759), 85.

28. A. Dale, *James Wyatt* (Oxford, 1956), 25; Stillman in *Art Quarterly*, 195; and *Mausoleen des 18. Jahrhunderts in England*, 90–96.

29. Dale, *James Wyatt*, 25–26; Stillman in *Art Quarterly*, 194–95; *Mausoleen des 18. Jahrhunderts in England*, 97–104; "The Brocklesby Mausoleum," *Country*

Life 181 (Dec. 3, 1987): 240; and J. Lord, "The Building of the Mausoleum at Brocklesby, Lincolnshire," *Church Monuments* 7 (1992): 85–96.

30. Stillman in *Art Quarterly*, 196; *Mausoleen des 18. Jahrhunderts in England*, 117–24; and The National Trust, *Blickling Hall* (London, 1987), 69.

31. H. Walpole, *Hieroglyphic Tales* (*1785*), The Augustan Reprint Society 212–13, intro. by K. W. Gross (Los Angeles, 1982), 42, and J. Britton and E. W. Brayley, *The Beauties of England and Wales*, vol. 1 (London, 1801), 188.

32. P. Gosse, *Dr. Viper: The Querulous Life of Philip Thicknesse* (London, 1952), 223–24, and E. Sheridan, *Betsy Sheridan's Journal*, ed. W. Le Fanu (Oxford and New York, 1986), 89.

33. *The Gentleman's Magazine* 78, pt. 2 (1808): 662 and 849, and Thiselton-Dyer, *Old English Social Life*, 164. Regarding Wilkinson and Thomas Paine, see [Great Britain], Hist. Mss. Comm., *The Manuscripts of Lord Kenyon* (London, 1894), 536–37.

34. F. Shoberl, *The Beauties of England and Wales*, vol. 14 (London, 1813), 121 in the section on Surrey.

35. W. H. Shercliff, ed., *Wythenshawe*, vol. 1 (Didsbury, 1974), 232–33.

36. R. A. Etlin, *The Architecture of Death* (Cambridge, Mass. and London, 1984), esp. 310–35 for the cemetery of Père-Lachaise. For English cemeteries, see J. S. Curl, *A Celebration of Death* (London, 1980).

Chapter V

1. [Great Britain], *Calendar of State Papers, Domestic Series, 1629–1631*, ed. J. Bruce (London, 1860), 121–22, no. 69, and 165–67, nos. 48 and 54. See especially C. Avery, "Hubert Le Sueur, the 'Unworthy Praxiteles' of King Charles I," *Walpole Society*, vol. 48 (Oxford, 1980–82), 146–47, 176–77, and 201–202, and V. B. Redstone, "The Diary of Sir Thomas Dawes, 1644," *Surrey Archaeological Collections* 37, pt. 1 (1926): 15 and 26.

2. J. W[orlidge], *Systema Horti-culturae* (London, 1677), 66–67.

3. K. Downes, *Sir John Vanbrugh: A Biography* (New York, 1987), 353, and C. S. Smith, *The Building of Castle Howard* (London and Boston, 1990), 130–32.

4. G. B. Clarke, ed., *Descriptions of Lord Cobham's Gardens at Stowe* (*1700–1750*), Buckinghamshire Record Society, no. 26 (n.p., 1990), 15–17 (Perceval, 1724), 18–19 (E. Southwell, 1724), and 60–65 (Milles, 1735); also G. Bickham, *The Beauties of Stow* (London, 1750), 10. For inscriptions on other monuments, see ibid. For Cannons, see C. H. C. Baker and M. I. Baker, *The Life and Circumstances of James Brydges, First Duke of Chandos* (Oxford, 1949), 159; F. H. W. Sheppard, *Survey of London*, vol. 34 (London, 1966), 433; and R. Gunnis, *Dictionary of British Sculptors 1660–1851*, rev. ed. (London, 1968), 70.

5. J. Physick, *Designs of English Sculpture 1680–1860* (London, 1969), 56–57; J. Harris, "The Diana Fountain at Hampton Court," *Burlington Magazine* 111 (1969): 444–47; and J. P[hysick] in *The Anglo-Dutch Garden in the Age of William and Mary, Journal of Garden History*, VIII, nos. 2–3 (1988), 219–20. For Wrest, see also G. A. Mott and S. S. Aall, *Follies and Pleasure Pavilions* (New York, 1989), 123; for the date of Carpenter's work at Wrest, see R. Gunnis, *Dictionary of British Sculptors, 1660–1851*, rev. ed. (London, [1968]), 83. For Chelsea Physic Garden, see C. Wall, *A History of the Worshipful Society of Apothecaries of London*, vol. 1 (London, 1963).

6. [F. Hutcheson], *An Inquiry into the Original of our Ideas of Beauty and Virtue*, 2nd ed. (London, 1726), 44–45.

7. W. Stukeley, *The Family Memoirs of the Rev. William Stukeley, M.D.*, Publications of the Surtees Society, LXXIII (Durham, London, and Edinburgh, 1882), 210.

8. G. Clarke, "Signior Fido and the Stowe Patriots," *Apollo* 122 (1985): 248–51.

9. J. Colton, "Kent's Hermitage for Queen Caroline at Richmond," *Architectura* (1974): 181–91, and C. M. Sicca, "'Like a Shallow Cave by Nature Made': William Kent's 'Natural' Architecture at Richmond," *Architectura* (1986): 68–82.

10. J. Colton, "Merlin's Cave and Queen Caroline: Garden Art and Political Propaganda," *Eighteenth-Century Studies* 10 (1976): 1–20.

11. H. S. Hughes, *The Gentle Hertford* (New York, 1940), 153.

12. W. Mason, *The English Garden: A Poem*, rev. ed. (York, 1783), 59 and 222. See also J. W. Draper, *William Mason* (New York, 1924), 75, and B. Barr and J. Ingamells, *A Candidate for Praise* (York, 1973), 38.

13. "Kent's Monkey Business," *Country Life* 179 (Jan. 9, 1986): 58.

14. For Gibbs's work, see T. Friedman, *James Gibbs* (New Haven and London, 1984), 190–98 and 292–93.

15. [T. Whately], *Observations on Modern Gardening* (London, 1770), 225–26.

16. H. Walpole, *Selected Letters of Horace Walpole*, ed. W. S. Lewis (New Haven and London, 1973), 154–55, quoted in C. Hussey, *English Gardens and Landscapes 1700–1750* (London, 1967), 113.

17. A. Pope, *The Correspondence of Alexander Pope*, ed. G. Sherburn (Oxford, 1956), IV: 144, 170, 178, 181, and 191, and J. Vardy, *Some Designs of Mr. Inigo Jones and Mr. W^m. Kent* ([London], 1744), pl. 25.

18. For urns, see J. Heely, *Letters on the Beauties of Hagley, Envil, and The Leasowes* (London, 1777), II: 115 (Somerville), 117–21 (Lord Stamford), 138 (Shenstone's brother), and 175–77 (Shenstone's cousin, the youthful Maria Dolman); for seats, see 122 (Dodsley), 199–201 (Thomson), and 225* (Jago and Graves). For some letter comments, see W. Shenstone, *The Letters of William Shenstone*, ed. M. Williams (Oxford, 1939), 172 (urn

for Thomson, Sept. 25, 1748), 240–41, 244, and 246 (urn for Virgil's Grove, Nov. and Dec. 1749), and 264–65 (urn versus pyramid, Mar. 22, 1750).

19. Heely, *Letters*, I: 164–65 (Shenstone), 169–70 (Pope), and 221–22 (Thomson).

20. [W. Shenstone], *Shenstone's Miscellany 1759–1783*, ed. I. A. Gordon (Oxford, 1952), 34.

21. G. B. Hill, ed., *Johnsonian Miscellanies* (Oxford, 1897), II: 427–28, and S. Johnson, *The Letters of Samuel Johnson*, ed. R. W. Chapman (Oxford, 1952), II: 207 and 548.

22. S. E. Pybus, *Shugborough: A Guide to the Monuments* (Shugborough, 1984).

23. D. Lambert and S. Harding, "Thomas Wright and Stoke Park," *Garden History* 17 (1989): 68–82. For Werrington, see R. Pococke, "Travels through England," in *Early Tours in Devon and Cornwall*, ed. R. P. Chope (Newton Abbot, 1967), 207, and B. Jones, *Follies & Grottoes*, rev. ed. (London, 1974), 301–302.

24. [A. Young], *A Six Months Tour through the North of England*, 2nd ed. (London, 1771), II: 304.

25. J. Evelyn *The Diary of John Evelyn*, ed. E. S. de Beer (Oxford, 1955), II: 355–56.

26. C. Oman [Lenanton], *David Garrick* (n.p., 1958), 161 and 185–89, and M. Symes, "David Garrick and Landscape Gardening," *Journal of Garden History* 6 (1986): 34–49. For Walpole's letters regarding the temple, see H. Walpole, *Correspondence*, vol. 9, ed. W. S. Lewis (New Haven, 1941), 198–99 and vol. 35, (1973), 242; for the statue, see K. A. Esdaile, *The Life and Works of Louis François Roubiliac* (London, 1928), 123–26; and for the chair, see M. Snodin, ed., *Rococo: Art and Design in Hogarth's England* (London, 1984), 67.

27. *Grove-Hill: An Horticultural Sketch* (London, 1794) and J. J. Abraham, *Lettsom, His Life, Times, Friends and Descendants* (London, 1933), 295–320, illus. on page 312.

28. *The British Poets* (Chiswick, 1822), LIV: 188–202.

29. Esdaile, *The Life and Works of Louis François Roubiliac*, 36–40 (Handel) and 40 (Milton), and T. Hodgkinson, "Handel and Vauxhall," *Victoria and Albert Museum Bulletin* 1, no. 4 (Oct. 1965): 1–13.

30. [Victoria County History], *A History of the County of Stafford*, vol. 20 (Oxford, 1984), 206, illus. opp. 193; for the exhibition of the design, see D. Stillman, "Death Defied and Honor Upheld: The Mausoleum in Neo-Classical England," *Art Quarterly*, n.s., 1 (1978), 205.

31. E. Cecil, *A History of Gardening in England*, 3rd ed. (London, 1910), 219, illus. opp. 218, and G. Jackson-Stops, "New Deities for Old Parterres: The Painting of Lead Statues," *Country Life* 181 (Jan. 29, 1987): 92 and fig. 2.

For Carpenter's price list, see Gunnis, *Dictionary of British Sculptors, 1660–1851*, 83.

32. Earl of Ilchester, *Henry Fox, First Lord Holland* (London, 1920), II: 281 and 327; H. Honour, "An Epic of Ruin-Building," *Country Life* 114 (Dec. 10, 1953): 1968–69; and R. Jessup, "The Follies of Kingsgate," *Archaeologia Cantiana* 71 (1958): 1–13.

33. [Seeley], "Stowe: A Description (1797)" in *The Gardens at Stowe*, ed. J. D. Hunt (New York and London, 1982), 26; L. Whistler, M. Gibbon, and G. Clarke, *Stowe: A Guide to the Gardens*, 3rd ed. (n.p., 1974), 22–23; and M. Gibbon, "Stowe, Buckinghamshire: The House and Garden Buildings and Their Designers," *Architectural History* 20 (1977): 44. For a view of the Cook monument in 1805, see C. N. Gowing and G. B. Clarke, *Drawings of Stowe by John Claude Nattes in the Buckinghamshire County Museum* (n.p., 1983), 12, no. 71. For the Vache, see D. Watkin, *Thomas Hope, 1769–1831, and the Neo-Classical Idea* (London, 1968), 153, and Jones, *Follies & Grottoes*, 292.

34. K. Lemmon, "The Monuments of Wentworth Woodhouse," *Garden History* 5 no. 3 (winter 1977): 25–26; R. B. Wragg, "Four Monuments of Wentworth," *Transactions of the Ancient Monuments Society*, n.s., 23 (1978): 29–39; D. Stillman in *Art Quarterly* (1978): 198; M. J. Charlesworth, "The Wentworths," *Garden History* 14 (1986): 120–37; *Mausoleen des 18. Jahrhunderts in England*, 105–10; and M. Binney, "Wentworth Woodhouse, Yorks," *Country Life* 185 (Jan. 24, 1991): 60–63.

35. T. Jefferson, *Thomas Jefferson's Garden Book 1766–1826*, Memoirs of the American Philosophical Society, XXII, ed. E. M. Betts (Philadelphia, 1944), 112–13.

36. P. Gosse, *Dr. Viper: The Querulous Life of Philip Thicknesse* (London, 1952), 223.

37. C. Ripa, *Iconologia* (Siena, 1613), pt. 1: 296–97, and H. Peacham, *Minerva Britanna 1612*, English Emblem Books No. 5 (Menston, Yorkshire, 1969), 21.

38. G. Sandys, *Relations of a Iourney begun An: Dom: 1610* (London, 1615), 127–31.

39. J. Aubrey, *The Natural History of Wiltshire*, ed. J. Britton (London, 1847), 93. For Aubrey's description of the garden, see R. Blunt, *By Chelsea Reach: Some Riverside Records* (London, 1921), 261–63, and A. M. Charles, *A Life of George Herbert* (Ithaca and London, 1977), 61–65.

40. G. B. Clarke, ed., *Descriptions of Lord Cobham's Gardens at Stowe (1700–1750)*, Buckinghamshire Record Society, no. 26 (n.p., 1990), 16.

41. K. Downes, *Hawksmoor* (London, 1959), 221–22, and C. S. Smith, *The Building of Castle Howard* (London and Boston, 1990), 9 and 147.

42. A. Pope, *The Correspondence of Alexander Pope*, vol. 2, ed. G. Sherburn (Oxford, 1956), 517.

43. A. Oswald, "Ebberston Hall, Yorkshire," *Country Life* 116 (Oct. 7, 1954), 1158–61; Hussey, *English Gardens and Landscapes,* 65–69; and J. Harris, *The Artist and the Country House* (London, 1979), 191.

44. J. Badeslade and J. Rocque, *Vitruvius Britannicus,* vol. 4 (London, 1739), pls. 104–105; P. Willis, *Charles Bridgeman and the English Landscape Garden* (London, 1977), 60; and T. Friedman, *James Gibbs* (New Haven and London, 1984), 170–72 and 302.

45. J. Harris, "Views of an 18th-Century Garden: Hartwell House, Buckinghamshire," *Country Life* 165 (Mar. 15, 1979), 707–709, fig. 6.

46. Jones, *Follies & Grottoes,* 88–89; R. B. Wragg, "Four Monuments at Wentworth," *Transactions of the Ancient Monuments Society,* n.s., 23 (1978): 29–31, with letter of marquis of Oct. 1746; M. J. Charlesworth, "The Wentworths," *Garden History* 14 (1986): 120–30; and M. Binney, "Wentworth Woodhouse, Yorks," *Country Life* 185 (Jan. 24, 1991), 60–63. For Bishop Pococke's account in 1750, see R. Pococke, *The Travels through England of Dr. Richard Pococke,* Camden Society, n.s., 42, vol. 1, ed. J. J. Cartwright (London, 1888), 65–67.

47. R. Haslam, "Studley Royal, North Yorkshire," *Country Life* 179 (Mar. 27, 1986), 804.

48. Jones, *Follies & Grottoes,* 124 and Headley and Meulenkamp, *Follies,* 174.

49. See p. 118

50. P. Howell and T. W. Pritchard, "Wynnstay, Denbighshire—III," *Country Life* 151 (April 6, 1972): 851.

51. See p. 144

52. See p. 165

53. For some examples, see J. G. Mann, "English Church Monuments, 1536–1625," *Walpole Society,* vol. 21 (Oxford, 1933), 19 and pls. xix, xxiiib, xxivb, and xxvic; K. A. Esdaile, *English Church Monuments 1510 to 1840* (London, 1946), figs. 2, 14, 53, 62, and 64; and M. Whinney, *Sculpture in Britain, 1530 to 1830,* rev. ed. (London, 1988), figs. 17, 28, 35, and 78.

54. A. Bocchi, *Symbolarum quaestionum liber secundus* (Bologna, 1574), ciiii, symbolum xlviii. For the meaning of obelisks, see especially W. S. Heckscher, "Bernini's Elephant and Obelisk," *Art Bulletin* 29 (1947), 154–82.

55. R. Laneham, *Laneham's Letter Describing the Magnificent Pageants Presented Before Queen Elizabeth at Kenilworth Castle in 1575* (Philadelphia, 1822), 71.

56. J. Dent, *The Quest for Nonsuch* (London, 1962), 286–94 (Parliamentary survey of 1650) and fig. 6b (engraving of 1610).

57. R. Hewlings, "Ripon's Forum Populi," *Architectural History* 24 (1981): 39–52, with a thorough account of the revival of the obelisk form in eighteenth-century England.

58. D. Green, *Blenheim Palace* (London, 1951), 170.

59. Smith, *The Building of Castle Howard*, 130–32. For the 1731 inscription and for the later obelisks, see K. Downes, *Sir John Vanbrugh: A Biography* (New York, 1987), 193 and 465–66.

60. Sir J. Vanbrugh, *The Complete Works of Sir John Vanbrugh*, ed. B. Dobrée and G. Webb (London, 1924), IV: 129–60.

61. [Great Britain], Hist. Mss. Comm., *Report of the Manuscripts of His Grace the Duke of Portland*, vol. 6 (London, 1901), 96, and Smith, *The Building of Castle Howard*, 137–39. For Yorke's comment, see J. Godber, "The Marchioness Grey of Wrest Park," *Bedfordshire Historical Record Society* 47 (1968): 130. Another early obelisk, perhaps dating from 1714, is at Dunham Massey in Cheshire, see G. Jackson-Stops, "Dunham Massey, Cheshire—II," *Country Life* 169 (June 11, 1981): 1666.

62. C. M. Sicca, "Lord Burlington at Chiswick: Architecture and Landscape," *Garden History* 10 (1982): 42 and 62. See also M. I. Wilson, *William Kent* (London, 1984), 189 (1728 ms.) and J. D. Hunt, *William Kent: Landscape Garden Designer* (London, 1987), 69–70, 113, no. 8, 125, no. 27, 126, no. 30, and 130, no. 39.

63. D. R. Coffin, *The Villa d'Este at Tivoli* (Princeton, 1960), 20. For Stowe, see M. Gibbon, "Stowe, Buckinghamshire: The House and Garden Buildings and Their Designer," *Architectural History* 20 (1977), 38 and 44, and [B. Seeley], *Stowe: A Description* (Buckingham, 1777), 28 in *The Gardens at Stowe*, ed. J. D. Hunt (New York and London, 1982).

64. "Vanbrugh Revamped," *Country Life* 184 (April 26, 1990), 147.

65. C. Hussey, *English Gardens and Landscapes, 1700–1750* (London, 1967), 70–77 (Braham Park) and 132–39 (Studley Royal).

66. D. Green, *Blenheim Palace* (London, 1951), 173–77 and 277–78, and K. Downes, *Hawksmoor* (London, 1959), 206–10 and 262–64.

67. A. Pope, *Correspondence of Alexander Pope*, vol. 2, ed. G. Sherburn (Oxford, 1956), 239.

68. T. Friedman, *James Gibbs* (New Haven and London, 1984), 292. For his publication, see *A Book of Architecture* (London, 1728), xx–xxi and pls. LXXXV–LXXXVII. An obelisk at Wrest is pictured in a marginal vignette to the plan of Wrest published by J. Badeslade and J. Rocque, *Vitruvius Britannicus*, vol. 4 (London, 1739), pls. 30–33. Other vignettes on the Wrest plan depict a small obelisk in the opening in the woods identified as "The Duke's Square" and a small column bearing a pineapple in "The Lady Dutches's Square." For Kedleston, see Gibbs, *A Book of Architecture*, xviii–xix.

69. For Holkham Hall, see W. Hassall, "Views from the Holkham Windows," in *Tribute to an Antiquary*, ed. F. Emmison and R. Stephens (London, 1976), 310–12; M. I. Wilson, *William Kent* (London, 1984), 173–74; and J. D. Hunt, *William Kent, Landscape Garden Designer* (London, 1987), 79 and 139, no. 56. For Belton House, see J. Badeslade and J. Rocque, *Vitruvius Britannicus*, vol. 4 (London, 1739), pls. 88–89.

70. C. Hussey, "Hall Barn, Buckinghamshire," *Country Life* 91 (Mar. 20, 1942): 564–67, and (Mar. 27, 1942): 612–15, and Hussey, *English Gardens and Landscapes,* 24–26.

71. C. Aslet, "Why Farnborough's Views Must Be Saved," *Country Life* 179 (Dec. 1, 1983): 1856–57, and G. Jackson-Stops, *Farnborough Hall, Warwickshire* ([London], 1984). See also Pococke, *The Travels through England,* II: 239.

72. *The Gentleman's Magazine* 18 (Dec. 1748): 568. See also [J. Hanway], *A Journal of Eight Days Journey,* 2nd ed. (London, 1757), I: 137–38, and K. Woodbridge, "Stourhead in 1768," *Journal of Garden History* 2 (1982): 66 (Parnell's journal). For Spence's comment on Bridgeman, see R. W. King, "Joseph Spence of Byfleet, Part IV," *Garden History* 8, no. 3 (winter 1980): 101.

73. W. Shenstone, *The Letters of William Shenstone,* ed. M. Williams (Oxford, 1939), 191–92, letter LXXXVI (April 23, 1749) and 218–219, letter XCIX (Oct. 1749?). For Lady Luxborough's letters regarding the obelisk, see H. Luxborough, *Letters Written by the Late Right Honourable Lady Luxborough to William Shenstone, Esq.* (Dublin, 1776), 91, letter XXXIII (June 4, 1749), 96, letter XXIX (June 24, 1749), and 222, letter LXIV (April 16, [1751]).

74. G. Nares, "Hagley Hall, Worcestershire," *Country Life* 122 (Sept. 19, 1957), 546–49. See also [T. Martyn], *The English Connoisseur* (Dublin, 1767), I: 40, and J. Heely, *Letters on the Beauties of Hagley, Envil, and The Leasowes* (London, 1777), I: 124.

75. A. Hill, *The Works of the late Aaron Hill, Esq.,* 2nd ed. (London, 1754), 239–40.

76. M. R. Brownell, *Alexander Pope & the Arts of Georgian England* (Oxford, 1978), 142–45, and M. R. Brownell, *Alexander Pope's Villa* (London, 1980), 58, no. 60. For Pope's letters, see Pope, *The Correspondence,* III: 51 (Sept. 8, 1729 to Digby) and 453 (Mar. 22, 1735 to Fortescue) and IV: 150 (Nov. 28, 1738, Kent to Burlington).

77. Ibid., IV: 33–34. See also P. Martin, *Pursuing Innocent Pleasures: The Gardening World of Alexander Pope* (Hamden, Conn., 1984), 59–60 and 195.

78. [Victoria County History], *A History of the County of Oxford,* vol. 9, ed. M. D. Lobel and A. Crossley (Oxford, 1969), 173; Jones, *Follies & Grottoes,* 379; J. Cornforth, "Wroxton Abbey, Oxfordshire—II," *Country Life* 170 (Sept. 10, 1981): 854–57; and P. Edwards, "The Gardens at Wroxton Abbey, Oxfordshire," *Garden History* 14 (1986): 55. For Walpole's comment, see H. Walpole, *Correspondence,* vol. 35, ed. W. S. Lewis (New Haven, 1973), 74.

79. K. Lemmon, "Wentworth Castle: A Forgotten Landscape," *Garden History* 3, no. 3 (summer 1975): 54, and M. J. Charlesworth, "The Wentworths," *Garden History* 14 (1986): 128.

80. W. Pitt, *Correspondence of William Pitt, Earl of Chatham,* vol. 3, ed. W. S. Taylor and Capt. J. H. Pringle (London, 1839), 325–30.

81. J. G. Southworth, *Vauxhall Gardens* (New York, 1941), 52–53, and T. J. Edelstein, *Vauxhall Gardens* (New Haven, 1983), 19–20 and 26.

82. [T. Percy], *The Percy Letters,* vol. 7, ed. C. Brooks (New Haven and London, 1977), 64.

83. J. Harris, *Gardens of Delight: The Rococo English Landscape of Thomas Robins the Elder* (London, 1978), 19, fig. 34; M. Richards, "Two Eighteenth-Century Gloucester Gardens," *Transactions of the Bristol and Gloucestershire Archaeological Society* 99 (1981): 123–26; and J. Harris, "'Gardenesque': The Case of Charles Grevile's Garden at Gloucester," *Journal of Garden History* 1 (1981): 167–78.

84. Sir T. Clifford [-Constable] and A. Clifford, *A Topographical and Historical Description of the Parish of Tixall* (Paris, 1817), 63; S. E. Pybus, *Shugborough: A Guide to the Monuments* (Shugborough, 1984), unpaginated; and G. Jackson-Stops, *An English Arcadia 1600–1990* (Washington, D.C., 1991), 90.

85. Jackson-Stops, *An English Arcadia,* 106–107.

86. *Wren Society Publications,* vol. 5 (Oxford, 1928), 45–51.

87. Sicca in *Garden History* 10 (1982): 47. See also J. Gibbs, *A Book of Architecture* (London, 1728), pl. LXXXVII.

88. See above pp. 153–54. For the later monuments, see G. Bickham, *The Beauties of Stow* (London, 1750), 29–30, and [B. Seeley], *Stowe* (Buckingham, 1777), 21–23 and 29–30, in *The Garden at Stowe,* ed. J. D. Hunt (New York and London, 1982); Whistler, Gibbons, and Clarke, *Stowe: A Guide of the Gardens,* 17 and 34; and M. Bevington, "The Development of the Classical Revival at Stowe," *Architectura* 21 (1991): 160. See also *The Gentleman's Magazine* 18 (1748): 23.

89. A. Green, "Letters of Sarah Churchill, Duchess of Marlborough, on the Column of Victory at Blenheim," *Oxoniensia* 31 (1966): 139–45, and [D. Green], *Blenheim Park and Garden* (Woodstock, 1976), 14–16.

90. Friedman, *James Gibbs,* 163.

91. Sir G. Jellicoe, "Creative Conservation," *Journal of the Royal Society of Art* 128 (1980): 290; Friedman, *James Gibbs,* 184 and 292; and M. Laird, "'Our Equally Favorite Hobby Horse': The Flower Gardens of Lady Elizabeth Lee at Hartwell and the 2nd Earl Harcourt at Nuneham Courtenay," *Garden History* 18 (1990), 105.

92. J. Lees-Milne, *Earls of Creation* (London, 1962), 52–53, and Martin, *Pursuing Innocent Pleasures,* 92–93.

93. W. Shenstone, *Letters of William Shenstone,* ed. D. Mallam (Minneapolis, Minn. and London, 1939), 233; Pococke, *The Travels through England,* I: 226–27; and Heely, *Letters on the Beauties of Hagley, Envil, and The Leasowes,* I: 124 and 224–25. For Parson Allen's poem, see [W. Shenstone],

Shenstone's Miscellany (1759–1763), ed. I. A. Gordon (Oxford, 1952), 34 and 145.

94. Headley and Meulenkamp, *Follies,* 424, and P. Leach, *James Paine* (London, 1988), 185.

95. K. Lemmon, "Wentworth Castle: A Forgotten Landscape," *Garden History* 3, no. 3 (summer 1975): 54, and Pococke, *The Travels through England*, I: 65.

96. C. J. Feret, *Fulham Old and New* (London, 1900), III: 173, and Headley and Meulenkamp, *Follies*, 62–63.

97. J. Godber, "The Marchioness Grey of Wrest Park," *Bedfordshire Historical Record Society* 47 (1968): 61–62, and Headley and Meulenkamp, *Follies*, 204.

98. F. Grice, "The Park Ornaments of Croome D'Abitot," *Transactions of the Worcestershire Archaeological Society*, ser. 3, 5 (1976): 42.

99. J. Collinson, *The History and Antiquities of the County of Somerset* (Bath, 1791), I: 24–25; Jones, *Follies & Grottoes,* 363; and R. Dunning, "Appealing Pillar of State," *Country Life* 181 (Sept. 10, 1987): 166–67.

100. D. Williams, *Audley End: The Restoration of 1762–1797* (Chelmsford, 1966) and Headley and Meulenkamp, *Follies*, 346.

101. For Wynnstay, see P. Howell and T. W. Pritchard in *Country Life* (April 6, 1972): 852. For Hawkstone, see Sir R. C. Hoare, *The Journeys of Sir Richard Colt Hoare through Wales and England 1793–1810*, ed. M. W. Thompson (Gloucester, 1983), 193–94; R. Haslam, "Rescue of a Masterpiece: Future of Hawkstone Park, Shropshire," *Country Life* 177 (May 9, 1985): 1246; and "Crowning a Landmark," *Country Life* 185 (Nov. 28, 1991): 58.

102. D. Hey, *Buildings of Britain, 1550–1750: Yorkshire* (Ashbourne, 1981), 109; M. J. Charlesworth, "The Wentworths," *Garden History* 14 (1986): 134; and M. Binney, "Wentworth Woodhouse, Yorks," *Country Life* 185 (Jan. 24, 1991): 62.

103. P. Willis, *Charles Bridgeman and the English Landscape Garden* (London, 1977), 107 n. 17.

104. For a succinct and clear account of the family relationships, see J. M. Robinson, *Temples of Delight: Stowe Landscape Gardens* (London, 1990), 27–58.

Conclusion

1. H. Repton, *Sketches and Hints on Landscape Gardening* (London, [1795]), 72.

2. See Boulton's introduction to E. Burke, *A Philosophical Enquiry into the Origin of our Ideas of the Sublime and Beautiful*, ed. J. T. Boulton (Notre Dame, Ind. and London, 1958). For Ripa, see D. J. Gordon, "Ripa's Fate," in *The Renaissance Imagination*, ed. S. Orgel (Berkeley, Los Angeles, and London, 1975), 51–74.

3. [T. Whately], *Observations on Modern Gardening* (London, 1770), 150–51. See also J. D. Hunt, "Emblem and Expressionism in the Eighteenth-Century Landscape Garden," *Eighteenth-Century Studies* 4 (1970–71): 294–317 and J. Archer, "The Real Beginnings of Association in British Architectural Esthetics," *Eighteenth-Century Studies* 16 (1983): 241–64.
4. [Whately], *Observations on Modern Gardening*, 116–17.
5. T. Frost, *The Life of Thomas Lord Lyttelton* (London, 1876), 313–14.
6. J. Loudon, *A Treatise on Forming, Improving, and Managing Country Residences* (London, 1806), II: 360–61.

INDEX

255